D0882340

Taoist Master Chuang

Master Chuang.

Taoist Master Chuang

MICHAEL SASO

SACRED MOUNTAIN PRESS
2000

SACRED MOUNTAIN PRESS
P.O. Box 312
Eldorado Springs, CO 80025
(720) 304-0549

Cover design by Robert Curto

Publisher's Cataloguing-in-Publication
(Provided by Quality Books, Inc.)

Saso, Michael R.
Taoist Master Chuang / Michael Saso. – 1 st ed.
p. cm.
Includes bibliographical references and index.
LCCN: 00-90198
ISBN: 0-9677948-0-3

1. Chuang, Ch'en Teng-yun, 1911-1976.
2. Taoism. 3. Taoists. 4. Taoism—Rituals.
I. Title.

BL1940.C47S27 2000 299'.514'092
QBI00-249

To the cherished memory
of
PROFESSOR ARTHUR WRIGHT
(August 11, 1976)

and

MASTER CHUANG-CH'EN TENG-YÜN
(April 7, 1976)

pai jih sheng t'ien

Contents

Part II. The Teachings of Master Chuang

Illustrations

Figures

Acknowledgments

A great debt of thanks is owed to Professor Noritada Kubo, retired director of the Toyo Bunka, and to Professor Hiroji Naoe of Kyoiku University, Tokyo. Their comments and help corrected many errors. The encouragement of Professor Arthur Wright of Yale University and Professor Arthur Wolf of Stanford, who with Margery Wolf read an early unrevised version of the text, is deeply appreciated. Fr. Yves Raguin, S.J., kindly loaned the Fu-Jen University copy of the Taoist Canon to the project. Murdoch Matthew did an excellent and much-needed job of editing. Finally, the most profound expression of gratitude must be made to Master Chuang himself, who so graciously revealed his teachings and allowed me to sit equally with his sons, A-him and A-ga, during the lengthy evening lessons in ritual orthodoxy. In so doing, Chuang insisted, he was following a prophecy made to Chuang's spiritual ascendants by the sixty-first generation Master of Dragon-Tiger Mountain. According to the words of the Heavenly Master, Chuang would give the secrets of orthodoxy to western scholars. The following pages represent only a fraction of Master Chuang's esoteric knowledge, but an essential part nevertheless which has not been described before in a western language. The study can be pursued, it is hoped, in future works and by future students of religious Taoism.

Preface to the Second Edition

It is now twenty-two years since the first edition of Taoist Master Chuang was published. In order to free the meaning of Chuang's teachings from misunderstanding that may have arisen from negative and positive reviews, glosses have been added to the original, unaltered text, in the form of italicized inserts in Times-Roman 10 pt. type face. These inserts clarify which quotes are Chuang's words, and which are translations from the Taoist canon.

The Teachings of Taoist Master Chuang represent an oral tradition, passed down for thirty-five generations, from Hua Shan in west China, (the late T'ang dynasty), Mt. Wu-tang (Wudang) in Hupei (Hubei) during the Ming dynasty, and the city of Chang-chou (Zhangzhou) in Fujian Province, during the Ch'ing (Qing) dynasty, when Chuang's ancestors, who were mandarins, moved to Hsinchu city in Taiwan. Chuang's ideas often differ significantly from what western scholars write and say about Taoism. They are both interesting and valuable in their own right, representing an oral tradition not found in other published western sources.

It was my privilege to bring Chuang's mijue (esoteric) texts back to Lunghu Shan and Mao Shan in 1986-1988, and to the Taoist Master Min Zhiting of Hua Shan, from 1990-1998, as Chuang requested before his death. Chuang's manuals and teachings were found to be identical to those of these modern mainland Taoist masters.

Michael Saso, Beijing, Oct., 1999

Introduction

Master Chuang describes the Taoist Canon

The teachings of Master Chuang are concerned with religious Taoism, a movement which began during the Han dynasty (the second century B.C. to the second century A.D.) in China and continues to flourish in the present. Taoism is an esoteric religion; that is, it has a body of secret teachings meant for the highly trained specialist, as well as a body of common doctrines meant for the men and women of China's cities and villages. The two doctrines are complementary, fulfilling rather than contradicting each other. The esoteric aspect of religious Taoism proposes a method for purifying and emptying the inner man, in preparation for mystical contemplation. The purpose of the meditative ritual of the Taoist is to bring about union with the transcendent, ultimate Tao of the Wu-wei. After winning salvation for himself, the Taoist master turns to help all men and women attain union with the Tao, either through meditative ritual in the present life or funeral ritual for those who die without attaining union. The exoteric or ordinary aspect of religious Taoism teaches the yin-yang five-element cosmology, the basis of the faith of China's masses.

Though Taoists built great monasteries, known as Kuan, for men or women to lead lives of austere celibacy, they also took up the duties of ordinary citizens, lived by the firesides of China's cities and villages, married, and bore children. Meditating in private, they also came forth to play the role of ritual expert in China's popular religion, when called upon by their fellow villagers. Many of the village Taoists were literati, trained in the classics and expert in literary composition. The texts of the *Lao-tzu* and the *Chuang-tzu* were their daily companions.

It must be said in the very beginning, however, that religious Taoism and philosophic Taoism are not identical. There are today many modern scholars, expert in explaining the *Lao-tzu* and *Chuang-tzu*, who are rightfully opposed to identifying religious Taoism with the teachings of these two early Taoist works. The Taoist priest too would assert that there are many philosophers and scholars who would qualify as Tao-chia (scholarly experts in Taoism) but not as Tao-chiao (experts in religious Taoism). To the religious Taoist, the *Lao-tzu* and the *Chuang-tzu* are basic texts used to teach novices the first steps of religious perfection. After novices are given a set of five, eight, or ten vows to observe, they are immediately given copies of the *Lao-tzu* and the *Chuang-tzu* to study and follow as a guide for daily living.

Young Taoists are taught that they must be humble, unassuming, and selfless, uninterested in the wealth, fame, or social advancement of the literati or the merchant.[1] They are told that they may never use their marvelous powers over nature for anything but the good of man. A heterodox Taoist is one who uses black magic for the detriment of man. An orthodox Taoist works solely for good while personally practicing the teachings of the *Lao-tzu* and the *Chuang-tzu*. It is specifically this latter work which is used to teach young Taoists the secrets of mystic prayer. The first seven chapters, known as the *Chuang-tzu Nei-p'ien* are considered essential to the training of a novice in contemplation.[2] As early as the fifth century A.D. the Taoists developed a ritual meditation based on the words made famous by the early chapters of the *Chuang-tzu*, the "fast of the heart" (Hsin-chai) and the notion that the Tao abides only in the heart or mind that has been made empty.

If the training of a Taoist in contemplative prayer is rigorous and exacting, the role he or she (for both men and women can become Taoists) must perform is self-effacing and demanding. The religious Taoist is at the beck and call of the common man at any hour. In the manner of a spiritual mandarin, the Taoist acts as a mediator between the invisible world of the spirits who govern nature and the visible world of men. From a family or temple altar purified by offerings of sweet incense, wine, fruit, and flowers, he ascends to the highest heavens to ask blessing for the community of men and women around him. He composes lengthy literary documents to the spirits who control nature, regulating the seasons and blessing crops and children. He descends into the darkness of hell (adopted from Buddhism) to free the souls of the deceased members of the community from the bureaucratic punishments inflicted by politicians eternally damned.

In his role as expert in China's popular religion, "the faith of the masses," the Taoist appears as a proponent of the yin-yang five-element theory of the cosmos, a philosophy worked out after the writing of the *Chuang-tzu* and the *Lao-tzu* and now an essential part of religious Taoism. Thus the exoteric or public doctrines of religious Taoism are seen to derive from a common body of knowledge known to all, and the Taoist is the expert and theologian of Chinese popular religion. He acts as teacher and counselor for the masses, while maintaining in private the esoteric and secret meditations and rituals of his own inner meditation.

Religious Taoism is a newly recognized field of research among China experts. Only in recent years has it been thought worthy of study by university professors and scholars of Chinese religions. The neglect can be partially ascribed to the secrecy with which the Taoists maintained their esoteric doctrines. The Taoist Canon, a massive collection of works in 1,120 volumes, was not available for scholarly study until modern times. The present edition of the Taoist Canon was commissioned during the reign of the Ming dynasty Emperor Cheng-t'ung, 1436–1450. About 1447, 1,057 volumes were printed by woodblock. During the reign of the late Ming Emperor Wan-li (1473–1620) a 63-volume supplement was added to the Canon, about 1607. It was not until 1924–1926 that a modern photo-offset edition of the Canon was printed by the Commercial Press in Shanghai and made available to some of the larger scholarly libraries in the West. Finally in 1962, the I-wen Press in Taipei produced an inexpensive photocopy edition of the Canon, which is now found in almost every major university library where Chinese studies are taught. Thus even the possibility of studying religious Taoism is very recent.

A second problem in studying religious Taoism was and is the antipathy felt by many Chinese scholars toward Taoism and even Buddhism; the overwhelming majority of scholarly endeavour both in China and the West has been concerned with the intellectual and moral teachings of Confucianism. Since the men who wrote Chinese history were for the most part (at least publicly) Confucian, the Taoist was always relegated (with women) to the last place in the biographies of famous people in the dynastic histories. This is not, of course, to deny the Taoists' profound influence at the Chinese court, nor that of their Buddhist confreres. Nevertheless the Confucian literati felt politically compelled to maintain their hegemony as leaders in the courts of the imperial Chinese government. Eternally on the watch lest the separation of church and state be broken by an emperor who overindulged his religious interests at the expense of good government, the Confucians believed that the balance of powers that maintained China in stability through so many millennia was dependent on keeping the Confucian mandarin on the top, and the Buddhist and Taoist toward the bottom, of the political and social pyramid. In modern times, however, especially after the famous May 4 movement in 1918, many Chinese intellectuals have consciously rejected the entire past in favor of the scientific modernization necessary to maintain China's greatness.

Finally, Taoists and their role in Chinese popular religion have been brought to the attention of the West by social scientists (ethnographers and anthropologists) in the field of Chinese religion and society. Where the historian and the humanist were overwhelmed by the abundance of written materials describing the literate Confucian past, the social scientist found the Taoist visibly active in the villages and cities of the Chinese present. Whether in Taiwan, Hong Kong, Penang, or Singapore, even in Honolulu City, Hawaii, the role of the Taoist was clearly evident in the practice of festival, burial, and temple and home ritual.

Many of the problems in interpreting the newly available Taoist Canon were solved by field work with Taoist priests, who could explain and punctuate passages insoluble to the scholar unfamiliar with esoteric Taoist terminology. The Taoists not only knew how to explain the Canon, but had manuals in their libraries far more explicit than the materials found in the printed Ming dynasty version. By studying with a Taoist priest, it was possible not only to give meaning to the seemingly haphazard order of the 1,120 volumes of the Canon, but to find supplementary materials that had not been previously published or were in clearer form than the printed sources.

To illustrate, one need only take a cursory glance at the Ming dynasty Taoist Canon.[3] Traditionally, the canon has been divided into seven sections, the first three Tung, or arcana, which were described by Lu Hsiu-ching, who died in 471, and the four Fu, or supplements, which were added shortly after. The *Three Arcana* are called the (1) Tung-chen Pu, or arcana of the realized immortal, (2) Tung-hsüan Pu, or arcana of the mysterious, and (3) Tung-shen Pu, or arcana of the spirits. The first, Tung-chen section of the Canon is supposed to contain the teachings of the elite Taoist monastic group, the Shang-ch'ing (Highest Purity) sect, founded in 370 atop Mao Shan (Mt. Mao) in Kiangsu province, central China. The second, Tung-hsüan section of the Canon contains the texts of the Ling-pao order, the popular ritual-oriented Taoists of third and fourth century China, who created the great liturgies of renewal and burial. The third, Tung-shen section of the Canon is named after a manual used by the former Ling-pao Taoists, that is, the *San-huang Wen*, the *Writ of the Three Emperors*. But it also contains the teachings of the third early group of Taoists, the Meng-wei (Heavenly Master) sect.

Each of the first three sections of the Canon is divided into twelve subsections:

1. Pen-wen	basic doctrines and writings
2. Shen-fu	talismanic charms for commanding spirits
3. Yü-chüeh	esoteric secrets and rubrical directions
4. Ling-t'u	spiritual charts and maps, illustrations
5. P'u-lu	lists of spirits' names and titles
6. Chieh-lü	vows and rules for the initiate
7. Wei-yi	liturgies of renewal and burial
8. Fang-fa	shorter rites of magic, cures, and blessings
9. Chung-shu	miscellaneous magic and incantations
10. Chi-chuan	biographies of famous Taoists
11. Tsan-sung	hymns and medodies
12. Piao-tsou	documents, memorials, and rescripts

The last four sections of the Canon, or the Szu-fu supporting passages, are not divided into twelve subsections as are the *Three Arcana* above. The four supplements not only contain ritual, which adds to the materials of the first three sections of the Canon, but also include books of alchemy, breath control, Taoist philosophy, and dictionaries of Taoist lore.

The fourth section of the Canon is called the T'ai-hsüan Pu, or the section of the Great Mystery. It is said to support the first arcanum, the Tung-chen Pu; that is, it supplements the teachings of the first great monastic sect, the Mao Shan Highest Purity order. The fifth part of the Canon, the T'ai-p'ing Pu, or Great Peace, is supposed to supplement the second arcanum, the Tung-hsüan Pu, the teachings of the Ling-pao order. The sixth section of the Canon called T'ai-ch'ing Pu, or the Great Purity, is supposed to support the third arcanum, the Tung-shen Pu. Finally, the seventh and last section of the Canon is the repository of the teachings and holdings of the Heavenly Master sect, the Cheng-i or Orthodox One order of antiquity.

Here in schematic form is the structure of the Canon:

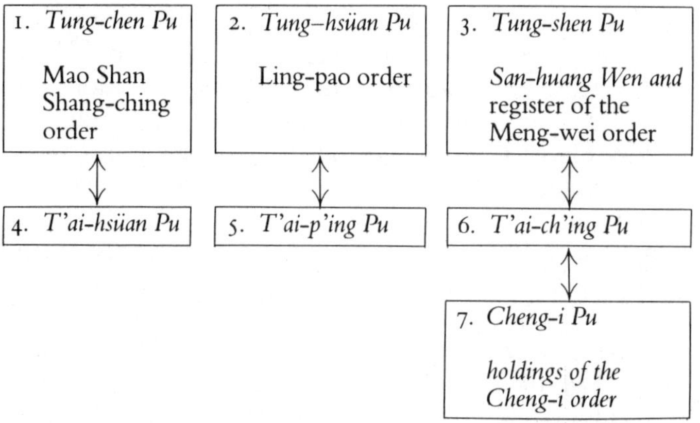

Having established a theoretical structure for the Canon, the Taoists of the Ming dynasty seem to have brought their documents to the Cheng-t'ung emperor in such haphazard order that the imperial court as well as the Confucian scholars were totally confused about which documents belonged in each of the seven categories. Thus, one would expect to find the major documents and teachings of the contemplative Mao Shan order in the first section of the Canon. But instead, one finds at the very beginning of the Pen-wen, or basic teachings, of the first section, the basic document and teachings of the Ling-pao order in the Ling-pao Wu-liang *Tu-jen* Shang-p'in Miao-*ching*, with a commentary in sixty-one chapters. Next, one finds the *Ta-tung Chen-ching*, one of the basic texts of the Mao Shan Shang-ch'ing sect, immediately followed by two documents taken almost bodily from the Buddhist Canon, the *Hai-k'ung Chih-tsang* and the Pen-hsing Ching. Also in the first section are found the basic doctrines of the various thunder magic sects that are the Taoist counterparts to the vajrayana of tantric Buddhism, the manual of interior alchemy known as *Yin-fu Ching*, more texts and commentaries of the *Tu-jen Ching*, commentaries on the *I-ching* (*Book of Changes*)—texts and documents which in fact cover almost every aspect of religious Taoism.

In the second section of the Canon, which should have been exclusively devoted to the Ling-pao tradition, one finds the basic texts of the first, Tung-chen section, the Yellow Court Canon, and the magnificent work of the ninth master of Mao Shan, the *Teng-chen Yin-chüeh* of T'ao Hung-ching. The great liturgical sections of the Tung-hsüan Pu do actually contain the rituals of the Ling-pao order, including the beautiful chiao festivals of renewal and the chai Yellow Registers for burial. In the third section of the Canon, the Tung-shen Pu, the *San-huang Wen*, or *Writ of the Three Emperors*, is the remnant of a strange text, a cryptic document mentioned first in the apocryphal texts of early Han China. The *San-huang Wen* was suppressed during the T'ang dynasty for certain excesses in its use by Taoist monks and nuns. Since the text obviously belonged to the Ling-pao sect of Taoist practitioners, its use to name the third section of the Canon points to the central role played by Ling-pao Taoists from the very beginning in the formation of the Canon. The third Tung-shen section contains commentaries on the *Lao-tzu* and the *Chuang-tzu*, the registers and rituals of the Heavenly Master sect, and documents deriving from the military Pole Star sect from Wu-tang Shan in Hupei province.

The eclectic nature of the canon can be further seen in the four supplements. The fourth, T'ai-hsüan Pu, does indeed contain one of the basic documents of the first monastic order, the famous *Chen Kao*. Along with this document, which supports and supplements the teachings of the first Mao Shan monastic order, are texts of internal alchemy, a grand encyclopedia of Taoist lore (the *Seven Cloud Tally Box*), and texts of alchemy. The fifth, T'ai-p'ing Pu, further supports the second, Ling-pao section of the Canon with the basic *T'ai-p'ing Ching*, the *Canon of the Great Peace*. Also in the fifth section of the Canon is one of the earliest and most valuable of the canonical texts, the *Wu-shang Pi-yao*. This partially incomplete text can be safely dated to the sixth century, and its teachings figure prominently in the doctrines of Master Chuang, as explained in the main body of the present work. The sixth and shortest section of the Canon contains the *T'ai-shang Kan-ying P'ien*, a morality treatise widely used in China's popular religion, and the works of the most famous Taoist philosophers.

The seventh and last section of the Canon is named after the Orthodox One, or Cheng-i sect. Known from the earliest times as the Heavenly Master sect as well as the Meng-wei (Auspicious Alliance) order, the twenty-four basic registers or Lu which identify the Taoist of the Cheng-i order are found in clear and explicit form in this last section of the Canon.[4] The Cheng-i section, in fact, represents the holdings of the Heavenly Masters, the successors of the first Heavenly Master Chang Tao-ling in the southern headquarters of orthodox Taoism at Dragon-Tiger Mountain (Lung-hu Shan) in the province of Kiangsi. Commissioned by the imperial government from Sung times to give licenses of ordination to local Taoist priests, the Heavenly Master at Dragon-Tiger Mountain kept in his possession the main books and paraphernalia of the various Taoist orders of south China whose members came to the sacred mountain to be licensed. Thus one finds in the seventh section of the Canon the registers of the Meng-wei order, the Ling-pao order, the Pole Star sect, the various Thunder Magic sects, and the ubiquitous Shen-hsiao sect of the Sung dynasty charlatan Lin Ling-su.

To the lay reader unfamiliar with the complexities of the Taoist Canon or the various sects and orders of religious Taoists, the above brief description is both confusing and brusque. The introduction of Master Chuang, in chapter 1 of this work, will bring order into the seeming confusion. In fact, the first three early Taoist movements are clearly defined in Master Chuang's teaching. Though called by various names, a marvelous doctrinal unity was preserved by all the early Taoist groups until the middle of the Sung dynasty. The attempts to pull away from orthodoxy or to separate from the mainstream of Taoist tradition were curbed by the Heavenly Masters through their right to grant official licenses of ordination. As seen in the documents of Master Chuang and as will be explained in chapter 5, the various sects of Taoists are carefully graded. The status and rank of a Taoist at the time of ordination is awarded according to conformity to the teachings of the Heavenly Masters. In an ordination manual used by the Heavenly Masters at Dragon-Tiger Mountain from the mid-Sung dynasty (ca. 1120) until the present, the grades of ordination are:

Grade one:	Knowledge of the teachings and meditations of the Mao Shan Shang-ch'ing sect, the *Yellow Court Canon*.

Grades two and three:	Knowledge of the teachings and meditations of the Ch'ing-wei, Thunder Magic, sect (tantric Taoism).
Grades four and five:	Knowledge of the rituals of the orthodox Meng-wei sect, the twenty-four registers of the Heavenly Masters.
Grades six and seven:	Knowledge of the rituals of the Ling-pao sect, the fourteen registers of popular Taoism.[5]

The manual further indicates the kinds of Taoists, that is, the sects and orders of Taoists, who come to Dragon-Tiger Mountain for ordination. For each of the orders, the Heavenly Master provides teachings and instructions in their own sect and in its proper doctrines. Thus if a Taoist from the highly rigorous monastic order known as the Ch'üan-chen sect approaches the Heavenly Master, the integrity of his own order and its practices are maintained. But the rank at ordination will be given according to the monk's knowledge of the above registers or doctrines. There are of course almost a hundred local sects and orders of Taoist men and women who approach the Heavenly Master for documents of ordination. The main sects are:

1. The Mao Shan Shang-ch'ing sect, the basic doctrines of which are to be found in the *Yellow Court Canon*. Meditations of mystical union are the specialty of this order, based on the writings of the *Chuang-tzu*.
2. The Hua Shan Ch'ing-wei, or Thunder Magic, sect from west China. The powerful exorcism and purification rituals of this order are used to oppose evil black magic.
3. The military Pole Star sect from Wu-tang Shan in

Hupei province. The use of Kung-fu bodily exercises, military prowess involving spirits as well as weapons, and Pole Star magic are proper to this early order.

4. The orthodox Heavenly Master Cheng-i sect, also called Auspicious Alliance Meng-wei sect, with headquarters at Lung-hu Shan in Kiangsi province. The Taoists who belong to the order but live by the firesides of village and city China call themselves Jade Pavilion (Yü Fu) Taoists as a sort of identifying secret title.
5. The popular Shen-hsiao order founded by Lin Ling-su during the reign of the Sung Emperor Hui-tsung, ca. 1116, in central and south China. The Taoists of this sect were at first considered heterodox, proponents of a kind of black magic for harming people. But according to tradition, they were drawn back into orthodoxy by learning of Thunder Magic from the famous thirtieth generation Heavenly Master. To all of the minor local Taoists coming to Lung-hu Shan for ordination, the Heavenly Master awarded a license and gave instructions in this form of late Sung dynasty Taoism.

The teachings of Master Chuang deal with the above themes in an intimate and lively fashion. Trained from youth in the secrets of Meng-wei orthodox Taoism as well as in the elite exorcisms of the powerful Ch'ing-wei Thunder Magic, Master Chuang imparts in the following pages the secrets of esoteric religious Taoism. In chapter 1, the sources of Chuang's teachings are traced to the beginnings of religious Taoism. A brief but fairly complete history of the origins of religious Taoism and its development into the Sung dynasty is given. In chapter 2, the history of the transmission of Chuang's teachings from mainland China to Taiwan is recounted from local archives and from sources found in Chuang's extensive library. In chapter 3, the role of Chuang in the community, his effect on his neighbors, and the respect engendered by his battle against evil and prayers for public blessing are described. The first three chapters comprise part I of the book and define Master Chuang and his role in society.

Part II, chapters 4 through 6, deals with the teachings of Master Chuang in detail. Chapter 4 describes the terrifying Tao of the Left, the black magic of the Six Chia spirits, attributed to Mao Shan in Kiangsu. Chapter 5 gives a general description of the Tao of the Right, the beautiful rituals of orthodox Taoism. The second part of the chapter teaches the method of performing one of the earliest meditations of orthodox Meng-wei Taoism, the Fa-lu rite of mandala building. Chapter 6 describes the rites of tantric Taoism, the famous Five Thunder method, which became popular during the Sung dynasty. The ability to perform thunder magic is highly prized by the orthodox Taoists and a high rank at ordination is awarded for the mastery of its secrets. Thunder magic is used to counteract the harmful black magic described in chapter 4. As has been observed, the term orthodoxy is applied to Taoists who spend their lives in doing good for their fellow men and women of the Chinese community and who follow the texts and rubrics of classical canonical Taoism descending from antiquity. Heterodoxy describes Taoists who practice harmful black magic to the detriment or harm of others. But from the viewpoint of an outsider, a marvelous unity is seen to exist among Taoists. In spite of the diversity of sects and rubrics, the mystic experience of unity with the transcendent Tao and the power over nature resulting from such a union draw all Taoists together in a camaraderie transcending sectarian difference. "Yü Tao ho I" (to be joined as one with the Tao) is the Taoist key to ecumenism.

PART I
Master Chuang

1. Historical Origins

Taoist History as told by Master Chuang

Introduction

Master Chuang is a Taoist of the Heavenly Master sect who lives in modern north Taiwan, an island whose people often seem more interested in the industrial present than in the past glories of traditional China. His teachings are concerned with classical religious Taoism, a system of beliefs that originated in the first half of the second century A.D. and has continued to evolve, grow, and proliferate until the present. To Master Chuang the historical origins of his religious beliefs are a matter of faith, unshaken by the opinions of historians.[1]

To Master Chuang, religious Taoism was indisputably established by Chang Tao-ling, the first Heavenly Master who founded the Orthodox One, or Heavenly Master, sect about A.D. 142, toward the end of the Han dynasty. The basic doctrines of Chang Tao-ling concerned the twenty-four Auspicious Alliance registers, or lists of spirits by names and descriptions, that the Taoists of his order were empowered to summon and command.[2] Master Chuang also owes a deep sense of allegiance to the Mao Shan Highest Purity order, a meditative sect founded in the fourth century near Nanking in the central province of Kiangsu. To this order is ascribed the difficult text known as the *Yellow Court Canon*, used by Chuang as a manual for meditation.[3] Next in the honor and prestige associated with its magic is the tantric Taoist order called Ch'ing-wei, or sometimes the Heavenly Pivot sect. Chuang puts its origins in the T'ang dynasty and associates it with the famous western peak, Hua Shan.[4] Directly after the Ch'ing-wei sect Chuang ranks the Pole Star (Big Dipper) or Pei-chi Taoists, the famous military Kung-fu experts associated with Wu-tang Shan in the province of Hupei.[5] His own Cheng-i Meng-wei (Orthodox One–Auspicious Alliance) sect is ranked fourth, after the three monastic centers mentioned above.

In fifth place, Chuang puts the Shen-hsiao order, a Sung dynasty sect that began in Fukien, the province of orgin for the majority of Taiwan's Chinese population. For two reasons, the Shen-hsiao sect is not as respectable as the first four orders. First, says Chuang, its rituals are a "ministry of imitation," weak replicas of the stately orthodox rituals of the earlier orders. They lack the meditations of inner alchemy that are essential to the traditional orthodox orders.[6] Second, its Taoists sometimes practice black magic to harm men or women of the community and thus some of its practices are classified as hsieh, or heterodox.[7] The Shen-hsiao order was, however, brought under the wings of orthodoxy. Its beneficent rites are now a part of the repertory of the Heavenly Master, who grants licenses of ordination in its rituals, along with those of the higher four orders.[8]

Chuang is not unaware of the monastic Ch'üan-chen order or the other great Taoist movements of Chinese history. His own master, Lin Hsiu-mei, was a devout practitioner of the meditations of Ch'üan-chen Taoism.[9] The teachings professed by Chuang are most intimately related to the first four doctrines mentioned above, that is, the Mao Shan *Yellow Court Canon*, the Ch'ing-wei tantric rites, the Pole Star (Big Dipper) Kung-fu exercises, and the stately rites of renewal and burial of the Orthodox One–Heavenly Master sect. The doctrines of these sects are Chuang's rightful inheritance.[10]

Though there have been a number of excellent treatises published in Japanese and Chinese within the last two decades on the history and the doctrines of religious Taoism, there has been very little published in western languages and no overall work. The brief overview of

Taoist history given here is meant only to acquaint the reader with some of the names, movements, and historical origins of topics to be discussed by Master Chuang. All the sources are in either Japanese or Chinese; many are from the cryptic Taoist Canon itself, a source that is certainly not critical. Its biographies are, in fact, hagiographic and filled with pious legend. My outline is therefore a first attempt to list the origins of the teachings of Master Chuang.

1. THE FIRST TAOISTS (The Ch'in and early Han period, 220 B.C.–24 A.D.)

Though religious Taoism did not begin as an organized movement until the declining years of the Han dynasty, that is, the second century A.D., historians agree that the court magicians, or fang-shih, of the early Han dynasty and the violent years which preceded the Han (ca. 221 B.C.) were the precursors of the first Taoists.[11] The infamous Ch'in Shih Huang-ti, the man who united China under a strict military rule and called himself the First Emperor, spent his declining years in search of Taoist formulae for longevity. He died on a trip to the eastern coast of China, and his body was spirited back to the capital, bringing about the fall of the Ch'in and the rise of the Han.[12]

Legend says that Liu Pang, who founded the Han empire in A.D. 206, was assisted to victory by the magic of a Taoist named Chang Liang.[13] Chang used a talismanic manual received from Lao-tzu, who appeared in the guise of "the Duke of the Yellow Stone." The founder of Heavenly Master sect Taoism at the end of the Han period, Chang Tao-ling, was said to be the eighth generation descendant of Chang Liang.[14] The sixth emperor of the Han dynasty, Wu-ti, or the military emperor, surrounded himself with fang-shih (court magicians) and established state cults to Huang-ti, Hou-t'u, and T'ai-yi, spirits worshipped in later religious Taoism.[15] Both court ritual and popular religious practices during the Han dynasty helped to form and to influence religious Taoism at the end of the Han period.

Chinese and Japanese historians point to the importance of a strange and little studied apocryphal literature, the *Ku-wei Shu*, in the formation of early religious Taoism.[16] The *Wei* apocrypha were popular during the reign of the usurper Wang Mang, who ruled from A.D. 9 to 23, in the middle of the Han period. The emperor Kuang Wu-ti, who restored the Han dynasty in 25, used the *Wei* Apocrypha and especially the *Ho-t'u*, or magic chart of the river, to justify his rule.[17] During the later Han period the *Ho-t'u* and its sister chart, the *Lo-shu* (writings that came out of the Lo River on the back of a turtle), became an accepted branch of scholarly study. Their use is frequently mentioned in the *Hou Han Shu*, the history of the later Han dynasty.[18] During the Sui dynasty (589–618), however, the *Wei* apocrypha were condemned and their connection with religious Taoism was forgotten.[19]

It is useful to examine briefly some of the *Wei* apocryphal texts to see how much of religious Taoism was in fact drawn from these popular sources. The important early Taoist text, the *San-huang Wen*, or *Writ of the Three Emperors*, is mentioned in the *Wei* apocrypha.[20] The fragmentary texts remaining from this collection are not consistent in describing who the Three Emperors were. They are sometimes said to be Fu Hsi, the heavenly emperor; Nü Kua (the wife of Fu Hsi), the earthly emperor; and Shen Nung, the emperor of mankind. In another text the heavenly emperor is called Fu Hsi, the earthly emperor is Shen Nung, and the emperor of man is Huang-ti.[21] The three emperors are described as having twelve heads, eleven heads, and nine heads, respectively, but the term "head" is interpreted as a single ruler in a dynastic succession of emperors. Thus the Heavenly Emperor was a dynastic reign of twelve kings, the earthly emperor a series of eleven kings, and the emperor of humanity a series of nine kings. The *Writ of the Three Emperors* was assumed into the texts of religious Taoism, and the connections with the *Wei* apocrypha forgotten.[22]

A second central theme of religious Taoism is the worship of the five heavenly rulers, Wu-ti. The five emperors are taken to be personifications of the primordial stuff of the cosmos, the five movers or five elements. The doctrine is taken from the yin-yang five-element cosmology, and is found in adapted form as a part of court ritual in the Yüeh-ling, or Monthly Commands chapter, of the *Book of Rites*.[23] Chang Tao-ling, the founder of Heavenly Master sect Taoism, is said to have used the Monthly Commands chapter in forming his sect in west China. The later texts of religious Taoism found in the Canon show that the names given to the five heavenly emperors coincide with the esoteric titles found in the *Wei* apocrypha; that is, the Taoist texts are similar to rituals found in the classical *Book of Rites*, with names taken from the *Wei* apocryphal texts.[24]

One of the central documents of religious Taoism, the *Ling-pao Five Talismans*, is also cryptically mentioned in the apocryphal *Ho-t'u* texts.[25] The apocryphal texts themselves do not explicitly state that the Five Talismans are a *Ho-t'u*. The following story, relating how the *Ho-t'u* was given to Yü the Great as a talismanic means to control the floods,[26] is changed in later Taoist legends to say that the *Ling-pao Five Talismans* were given to Yü to use in controlling the flooding waters, in the same textual context.

In the story, the *Ho-t'u* is described as a talismanic chart painted in red characters on a green background. It depicts the course of the Yellow River, beginning at Mount K'un-lun and flowing to the sea. At each of the great curves in the river a star in the heavens controls the water for a thousand li. The river flows consecutively in the five directions, east, south, center, west, and north, finally emptying into the P'o Sea in the east. The person who possesses the chart can control the flow of the river, the stars, and the elements. When the *Ho-t'u* is revealed, it is always brought out of the Yellow River by a spirit horse or dragon. Phoenixes are seen in the royal temple, and vapors of five colored lights come forth from the river. The spirit of the Yellow River who announces the chart is described as having a man's head and a fish's body.[27]

The three ancient rulers—Yao, Shun, and Yü—are each given a *Ho-t'u* which enables them to establish a successful rule. Yü uses the magic chart to control the floods and, when finished with the powerful talismans, he is told to bury them atop Mao Shan in Kiangsu.[28] Thus there can be seen in the mid-Han period a definite association between the later center for Taoist legerdemain and the apocryphal descriptions of the *Ho-t'u*. The *Ho-t'u* is called a chen-wen, realized or true writ, the name used exclusively by later Taoists to describe the Ling-pao talismans.[29]

Abruptly the apocryphal text shifts to the evil King Ho-lü of the kingdom of Wu. In search of a magic means to conquer the kingdoms of Yüeh and Ch'u, Ho-lü climbs Mao Shan to find the chen-wen talismans. There he encounters master Lung-wei and commands him to go into the secret recesses of the mountain and bring out the true writs. The text states explicitly that there are 174 characters (tzu) in the writ.[30] Master Lung-wei complies, but King Ho-lü cannot understand the text. The king takes it to Confucius and tells a lie, saying that a red bird brought it.[31] Confucius is not fooled, and quotes a rhyme sung by the children of the western sea:

The King of Wu went out one day
To see a cloud filled lake.
He met old master Lung-wei
Who lived upon a peak.

Climbing up north Mao Shan
He came upon a cave.
There was built a secret room
The writs of Yü to save.
The heavenly rulers great writs
Are forbidden to narrate;
He who would receive them
Six hundred years must wait.
He who takes them out by force
Will ruin his own kingdom.

The myth and the poem are found in four different sources, one a fragmentary historical text called the *Yüeh-chüeh Shu* (*The Demise of the Yüeh Kingdom*),[32] one from the Buddhist Canon, and two from the Taoist Canon.[33] The most interesting of these later references is the diatribe against Taoism quoted by the T'ang dynasty Buddhist Hsüan Yi in the *Chen-cheng Lun*.[34] In this T'ang dynasty text, the Buddhist master laughs at the notion that the *Ling-pao Five Talismans* are a source of blessing. If possession of the famous Taoist charms is so efficacious, the Buddhist says, why did they cause the fall of the kingdom of Wu?[35]

It is apparent, therefore, that the association of the *Ling-pao Five Talismans* of the Taoists with the *Ho-t'u* of the apocryphal texts was still made in the T'ang period, even after the apocrypha and the *Ho-t'u* were condemned during the preceding Sui period. The *Introduction to the Ling-pao Five Talismans*,[36] a very early text in the Canon, also recounts the story of Ho-lü. The writer refers to the *Ho-t'u*, specifically, when recalling the story. On the final page of the Taoist canonical text, the Ling-pao basic sources are said to be:

1. The hidden secret talismans of the *Ho-t'u*;
2. The *Lo-shu* found on the carapace of the flying turtle;
3. The *P'ing-heng*, or seven stars of the dipper.[37]

Both the *Ho-t'u* and the *Lo-shu*, therefore, along with the Pole Star and the rituals surrounding its central place in the northern heavens, were considered to be predecessors of Taoist Ling-pao liturgy.[38]

The influences of Han dynasty religious practices on religious Taoism go far beyond the few examples cited in the preceding pages. Scholars who have studied the period agree that the popular conjurers (chou) and their charges, the possessed wu mediums of feudal China who also figure prominently in the religion of the Han, became associated with a branch of religious Taoism.[39] But the use of possessed mediums in popular ritual is not admitted by the orthodox Heavenly Master sect professed by Master Chuang. The two professions—that of the stately, literary, orthodox Taoist, and that of the frenzied possessed medium—were distinguished by two separate ministries almost from the beginning of religious Taoism.[40] In modern times, the possessed mediums and the Taoists who control them are called Redhead—that is, they belong to a branch of Taoists and a style of ministry called Redhead in popular usage.[41] The Taoists who do not employ medium possession and who follow the strict canonical rules, literary documents, and meditations of ritual alchemy are called Blackhead. A distinction between the literary and the military, elite and popular religious Taoism seems to have been made in the very beginning,[42] as can be seen from an examination of the two earliest Taoist movements.

2. THE BEGINNING OF RELIGIOUS TAOISM (The Later Han and three Kingdoms Period, A.D. 25–264)

The first saintly man associated with the founding of religious Taoism is the semi-legendary Yü Chi, a mystic and visionary who was born in the area known as Lang Yeh in the province of Shantung, northeast China. Perhaps during the reign of the Shun-ti emperor (126–145), Yü Chi was visited by spirits while standing by a river near a place called Ch'ü-yang.[43] The spirits gave him a book, called the *T'ai-p'ing Ch'ing-ling Shu*, *The Great Peace Book of Pure Commands*. It had 170 chapters and its doctrines consisted of texts taken from the Yin-yang Five Element theory of the Cosmos, the sayings of the Fang-shih or Tao-shih of the mid Han period, and a new method for commanding spirits to bring blessings and cure illness.[44] According to the message of Yü Chi's prophetic book, heaven had forgotten the principles of yin and yang, thus losing the Tao. Earth had lost the proper functioning of yin and yang, and was experiencing natural diasters. The rulers and ministers of state had neglected the proper balance of yin and yang and were not acting according to the seasons and ways of nature; they were in danger of losing the succession of rule. The loyal minister Hsiang K'ai, whose biography is found in chapter 60 of the later Han dynasty history, was concerned enough to bring the book to the court of Huan-ti (who reigned 147–168).[45] But Huan-ti put the prophetic book aside, not realizing that within two decades it would fall into the hands of the Taoist rebel Chang *Chiao*, leader of the Great Peace movement, also known as the Yellow Turban rebellion.[46]

There is no doubt of the deep and lasting influence of Yü Chi's book on the formation of religious Taoism. Besides being the basic manual of the Yellow Turban rebels, it also influenced Chang Tao-ling, the founder of the orthodox Heavenly Master sect; Ko Hsüan, who is later credited with forming the Ling-pao sect; and the founders of the third early order known as Mao Shan.[47] Though the origins of the three early Taoist movements are shrouded in legend, as is the authorship of the *T'ai-ping Canon*, the doctrines attributed to Yü Chi are still found in religious Taoism. The present text of the *Great Peace Canon* has only 119 chapters and many obvious lacunae. It is found at the head of the fifth section of the Taoist Canon, and is used as a title for the entire section, as supporting the doctrines of the Ling-pao Canon.[48]

The second great holy man and mystic to whom the founding of religious Taoism is attributed is the first Heavenly Master Chang Ling, known also as Chang Tao-ling.[49] Chang was born in the state of P'ei, on the northwest corner of Kiangsu province and the border of Anhwei. Two very sparse accounts of his life are found in the dynastic histories, the first in the biographical section of the *Wei* history, the second in the *Hou Han Shu History of the Later Han.*[50] In these biased Confucian sources, Chang is said to move from his home in Kiangsu to Szechuan province in west China, in search of formulae of longevity, inner alchemy, and macrobiotic practise. While in Szechuan, he composed Taoist books[51] that led the people astray. All those converted to the sect were made to pay five bushels of rice. The Confucian historians gave them the derisive name, "Five Bushels of Rice thieves."[52]

Chang Tao-ling flourished after the time of Yü Chi, during the years of the Shun-ti reign (126–145). The earliest accounts of his doctrines speak of the composition of twenty-four books of talismanic writings (fu-shu)[53] and the dividing of his theocratic kingdom into twenty-four chih or administrative districts, with a chi-chiu, or grand libationer, at head of each division.[54] The *Yüeh-ling* chapter of the *Book of Rites* and the *Ling-pao Five Talismans* were used to compose his liturgies.[55] Finally, Chang was credited with creating a ritual which characterizes his sect and its successors until the present day. Documents were composed after the model of memorials and rescripts of the imperial court. The documents were addressed to the rulers of the three realms—heaven, earth, and underworld—to cure illness and win blessings for the people.[56]

A third biography of Chang Ling is found in the Canon.[57] This account may be modeled on a work missing from the Ming-dynasty Taoist Canon, the *Shen-hsien Chuan*, attributed to the third- and fourth-century eccentric, Ko Hung.[58] The Ming dynasty version relates that Chang Tao-ling was a student of the classics when young. He became enamored of the doctrines of longevity in the works of the alchemists, and depleted his family's fortunes in searching for life-prolonging macrobiotic formulae. He is said to have discovered the "Nine tripods of the Yellow Emperor for preparing the elixir of life," but in the process, he became so poor that he had to till the soil and herd cattle for his livelihood.

It was then brought to Chang Tao-ling's attention that in the kingdom of Shu (Szechuan) lived a simple and good people who were easy to convert. Chang immediately gathered some of his followers and went there. He took up residence on the slopes of the mountain where the ku-bird sings (Mount Ku-ming). A host of heavenly spirits appeared and revealed to him a doctrine by which the sick could be cured and the land governed in a kind of communal theocracy. It was probably at this time that the book of the twenty-four registers was written. Converts flocked to the new religion and their contributions supported Chang's alchemical experiments. He was soon able to concoct a formula for longevity, which led to immediate dissolution (death) and immortality. Reminiscent of the accounts of the Boddhisattva in Mahayana Buddhism, Chang drank only half of the potion, thus remaining behind to preach his new doctrines of salvation. After consuming the portion of the drink, Chang was able to be in two locations at once. Visitors and disciples often saw the master rowing a boat on the lake in front of his retreat while speaking to visitors in the guest pavilion.

The rituals by which Chang governed the villages of Szechuan were expanded by his grandson and successor Chang Lu, whom many scholars feel to be the first systematic organizer of Taoism in West China. Classical sources were used to reconstruct a theocratic kingdom from the ruins of the decaying Han empire.[59] Taxes were levied, roads repaired, marshes drained, and crops increased. Portions of the grain crops were stored for the poor and the weary traveler. People who committed public offenses were made to confess their sins publicly and to repair a section of a road in penance. If Ko Hung's account is to be trusted, the early Taoists appear as men of learning and intellectual attainment, trained in chemical experiment and classical learning. Their intent was to found a golden age in the provinces of the floundering Han empire. As Professor Rolf Stein has observed in a masterful article on Taoist movements at the end of the Han, the political divisions of Chang Tao-ling's twenty-four spiritual bishoprics were not unlike the well-functioning village leadership of an earlier Han local administrative system.[60] The leaders of early Heavenly Master sect Taoism were indeed the elite of provincial society.

The writings of Yü Chi, as mentioned above, were also the basis of a second popular but ill-fated Taoist movement that was to meet a bloody end. In the eastern provinces of China a man named Chang Chiao (no relationship to Chang in the west) founded a sect based on the *T'ai-p'ing Ching*, the *Way of the Great Peace*, of Yü Chi.[61] Chang Chiao's brand of Taoism, similar in many respects to the Five Bushels of Rice sect in the west, was different in one important aspect. The followers of Chang Chiao were considered by late Han officials to be rebels intent on overthrowing the court of Han and setting up a new kingdom of Huang-lao (Huang-ti and Lao-tzu, or, according to some commentators, Lao-tzu as Emperor). According to the teachings of Chang Chiao, the Blue Heavens (the religion and rule of Han) were dead, and the Yellow Heaven (the era of the Great Peace rebels) was soon to be established. The beginning of a new sixty year cycle, that is, the Chia-tzu year, A.D. 184, would see the establishment of the new peace. But instead, in a quick and savage reprisal, mandarin, martial commander, and court arose to obliterate the leader and his converts. The Way of the Great Peace ended in the massacre of its leaders and their myriad followers. Taoism would thereafter be a spiritual rather than a political movement in Chinese history. The Way of the Great Peace was renamed the Yellow Turban Rebellion for the color of the kerchiefs that Chang Chiao's troops wore to their death.[62]

In the official dynastic histories, the sparse details and certain common features may make the original Taoist movements seem almost identical. Closer scrutiny, however, shows that the two were in fact distinct, separated not only by the plains of east China and the hilly country of the west but by two distinct styles of religious ritual, some of which still distinguish Taoist sects today.[63] Thus, both the Great Peace movement in the east and the Heavenly Master sect in the west worshipped Taoist divinities. But while the eastern group simply honored Huang-lao (The Yellow, or Imperial Lao-tzu), the west required a specific devotional reading of the Lao-tzu *Tao-te Ching* for membership in the sect. Both movements set up religious theocracies, but the eastern Great Peace movement divided China's eight central and eastern provinces into thirty-six commanderies with a general at the head of each. The Heavenly Master Taoists in the west divided their kingdom into twenty-four bishoprics, each led by a grand libationer. A group of elders, "surveyors of merit," were put in charge of local village administration. The system, as has been noted, resembled Han local administration in its age of prosperity.

Both sects considered sickness and disaster to be caused by sinful acts. The Great Peace movement required its penitents to meditate on their sins in "Pure Rooms," while the Heavenly Master sect developed a ritual of repentance. The devout were made to write out their sins on three documents; the one for the heavens was burned, the one for the earth was buried, and the one for the underworld was dropped in the water. Thus one sees a definite literary, scholarly spirit in the Heavenly Master sect and a military, popular, almost heterodox bent to the way of the Great Peace. The Great Peace movement clashed openly with the civil government and ended in a bloody conflagration; the grandson of Chang Tao-ling, Chang Lu, surrendered his territories to the conquering forces of Ts'ao Ts'ao and the Wei kingdom in the north. He was rewarded with a noble rank, and his theocratic kingdom continues until the present. Thus the two movements can be distinguished by the tendency of their ritual and political activities: the one military and the other literary in religious intent.[64]

It is interesting to note a further difference in the color symbolism of the two movements. The three basic colors of the meditative system attributed to Chang Tao-ling are black (hsüan), yellow (huang), and white (pai).[65] Black, the color of the sky just before dawn or the winter solstice before the rebirth of yang in the cosmos, is the color of the deities of the heavens, the symbol of primordial breath within the microcosm of man. Yellow is the color of earth, of gold, and of the spirit within the center of the microcosm in man. White is the color of the late afternoon, of the watery underworld, and of the seminal essence in the lower parts of man.[66] The *T'ai-p'ing Ching* of Yü Chi, on the other hand, takes a different view of the basic colors. Blue-green is made the color of yin, or north, and red the color of yang, or south. The two systems are not contradictory but complementary, as the military and the literary were meant to complement each other in the visible imperial system.[67] The *Chen Kao*, a compilation of the basic texts of the Mao Shan order in the sixth century by T'ao Hung-ching (see below), ecumenically uses both the colors of the *T'ai-p'ing Ching* and the colors of the Heavenly Master order for its symbols.[68] It is also interesting that the common people often classify Taoists who are literary, classical, or orthodox as Black and those who are military, popular, or exorcist- or cure-oriented as Red. Most important for our present purposes, however, is to note that the two traditions were present from the very beginning of religious Taoism.[69]

The temporal kingdom of Chang Tao-ling was surrendered by his grandson in the year 215, a few years before the final fall of Han and the establishment of the short-lived Kingdom of Wei. By the year 317 and the publication of Ko Hung's *Pao-p'u-tzu* (*He Who Embraces Simplicity*), the main themes in religious Taoism had been established, and the books later expanded into the Canon were already known, if only in nuclear form.[70] Thus in the valuable bibliography of books possessed by Ko Hung, there is mentioned the *Yellow Court Canon*, which will become the basic text of the Mao Shan monastic order, and the *Tu-jen Ching* and the *Ling-pao Five Talismans*, which are central to the Ling-pao order. Surprisingly, the Meng-wei or Auspicious Alliance registers of the Heavenly Master sect are not mentioned although we know from other sources that they were already extant.[71] The formation of a first Taoist Canon was completed by 471, a hundred and fifty years after Ko Hung's publication of the *Pao-p'u-tzu*.

(Chuang's version of Taoist history differs significantly from the studies of western scholars)

3. THE FORMATION OF THE FIRST TAOIST CANON (The North-South Period, A.D. 265–581)

There is no doubt that the coming of Buddhism to China during the Han dynasty and its widespread acceptance during the north-south period (265–581) had a profound influence on the formation of religious Taoism. Perhaps two of the deepest impressions were in the emphasis Taoism came to place on burial ritual and the notion of universal salvation. That man should be involved in the care of all souls, not only in the rites for his own ancestors, was a revolutionary thought in the history of Chinese religious expression. Somehow between the sparse accounts of the Han and Wei dynasty histories and the gathering of the first Taoist Canon before the death of Lu Hsiu-ching in 477,[72] a magnificent ritual of cosmic renewal (Chiao) and communal rites for the dead (Chai) were worked out in something like first draft form.[73] Through a combination of ancient court ritual from the *Book of Rites*,[74] Buddhist canons of merit and repentance as in the *Avalambana* (Chinese: *Yü-lan-p'en*), and the liturgies of the early Taoist popular movements, an esoteric ritual was created and universally accepted as basic to all Taoist orders by the end of the fifth and beginning of the sixth centuries. Three different expressions of these rituals were incorporated into the first Canon, called the *San-tung* or the *Three Arcana* by its compiler, Lu Hsiu-ching.[75]

The first of the arcana, the *Tung-chen Pu*, or the arcana of the realized immortal, supposedly evolved around a group of literati-mystics atop Mao Shan in the province of Kiangsu. The sect was called the Shang-ch'ing movement, that is, the Highest Pure order. Its organization was monastic in spirit and the first Taoist monasteries of the sect were established atop the several peaks of the Mao Shan range, which is near the modern city of Nanking in central China.[76] The second arcana, the *Tung-hsüan Pu*, arcana of the mysterious, derived from a variety of sources, including the classic rituals of the *Book of Rites* and the early Han dynasty *Wei* apocrypha. The collectanea, containing the varied Ling-pao scriptures, became the basis for the later magnificent liturgies of the *Tung-hsüan* section of the Canon. The third arcana, *Tung-shen Pu* (arcana of the spirits), became the repository for the *Three Emperors Writ* and the spirit-summoning methods on Fa-lu of the early Heavenly Master sect, among many other materials found in its pages. All Taoists were required to learn the Fa-lu and Ch'u-kuan rites for summoning spirits, a meditation used at the beginning of orthodox ritual from the formative period until the present. The formation of the canon is seen in the diagram opposite.[77]

Formation of the First Taoist Canon ***(chart drawn by Chuang)***

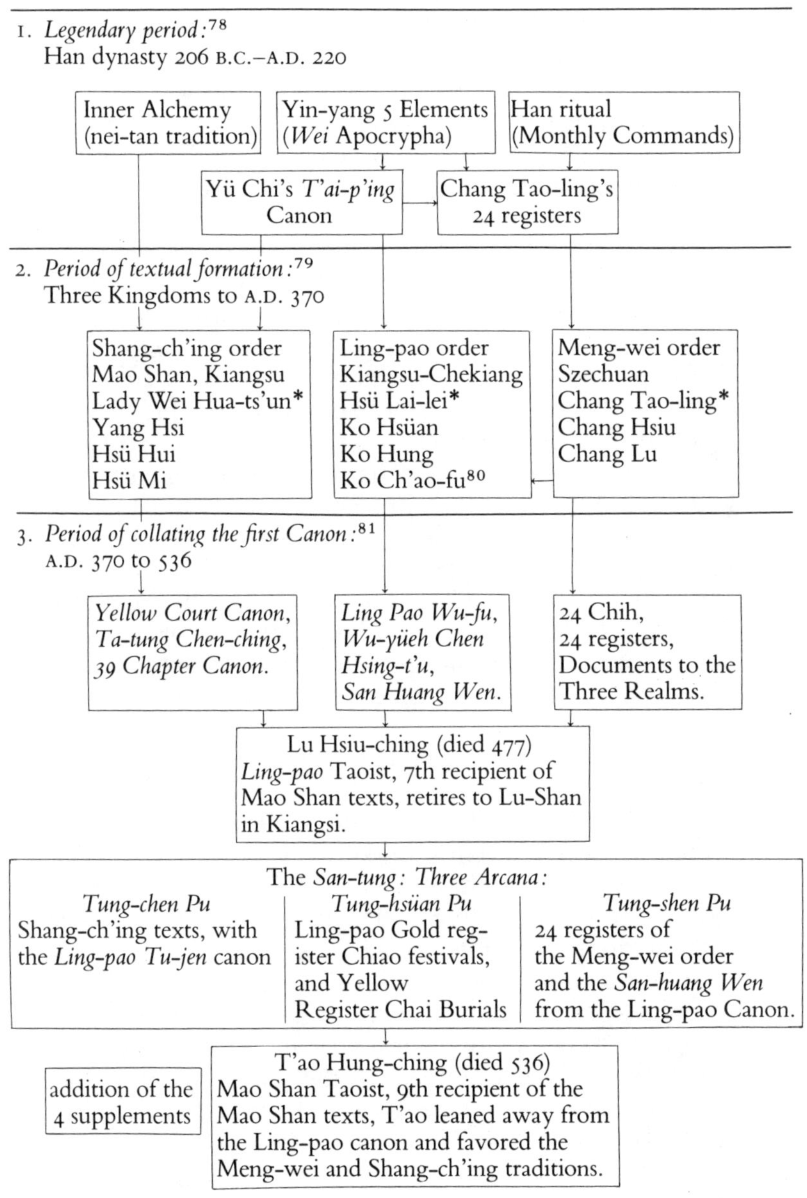

(*indicates a semi-legendary person)

Referring to the diagram, the three traditions are seen to flow almost as a single entity into the final form of the Canon. It is possible that the Shang-ch'ing sect through its semi-legendary lady founder may have been closely allied in its origins to the third Meng-wei tradition, as will be suggested in the following pages.[82] Furthermore, the basic rite of the Meng-wei tradition, the fa-lu, is used by all three traditions as an introduction to orthodox ritual.[83] The Taoist sects of the three formative centuries were thus separated more in space than in doctrine or practice.

The first of the traditions, the monastic Shang-ch'ing (Mao Shan) order has received by far the most attention from historians, undoubtedly because of the high social standing of the literati-scholars who were converts to its meditative practises. The Meng-wei tradition has received the least historical attention, and piecing together its earliest roots is indeed difficult. The tension between the refined scholar who practises inner alchemy for self-perfection and the demand of the masses for popular salvational liturgy runs like a major theme through the long history of Taoism. Until the Sui dynasty, an elite, scholarly tradition maintained itself above the popular vulgar masses.[84] But the development in the T'ang of a new Neo-confucian metaphysics, the secularism of the late Sung intellectual, and other historical developments eventually resulted in victory for the forces of popular, magical ritual, exorcism, burial, and festival. Whatever the status of Taoism in the minds of China's intellectuals today, from the second to the sixth centuries, it was a favorite topic in literate court circles.[85]

The Meng-wei tradition, for all the difficulties encountered by the scholar attempting to find traces of its existence in the writings of early historians, was firmly established by the beginning of the third century in the area of Han-chung, in Szech'uan. The twenty-four spiritual bishoprics of Chang Tao-ling, and the twenty-four "chapters" of the book revealed by spirits, appear in the earliest Canon as a series or register (Lu) of spirits' names and summons.[86] In order to perform ritual properly, the Taoist was required to memorize these spirits' appearance, clothing, secret names, and even the sort of perfume used on their apparel. In the performance of public ritual as well as in private meditation, the vision was to be formed in the mind of the adept with immense care that every detail of the garb, countenance, coiffure, and so forth, was complete and accurate. The secrets were passed on by word of mouth, or kept in the rare written record, lu, the register of the spirits. A special rite was used to send forth the spirits (ch'u-kuan) and a mandala-like meditation preceding it (fa-lu, lighting the incense burner) was performed at the beginning of all orthodox ritual.[87] The fa-lu is found in the earliest Taoist texts, and glosses attribute it to the teachings of Chang Tao-ling in Han-chung at the end of the Han dynasty.[88] The method of performing the fa-lu in the classic orthodox tradition tracing from the fourth and fifth centuries is taught by Master Chuang in chapter 4 below. Though Meng-wei Taoism was widespread enough to have influenced Wei Hua-ts'un, the lady founder of the Mao Shan Shang-ch'ing order, there are very few references to those who practiced it or spread its doctrines in the writings of the third to fifth centuries. Thus the oldest of the traditions of religious Taoism is the least represented in the Confucian annals of early religious Taoism, most probably because the literate class did not spread its doctrines.

The second of the great early traditions, the Ling-pao texts and scriptures, are also not as well attested in historical writings as are the works of the prestigious Shang-ch'ing founders.[89] One of the basic texts of the tradition, the *Ling-pao Five Talismans*, was (like the Fa-lu rite mentioned above) found in wide use among all early Taoist masters. One of the more popular rituals in which the five talismans are used, the so-called Su-ch'i, makes use of formulae found in the Monthly Commands chapters of the *Book of Rites* to renew and bless the cosmos. Though Ko Hung in his *Pao-p'u-tzu* mentions the *Ling-pao Five Talismans* as being efficacious charms to carry on the person as a defense against evil, he does not mention a liturgy such as the Su-ch'i, which uses them for a sort of cosmic renewal. Historians do record that Ko Hung's grand nephew Ko Ch'ao-fu multiplied the Ling-pao scriptures, forging texts and the like, in order to sell them for a profit.[90] It could be surmised that between the time of Ko Hung's writing and the gross profiteering of the grandnephew, a liturgy of renewal (the canonical Chiao Gold Registers of the Canon) had been created. But since Ko Hung does not mention Meng-wei rituals either, one must conclude that the eccentric scholar was more interested in the formulae of alchemy and macrobiotics than the content of liturgies performed for the vulgar masses. The very fact that forged copies of Ling-pao rituals could be sold supposes a fine market in the fourth century for popular liturgy. Lu Hsiu-ching, when compiling the first Canon in the fifth century, was careful to edit out the forgeries of Ko Ch'ao-fu,[91] which suggests that a detailed Ling-pao liturgy of sorts had been worked out by the end of the third century, even though Ko Hung does not mention it in his *Pao-p'u-tzu*. The Ling-pao liturgies are among the most detailed sections in the present Taoist Canon. Their composition can be conservatively assigned to the fifth century before Lu Hsiu-ching compiled the first Canon.

The third of the great Taoist traditions formulated before Lu Hsiu-ching's Canon is the Mao Shan Shang-ch'ing scriptures.[92] Where the historical origins of the Meng-wei registers and the Ling-pao scriptures are difficult to piece together, the Shang-ch'ing scriptures are clearly and accurately described from their fourth-century revelation to their sixth-century critical edition by the great scholar T'ao Hung-ching. The founding of the Shang-ch'ing (Highest Pure) Mao Shan sect is attributed to a woman, Wei Hua-ts'un (251–334).[93] She was the daughter of a literatus-scholar and the wife of an official. In her youth, she was given a classical education and was learned in Taoist texts, receiving the ordination of a libationer in the Meng-wei tradition. Married at twenty-four, she bore two sons, whom she took to the south of China to escape the wars of the times. After both sons had become officials, Wei Hua-ts'un turned to spiritual pursuits. She was visited by a host of immortals, who revealed to her the basic scriptures of the Shang-ch'ing tradition, including the *Yellow Court Canon*[94] and the *Ta-tung Chen-ching*. After her death, her eldest son passed on her teachings to a young official of the court of the eastern Chin dynasty, Yang Hsi.

In the second year of the Hsing-ning reign (Chin Ai-ti, A.D. 364) Yang Hsi began to have nocturnal visitations from the spirit of Wei Hua-ts'un, dead some thirty years.[95] The visions took place atop Mao Shan in Kiangsu province. The noble lady directed that two friends of Yang Hsi attend the seances as scribes—Hsü Mi, an army official, and his younger *relative* Hsü Hui. First acting as scribes, the two later received visions themselves and became Taoist adepts. A host of Taoist immortals came with Wei Hua-ts'un and joined in dictating the revelations that had originally been given to the libationer during her earthly life. It is not difficult to understand the need for supernatural authority to support the strange new books and methods that Yang Hsi had received from Wei Hua-ts'un's eldest son. The nocturnal visions can be taken either as true trance possessions, in which Yang-Hsi acted as a medium, or as dictations of texts memorized by Yang Hsi and chanted during the rituals of meditative alchemy. If it were true that the visions of Yang Hsi and his colleagues were mediumistic possessions, then the roots of Mao Shan would have to be seen as a form of lowly, even heterodox, popular religion.[96] The same must be said for the theory that Yang Hsi's dictations took the form of the planchette spirit-writing seance. In such a seance, the demon was thought to possess a small chair with a pen attached to one leg; as the scribes hold the possessed chair, the spirit was thought to occupy the seat and cause the leg of the chair to inscribe characters on a piece of paper or in a box of sand held under the moving instrument.

The very literary style of Yang Hsi's writings, and the excellent penmanship of the two Hsüs, seem to argue against the medium possession theory. T'ao Hung-ching was able to identify the handwriting of Yang and the Hsüs a century and a half later by the fine calligraphy and the excellent literary composition. The revelations of Wei Hua-ts'un must be placed with the orthodox classical tradition of Taoist ritual meditation. The appearance of the spirits, the minute descriptions of their clothes, their words, and even the composition of the texts already reported by Ko Hung in the *Pao-p'u-tzu* argue for the orthodoxy of Yang Hsi's visions. The basic *Huang-t'ing Wai-ching* (the appendix to the *Yellow Court Canon*), which now appears as the earlier of Yellow Court texts, is in fact directions for elite meditations of inner alchemy. The *Huang-t'ing Nei-ching*, or the new revelations of the *Yellow Court Canon* attributed to Wei Hua-ts'un, is in fact a register or Lu naming and describing a new list of spirits proper to the Shang-ch'ing sect and its ritual meditations. The Mao Shan monastic sect was in its beginnings an order founded for and by the highest literati class in the courts of the southern kingdoms. The Yang and Hsü revelations became the center of interest of an elite court society.[97]

News of the revelations atop Mao Shan soon spread widely in the kingdoms of south China. The original writings of Yang and the two Hsüs were borrowed, copied, forged, and stolen by various interests among the literate elite families. After a lengthy search for the lost documents, T'ao Hung-ching (456–536) was able to piece together from hearsay as well as fragmentary documentation the odyssey of the Shang-ch'ing texts. A critical edition of the fragments was published in the *Chen Kao*, a work still appearing in the Taoist Canon.[98] In chapter nineteen of the work, the following almost humorous account is recorded of high society's attitude toward the texts and T'ao Hung-ch'ing's recovery of the lost documents.

After the death of Hsü Hui in 370 and the approaching demise of Hsü Mi (376), the written records of Yang Hsi's visions were entrusted to Hsü Mi's seventeen-year-old son, Hsü Huang-min. Since the transmission of documents was enough to constitute a Taoist adept, it was thought that Hsü Huang-min would follow his father and uncle and put into practice the esoteric teachings of the new revelations. But Hsü Huang-min proved inept as leader and propagator of the new sect. The beautiful calligraphy of his father and uncle and Yang Hsi, contained in trunks full of written scrolls inherited from his father, were soon dispersed throughout the kingdoms of south China. Hsü Huang-min, frightened by the wars of the time, moved away from Mao Shan to a district called Shan in Chekiang province. There his grandfather and his uncle Hsü Mai had been highly respected public officials. Hsü went to live with two pious laymen, Ma Lang and his cousin Ma Han, who had been friends of his grandfather. Ma Lang was especially delighted that the young Hsü had brought along the valuable manuscripts containing the revelations. He took charge of the trunks and tried to keep the precious contents in good condition.

The Ma family was soon importuned, however, by callers from the literati-official class of the region, who came inquiring about the famous documents. Unfortunately, Hsü Huang-min gave or loaned the scrolls indiscriminately to all callers, thus causing great concern to the Ma brothers. Some who borrowed the books did not care for them with proper respect and dignity and soon died. When he attempted to read one of the books, a certain Wang Ch'ing saw fire come down from heaven and destroy it.[99] In a gloss of the *Chen Kao*, T'ao Hung-ching relates that the unworthy who received the Shang-ch'ing scriptures without proper instructions and rites of transmission were punished by the heavens. The revelations of Yang and the two Hsüs were not meant for popular dissemination.[100]

There also came a refined scholar named Wang Ling-ch'i to the home of Ma Lang and begged Hsü Huang-min to allow him to have copies of the scriptures.[101] Hsü refused but Wang Ling-ch'i waited outside Ma Lang's home in the snow until Hsü relented. It must be remembered that the Ling-pao scriptures, the books of macrobiotic diets and the alchemical formulae for "instant longevity" were very popular from the north-south period through the Sui into the T'ang dynasty. The demand for macrobiotic manuals in particular offered a ready fortune for the adept who could produce the latest book on Taoist hygiene or Taoist magic. The motives of Wang Ling-ch'i were not purely spiritual. Taking the prized manuals home, Wang was disappointed to discover that the Shang-ch'ing doctrines were lofty and difficult to follow. The meditations, the high literary style, and the complicated ascesis would not find easy acceptance in the ritual-loving world of Ling-pao scripture patrons. Wang therefore took note of the titles that Wei Hua-ts'un had promised to divulge at a later date and forged his own versions of these works, announcing that they had been revealed to himself in a vision. Hsü Huang-min was completely taken in by the forgeries. Ma Lang at first planned to purchase the new books of revelations, but in a dream saw a jade bowl fall from the heavens and shatter. From this he understood that heaven had not after all revealed the new books and called off the transaction.[102]

Hsü Huang-min then left the residence of Ma Lang to live with the Tu family in the distant city, Ch'ien-t'ang. He left behind the trunks of precious documents, now somewhat depleted, with strict orders to Ma Lang that no one was to open them or give any more of the documents away. Not even if a letter came from Hsü Huang-min himself was Ma Lang to open or remove a box. A few months later, Hsü Huang-min fell ill and sent a letter to Ma Lang asking that the trunks be sent to him at the Tu residence. Obedient to the earlier orders, Ma refused to let the boxes out of his house. Hsü's sickness worsened, and he died in 429.[103]

The pious Ma Lang, meanwhile, refused to let the Shang-ch'ing scriptures be taken out of their protective trunks. He appointed two elderly custodians to guard the door of the room where the treasures were kept, burn incense, and sweep the floor. The fortunes of the Ma family increased a hundredfold, because of the care and devotion with which he guarded the scriptures. As Ma Lang approached old age, he decided to have accurate copies of the texts made, lest they be lost to the ravages of time. A fine calligrapher and one-time friend of the family, Ho Tao-ching, was hired. The temptation of the prized texts proved too much for Ho, who sold many of the best copies to the public, gave transcriptions to his friends and disciples, and even substituted some of his own copies for the originals. Ma Lang discovered the treachery and was furious. More devastating than the thievery was the scandalous conduct of Ho Tao-ching, who had given copies of the sacred documents to two of his women followers. He was rumored actually to practise the vulgar fang-chung sexual techniques, a means to lōngevity specifically forbidden in the revelations of Wei Hua-ts'un. Outraged, Ma Lang dismissed the scribe and had molten copper poured over the locks of the trunks so that they could no longer be opened.[104]

The actions of Ho Tao-ching were ruinous to the pious

work of Ma Lang. Copies of Ho's manuals reached the court and an official named Lou Hui-ming went to the Ma household to claim the prized collection. When Ma refused to break the seals, Lou memorialized the court of Sung Wen-ti and in the year 465 had the trunks brought to the capital. On the way, the Shang-ch'ing scriptures were once more rifled. Lou Hui-ming opened the trunks and removed some of the contents. Thus the depleted collection of spiritual revelations finally came to light officially, where they were first examined by the court Taoists and then, on the recommendation of the emperor, turned over to Lu Hsiu-ching, who incorporated them in the first Canon and transmitted them to his successor Sun Yu-yüeh.[105]

T'ao Hung-ching, who, as Sun Yu-yüeh's successor laboriously collected the scattered documents from the literati who had avidly gathered them, noted that a great number of those involved in collecting the precious manuscripts were themselves Taoists.[106] Thus Lou Hui-ming and Shu Chi-chen, men employed by the Sung court, were accomplished Taoist masters. Lu Hsiu-ching and T'ao Hung-ching himself received imperial patronage. By the efforts of scholars like Lu and T'ao, the Taoist scriptures were collected, critically edited, and preserved as a canon.

The following scholars were directly involved in the transmission of the Shang-ch'ing scriptures:[107]

Wei Hua-ts'un	(252–334)
Yang Hsi	(330–387)
Hsü Mi	(305–376)
Hsü Hui	(died 370)
Hsü Huang-shih	(361–429)
Ma Lang	
Ma Han	
Lu Hsiu-ching	(died 471)
Sun Yu-yüeh	
T'ao Hung-ching	(456–536)

T'ao Hung-ching was able to piece together the original fragments of the Mao Shan revelations by identifying the beautiful handwriting of Yang and the two Hsüs and rejecting the forgeries of Wang Ling-ch'i. The fragments were put together in the *Chen-kao*, a scholarly presentation by T'ao the literatus for the elite society of the early sixth century. In his Chao-t'ai pavilion atop Mao Shan, T'ao Hung-ching lived the life of a renowned master. The three-story Chao-t'ai was a gathering place where T'ao ruled like a despot from the top floor, over a crowd of copyists and disciples on the middle floor, who in turn cared for the guest rooms and distinguished visitors on the ground floor of the grand residence.

The personality and influence on Taoism of the two great masters, Lu Hsiu-ching and T'ao Hung-ching, were entirely different. Lu Hsiu-ching was a master of the Ling-pao tradition, which he had received through Ko Hsüan and Ko Hung. He was also familiar with the Meng-wei registers, or the teachings of the three first Heavenly Masters, Chang Tao-ling, Chang Heng, and Chang Lu. Lu Hsiu-ching was an organizer and a synthesizer. It is most probable that by his time the liturgies of the Ling-pao tradition had been combined with the rites of spirit-summoning and spiritual memorials of the Meng-wei Heavenly Master tradition into a prototype of the chiao. Though Lu Hsiu-ching recognized the value of the Mao Shan revelations and accorded them the highest place in the canon of the *Three Arcana*, he came to them through the ministries of Sung Wen-ti and not by a previous conversion or dedication to the Mao Shan scriptures as such.[108]

T'ao Hung-ching, on the other hand, was a perspicacious man. He despised the loud and vulgar Ling-pao rites and did not hesitate to discourage their practice on Mao Shan.[109] Rightfully, he saw the degrading potential of the popularizing tendency in the Taoist movements; the popular rites were beneath the interests of the scholar who was the elite of China's ruling classes. The Shang-ch'ing scriptures, however, were the supreme Taoist teachings. T'ao, who had been a Buddhist, ranked the Shang-ch'ing revelations beside the *Lotus Sutra* and the *Chuang-tzu*. They were the Sarvayana (all in one vehicle); he thought of the three revelations as one doctrine revealing the highest of all causes.[110] To preserve itself in the religious conflicts of the north-south period, Taoism must remain the prerogative of the highest social classes. As history soon proved, the emphasis on the nonintellectual aspects of Taoism, an emphasis that the court preferred to the elite meditations of the scholarly hermit, was to result in its rejection by many literati.

The influence of T'ao Hung-ching on orthodox classical Taoist ritual is still deeply felt today. It was in the first chapter of his compilation, *Teng-chen Yin-chüeh*, that T'ao's opinions had an especially deep effect on future masters. More than in the practises of macrobiotic or chemical alchemy, T'ao Hung-ching taught as part of the Mao Shan tradition that the very act of ritual meditation, in which the spirits are summoned forth from the body and the very center of the microcosm emptied, was a workable method for finding immortality and longevity.[111] Thus, by carrying the doctrine of the *Yellow Court Canon* to its conclusion, T'ao put the final touch on the formation of the orthodox ritual practice. The meditations through which the Taoist purified his body and emptied even the spirits of the highest heavens, the meditations that prepared the microcosm for the encounter with the transcendent Tao—these gave efficacy to ritual and direction to the pursuit of immortality. Thus meditative alchemy was given a visible expression in liturgy, and liturgy in turn derived its power from the meditations that established the contact of the Taoist with the purest powers and forces of the ultimate heavens. The Ling-pao rites of the vulgar masses were an empty shell, a chanting of verses and ringing of bells. Orthodox ritual was a thing of power and beauty, expressing the very depths of the Taoist's meditations.[112]

4. GREAT TAOIST MASTERS (of the Sui and T'ang Periods A.D. 581–905) *(Taoists spoken of by Chuang)*

The teachings of T'ao, though preserved in the orthodox monastic rituals of the traditional classic orders, were superseded by his successor the tenth master of Mao Shan, Wang Yüan-chih.[113] This honored master, who lived through two complete cycles of sixty years to reach an incredible age of more than one hundred and twenty, was only eleven when T'ao Hung-ching died. He was instructed in Taoism by Tsang Ching, who unfortunately chose to train him in the *T'ai-p'ing Ching* and the popular chiao liturgies deriving from the Ling-pao tradition. Though he obviously knew the elite meditations of the Mao Shan Shang-ching sect, Wang chose to emphasize the liturgical tradition. The fame of Wang's liturgies spread throughout the Sui empire, and in 611 Wang met Sui Yang-ti, the second Sui dynasty emperor, who ordered him to perform a Ling-pao Chiao ritual atop the famous central peak, Sung Shan. Subsequently an official Taoist temple, Yü-ch'ing Hsüan-t'an, was constructed at the court in Loyang, and Wang was appointed its Master. He lived well into the T'ang period and died finally in 635, the ninth year of the Chen-kuan reign.[114]

During the lifetime of Wang the emphasis on public ritual superseded the elite ritual meditations of T'ao Hung-ching. The delight of the court in Wang's fancy Ling-pao rituals of renewal only echoed the popular Taoist movements which grew and expanded during the T'ang and the Sung. Ling-pao rites were patronized by China's village and urban masses, as well as by the nonintellectual imperial court. One can almost see the disapproving stares of the Confucian literati, opposing both the fascination of the emperors and the enthusiasm of the people for Taoism's great dramatic liturgies. The development of popular religious expression and the patronage of T'ang and Sung emperors contributed to Taoism's intellectual decline.[115]

If the preceding accounts of religious Taoism seem overly detailed, one need look no further than the Taoist Canon to grasp the importance given to the founding of the Mao Shan tradition. Much more attention is given to Mao Shan in its intellectual foundations than to the other forms of religious Taoist expression. In contrast, the summary outline of Taoism which follows is sparse; the material is relatively unstudied either in Chinese or other sources. The history of Taoism during the T'ang dynasty was that of a handful of great Taoist masters and a unique doctrinal ecumenism, all of which brought the urban and mountain centers together in a sense of camaraderie. The three arcana became the common possession of all Taoists. The Lu or registers of the various centers were shared and incorporated as a part of the Canon.

Three great masters whose names figure prominently in the Canon typify Taoism during the T'ang dynasty. The first, discussed here in this chapter, is the twelfth Mao Shan master, Szu-ma Ch'eng-chen (646–735), the descendant of a noble family. His biography appears in the T'ang dynasty official histories as well as in the Canon.[116] Six of his works appear in the Ming dynasty Taoist Canon, and chapter 924 of *The Complete Works of the T'ang* (*Ch'uan T'ang-wen*) is dedicated to his writings.[117] In that chapter a fine summary of the Shang-ch'ing Mao Shan teachings is found, in a discussion of the *Chuang-tzu* and its use in ritual meditation. According to Szu-ma Ch'eng-chen, the heart is to be emptied by meditation, for "only the heart which has been emptied can be the dwelling place for the Tao."[118] The doctrine is applied to the Ling-pao scriptures, that is, the exteriorizing of the spirits performed in Meng-wei and Ling-pao rituals are seen as preparations for uniting the Taoist with the Tao of the Wu-wei, that is, "nonact," or "transcendent act."

Some of the more startling occurrences in Taoism both before and after the T'ang period were the frequent and lengthy journeys of the masters. As if the powers of spiritual meditation conferred the ability to walk great distances with no effort, Szu-ma Ch'eng-chen is seen to be master of the central peak, Sung Shan; the southern peak, Heng Shan; the great Buddhist-Taoist center, Mount T'ien-t'ai in Chekiang; and his own home, Wang-shih Shan. He was an expert in Cheng-i orthodox Taoism, as well as in Mao Shan and Ling-pao Taoism. The two lesser forms of Pole Star magic and Thunder Magic were said by later writers to be part of his repertoire.[119] The Emperor Hsüan-tsung became a patron of Szu-ma Ch'eng-chen's Taoist arts and received the registers of the three Taoist orders (that is to say, a Taoist ordination) in A.D. 721.[120]

The second great Taoist of the T'ang period, whose works were ecumenical and to whom texts in the Canon are credited, was Chang Wan-fu (active ca. 712).[121] The extant writings of Chang Wan-fu show a clear continuity between the three original movements of the early north-south period and the Taoist unity of the T'ang. Volume 990 of the Canon contains a complete list of the registers and the times for transmitting them to the Taoist novice.[122] Chang, like his predecessors, unites all three of the orders—Meng-wei, Ling-pao, and Shang-ch'ing—into a single body of revealed doctrine. The young Taoist, beginning with the basic twenty-four Meng-wei registers, receives the *San-huang Wen*, the *Precious Ho-t'u Register*, the Chieh precepts and Chang documents of the *San-tung* (*Three Arcana*), the *Lao-tzu Tao-te Ching*, the *Ling-pao Five Talismans*, and the teachings of the Mao Shan Shang-ch'ing sect.[123] Chang

Wan-fu thus presents Taoism of the T'ang dynasty as an ecumenical union of monastic centers and great masters.[124]

The third great master of the T'ang period was the renowned Tu Kuang-t'ing A.D. 842–926). A favorite of both emperors and mandarins, Tu Kuang-t'ing is credited with having composed or contributed to twenty-eight works in the Canon.[125] A collection of his writings for the court are contained in *the Complete Works of the T'ang*.[126] As the last great master before the sectarian movements of the Sung dynasty, Tu Kuang-t'ing towers above his contemporaries and later generations as a scholar who commanded a view of the totality of religious Taoism. Tu left behind a grand summary of the unified system he envisioned in a number of important works in the Canon. In the *T'ai-shang Cheng-i Yüeh-lu Yi* (*T'ai-shang Ritual for Transmitting the Taoist Registers*), the orthodox traditional forms of religious meditation and ritual are clearly listed:[127]

1. The introductory ritual is given in the first section of the chapter. Tu Kuang-t'ing describes the classical, orthodox manner of initiating ritual (outlined by Master Chuang in chapter 5 below)—the solemn entrance of the Taoist into the sacred temple area, the offering of incense, the beginning of the meditation, the sounding of the drum, and the emptying of the microcosm in preparation for union with the Tao (See chapter 5, part 6, below).

2. The main body of the rite contains the registers of the classical orders. Tu Kuang-t'ing lists the twenty-four registers of the Cheng-i Meng-wei sect, the *Ho-t'u* registers, the Pole Star registers of military or exorcistic Taoism, the Liu Chia spirits (chapter 4) but does not yet mention the Thunder Magic sects, which developed in the Sung dynasty.[128]

3. The rite closes with the Taoist restoring the spirits to their places inside the microcosm, from whence they had been sent forth before the meditation of union with the Tao.

In a second work, which follows shortly after the rite for transmitting the registers of an orthodox Taoist, Tu Kuang-t'ing describes the ritual of the *Ho-t'u*, the magic chart used by Yü the Great to control the floods.[129] The *Ho-t'u* ritual differs in one important aspect from the earlier Yüeh-Lu liturgy. The rite for transmitting the Lu registers was meant for the Taoist priest alone and therefore was filled with esoteric meditations and allusions to union with the transcendent Tao. The ritual of the *Ho-t'u*, on the other hand, was meant to alleviate the sufferings of the common folk of village and countryside. Tu Kuang-t'ing begins by enumerating the uses of the *Ho-t'u* ritual. It is to control natural disasters, bring thunder and lightning under the Taoist's control, stop warring armies, and the like. The preparation of the Taoist altar is splendidly described: lanterns are set up representing the four directions, the eight trigrams, and the twenty-eight constellations. After the model of the *Ling-pao Five Talismans*, but in a much more complicated mandala, the entire cosmos is symbolically represented in scrolls, hangings, food offerings, and lanterns. With the altar arrayed, the ritual is performed according to the classical model outlined in the preceding paragraph and described more fully in chapter 5 below.[130]

With Tu Kuang-t'ing, the classical period of Taoist ecumenism and unity came to an end. During the following five dynasties and the Sung period, sectarianism and reformation threatened the structural unity of religious Taoism. But before the Sung dynasty revolution in Taoist orders, the seeds of change could be seen in the writings of some of the T'ang masters. This brief overview of the T'ang must include three of these precursors of change to indicate the direction from which growth was to come. Of the three masters, Li Ch'un-feng, an historical personage and early T'ang court Taoist, is easily identified in the Canon. Wang Tzu-hua and Tsu Shu-yüan, on the other hand, are almost legendary figures and their existence was hardly mentioned in historical writings before later Sung times. The sources of change, however, are clearly identifiable in the thunder ritual which was to become popular in the Sung period. Both the austere Ch'an (Zen) teachings and the tantric Buddhist sects, this latter with their colorful rituals, mudras, and mantric charms, were taken as the basis for many of the liturgical reforms in the Sung dynasty Taoist canon.[131]

Li Ch'un-feng was a Mao Shan Taoist who was active at the beginning of the T'ang period, about A.D. 632. Two works in the Taoist Canon are attributed to him, both of which describe the use of left-handed mudras, pseudo-Sanskrit mantras, and thunder magic to control and exorcise evil spirits.[132] The magic Pole Star rituals are highly developed in Li's two works, and the paraphernalia used in later Sung dynasty Thunder Magic are described in rudimentary form.[133] The style of magic described by Li is later developed into a distinct set of rituals associated with the Ch'ing-wei Thunder Magic sect.[134] Ch'ing-wei thunder magic is an essential part of the teachings of Master Chuang, and is described in chapter 6 below.[135]

The semi-legendary Wang Tzu-hua was born in 714 and died in 789. He resided on Heng Shan, a southern peak in Hunan province where he practised meditative ritual and allegedly developed a style of thunder rite called Ch'ing-ching magic.[136] The rituals of Wang were developed under the influence of the great Szu-ma Ch'eng-chen, and were supposedly influential throughout southeast China. His brand of Thunder Magic is mentioned by famous Sung dynasty masters such as Wang Wen-ch'ing and Po Yü-ch'an.[137]

Tsu Shu is a legendary figure active towards the end of the T'ang dynasty, Ca. A.D. 880. (note 138). Known in some traditions as a woman, s/he is said to have been born in Yung-chou, Kwangsi, to have had long black hair and a dark complexion, becoming an immortal at age 132 years. All of the Taoist schools credit her/him with founding the Ch'ing-wei (Qingwei) Tantric Vajra (Thunder magic) school of Taoism. S/he traveled extensively throughout China, to the city of Ch'ang-an, and the sacred mountain of the west, Hua Shan (note 139). The Ch'uan-chen (Quanzhen) Taoist Min Zhiting, who is a descendent of Zhengyi Taoists from Weibao Shan in Jizu Shan in Yunnan, teaches that she founded a form of Thunder ritual different from that of the Shenxiao school attributed to Wang Tzu-hua, and Lin Lingsu.

Whereas the Cheng-i (Zhengyi) and other Taoists of the "Three Mountains" (Lunghu Shan, Mao Shan, and Gozao Shan) schools use Thunder rites throughout the Chiao and Chai (Jiao, Jai) liturgies, Ch'uan-chen (Quanzhen) Taoists have an especially ornate rite used at the beginning of the P'u-to (Pudu) ceremony for "freeing all souls" which Min Zhiting claims differs from the Zhengyi (Chuang's) tradition.

5. THE AGE OF SECTARIAN DIVISION (The Sung and Yüan [Mongol] periods, A.D. 960–1341)

Historians agree that the Sung dynasty was a period of great intellectual and organizational change for China. Some historians even name the Sung dynasty as the beginning of China's modern period.[140] The great Japanese scholar Noritada Kubo, whose book *Chugoku no Shukyo Kaikaku* (*China's Religious Reformation*) is the classic work on Ch'üan-chen Taoism, compares Taoist sectarianism of the Sung with the Protestant Reformation in sixteenth- and seventeenth-century Europe.[141] The comparison is apt: the divisions in religious Taoism exceeded in sectarian quantity, if not in the fury of doctrinal debate, the protestant revolt in the west. Taoist sectarianism, although multiplied throughout the length and breadth of China so that each province and county had its own variety of Taoist expert, was not marked by the intensity of rivalry found in Europe.

Taoist rivalry, as will be seen in the teachings of Master Chuang, was limited to functional rather than doctrinal differences. That is, the disputes of the Taoist masters of the Sung and later times were not concerned with the basic doctrines of the Yin-yang Five Element cosmology, the Three Pure Ones, the Five Emperors, or the other common teachings of Taoist belief. Instead, the masters of the traditional orders opposed the use of ritual for harmful magic, the performance of liturgy purely for pecuniary gain and to the detriment of meditation, and the trend towards heterodoxy or popular sectarianism that brought down the wrath of the mandarin and the court on the heads of the beleaguered Taoists. Though Sung and Yüan Taoists may have argued about the proper color to be envisioned during a ritual meditation,[142] they presented a unified front when faced with outside opposition, whether Buddhist, mandarin, or imperial. Sectarianism therefore was exemplified by different forms of monastic living, the introduction of many new kinds of popular rituals, and a trend towards multiplying local and provincial level fraternities of Taoist brethren.[143]

The two greatest orders of the Sung dynasty were the Ch'üan-chen sect in north China and the Cheng-i or Heavenly Master sect in the south. The Ch'üan-chen sect represents the Taoist response to the influence of Ch'an or Zen Buddhism in China. Like the Ch'an monasteries of China, Ch'üan-chen Taoists aimed for a rigorous life of simple monastic discipline.[144] Like the Ch'an or Zen sect in both China and Japan, they eventually turned to the performance of popular ritual as a means of gaining support.[145] The Cheng-i sect, the successors of the first Heavenly Master at the end of the Han dynasty, experienced a renewal during the Sung period and became the court-sanctioned leaders of religious Taoism throughout south China. The hegemony of Cheng-i Taoism in liturgical matters continues to the present day.[146]

The founding of the Ch'üan-chen sect is attributed to Wang Chung-yang, who was born in 1113 in Ta-wei village, Hsien-yang county, Shensi province. The first monastery of the order was probably established in the Shantung province, the district of Ninghai.[147] The monastic headquarters of the order was later established in Pai-yün Kuan, Peking, where it is still maintained to the present day. Wang stressed Confucian and Buddhist doctrines as well as the texts of inner alchemy and self-perfection of religious Taoism. The Confucian *Canon of Filial Piety*, the *Lao-tzu Tao-te Ching*, the Buddhist *Pan-juo Hsin-ching* (*Prajña Pāramitā Hrdaya Sūtra*), and the *Ch'ang-ch'ing Ching* canon of religious Taoism were used by the order.[148] The influence of Buddhism on the Ch'üan-chen masters can be seen from the secondary title of the sect, Golden Lotus Orthodox Religion, (Chin-lien Cheng-tsung). The Ch'üan-chen sect was the parent organization for many later Taoist groups, including the Lung-men and Sui Shan sects of the north and the southern branch of Ch'üan chen Taoism founded by Chang Tz'u-yang.[149]

Other noted sects of the Sung period were the Chen-ta group of Liu Te-jen, the T'ai-i order of Hsiao Pao-ch'en, and the Ch'ing-ming sect of Ho Chen-kung. All three were flourishing at the beginning of the southern Sung period, between 1138 and 1140.[150] The last of the three, the *Ch'ing-ming* sect, claimed to originate from a third-century Taoist master named Hsü Hsun. Hsü Hsun was made to be one of the legendary founders of Thunder Magic and devotion to him was established at the court of the emperor Hui-tsung by 1112.[151] By far the most popular form of new magic during the Sung period was the prestigious thunder ritual, which was propagated by a number of noted Taoists and Taoist sects. Though historians have not yet established which of the thunder sects appeared earliest, it is certain that the patronage of Taoists by the emperor Hui-tsung encouraged the spread of the new form of magic.

In 1116 the Thunder Magic sect of Teng Yu-kung was introduced to the court of Hui-tsung, through the presentation of a systematic manual called *The Secret Method for Assisting the Nation and Saving the People.*[152] Teng called his sect the T'ien-hsin Cheng-fa and derived many of his teachings from the Cheng-i Heavenly Master.[153] The new doctrines of Teng were centered on the use of Five Thunder magic, that is, the power of thunder seen as a moving agent for the five elements. The sect used mudras and mantras modeled after the esoteric Buddhist orders, similar to those found in the later esoteric Buddhist sects of T'ien-t'ai (Japanese Tendai) and Chen-yen (Japanese Shingon) Buddhism. The use of pseudo-Sanskrit words, as foreshadowed in the writings of the T'ang master Li Hsiang-feng, and the various thunder mudras are clearly seen in the extant works of the *T'ien-hsin Cheng-fa* found in the Canon.[154] Some of the teachings of Teng will be found repeated by Master Chuang in chapter 6 below.

In 1117 the famous Taoist master Lin Ling-su was introduced to the court of Hui-tsung. Born in Yung-chia, Wen-chow district in southern Cheking, a step over from Fukien province where his doctrines were to become so popular, Lin Ling-su is credited with being a great propagator of Shen-hsiao style Thunder Magic in the Sung dynasty. So powerful a personality was Lin that he was given free access to the emperor, and his Shen-hsiao magic was awarded imperial patronage. The sect was given brief mention in the Sung dynasty official history, under the biography of Lin Ling-su.[155] Furthermore, a lengthy biography of Lin is found in *The Mirror of Perfected Immortals,* a Ming dynasty hagiography of famous Taoists. But Lin is given credit for none of the writings in the present Canon, although his biography mentions books he allegedly had written.[156] The Shen-hsiao order was destined to be the only Taoist sect that proved controversial to the Taoist masters themselves.

The Sung dynasty orthodox masters, as well as Master Chuang in the present, are somewhat ambivalent toward the Shen-hsiao order. One reason is that the Shen-hsiao masters are not consistent in their manner of performing meditation. Sometimes the orthodox colors are switched or new versions created without reference to the canonical tradition of the past.[157] At other times the Shen-hsiao Taoists perform ritual without regard for inner alchemy or any form of meditation.[158] Doubly reprehensible is the fact that the lower ranking local masters perform the stately Chiao and Chai liturgies with no real knowledge of the proper rites or of the true content of the ritual.[159] Such is often the case in modern Taiwan, where pecuniary motives have destroyed the spirit of generosity as well as devaluing the rubrical perfection in performing ritual that was typical of the Taoist sage in the past. Finally and perhaps worst of all from the orthodox Taoist's viewpoint, Shen-hsiao Taoists were and are sometimes accused of performing black magic. This last is true not only of Shen-hsiao Taoists but of Mao Shan and some other local orders as well.[160] In making such accusations, however, the critic immediately must add that there were many great Taoists of the Shen-hsiao order who have won the respect of all of their Taoist brethren.

Perhaps the most influential Taoist master of the southern Sung dynasty (1127–1278) was the gifted scholar, Pai Yü-ch'an.[161] Born on Hainan island of a literati family originally from Fukien province, Pai is credited with fifteen works in the Taoist Canon and is respected as one of the greatest masters of religious Taoism. A man of ecumenical breadth, Pai brought together the various sects and movements of his time and was considered the leader of Taoism in south China.[162] Among the many titles given to him are Propagator of Military Taoism, "Propagator of Shen-hsiao Taoism, and Master of Inner Alchemy." It is clear from his writings that he sought to give legitimacy to the Shen-hsiao rituals that were popular throughout his native Fukien province.[163] In a massive compendium of Thunder Magic literature, compiled from the writings of noted Taoist experts including Pai himself, are to be found a list of the various Thunder Magic sects of the Sung:[164]

1. Sanskrit Primordial Breath Thunder Sects (Ch'ing-wei sect)[165]
    a. Tung-chen (Mao Shan) Hun-t'un Thunder sect.
    b. Ch'ing-wei (Hua Shan and Fukien) Thunder sect.
    c. Ling-pao sect Thunder Magic, etc.
2. Ch'ing-hsü Thunder Magic, used by the T'ai-i sect.[166]
3. Shen-hsiao Thunder Magic, attributed to Wang Wen-ch'ing (born 1093),[167] friend of Lin Ling-su.
4. Yü-fu Thunder Magic, Cheng-i Heavenly Master sect.[168]
5. Pei-chi Pole Star Thunder Magic, Pole Star sect.[169]

Perhaps the most significant fact about the various kinds of Thunder Magic is the distinctive Lu that typifies each sect. Thus, the Mao Shan–related Ch'ing-wei sect uses a specific Lu, or register of spirits' names, and a style of pseudo-Sanskrit peculiar to its own order. The other sects were distinguishable from the Ch'ing-wei order by their own style of ritual as well as by their list of spirits summoned to perform Thunder Magic. The writer of the above list in the *Tao-fa Hui-yüan* suggests that there were many Taoists who used evil spirits and black magic, betraying the very purpose of Taoist ritual, which was meant to help and not to harm the people.[170]

The role of Pai Yü-ch'an was that of unifier and religious leader in the southern Sung period. The famous Ling-pao Taoist, Chin Yun-chung, a contemporary of

Pai, wrote against the Shen-hsiao order and against some forms of Thunder Magic in his *Shang-ch'ing Ling-pao Ta-fa*.[171] Because of the efforts of Pai and his disciples, the criticisms of Master Chin were no longer valid. Shen-hsiao Taoism became respectable. Since the various styles of Thunder Magic will be more fully described by Master Chuang in chapter 6, it is sufficient here to point out the complexity of Taoist movements in the late Sung and Yüan period and the need of historical scholarship to be nonpartisan as it traces development of Sung sectarianism. Pai Yü-ch'an sought to eradicate from Shen-hsiao Taoism the elements that brought criticism from his fellow Taoists. As a result he was given the honorific title, "Propagator of Shen-hsiao Taoism" (see note 163). It is interesting to note, however, that in signing his official Taoist statements, Pai Yü-ch'an did not use a Shen-hsiao rank but an orthodox Mao Shan Heavenly Master and Pole Star title.[172] The trend to learn as many registers as possible and to use the more prestigious in signing ritual documents can be seen in the southern Sung and the Yüan period. Taoists began to be ranked according to the number of registers that they could master.[173]

6. POLARIZATION AND POLITICAL DECLINE (Ming dynasty, A.D. 1638 to the present)

The Ming dynasty was noted from the beginning for its patronage of religious Taoism. The trends begun in the Sung period were confirmed and consolidated during the Ming. The present Taoist Canon was commissioned and completed by 1447, under the reign of the emperor Cheng-t'ung.[174] The trend toward sectarianism was brought under control by decree of the court. Three monastic centers in south China—Mao Shan in Kiangsu province, Lung-hu Shan, and Ko-tsao Shan in Kiangsi province—were given authority to grant licenses of ordination, without which the local Taoist masters were supposedly not permitted to practise. A manual called

Tao-chiao Yüan-liu, which is found in the libraries of Master Chuang and almost all Taiwan Taoists, explains how the licenses of ordination are given.[175] The heavenly masters of the three mountains were empowered by imperial authority to grant licenses of ordination in the following styles of ritual:

1. The Yü-ching or Mao Shan Shang-ch'ing style of meditative ritual.
2. The Ch'ing-wei or T'ien-shu style of Thunder Magic.
3. The Pei-chi or Pole Star style of military exorcism.
4. The Yü-fu or Cheng-i style of orthodox Chiao and Chai ritual.[176]
5. The Shen-hsiao style of popular ritual and exorcistic cure.

In the Tao-chiao Yüan-liu, each of these five styles of ritual are divided into nine grades of perfection, from the lowest grade nine, or Chiu-p'in, to the highest grade one, or I-p'in.[177] The grades are carefully listed, and the Taoist masters are required to sign their official documents, ritual memorials, and rescripts with the title given them at ordination. Thus the custom described at the end of section 5 above was standardized for southern Taoism by decree of the Ming emperors.[178] Furthermore, the Heavenly Master at Lung-hu Shan preserved a special manual in which the rite of ordination and the titles given to the Taoist masters were recorded. The manual is still in use by the present sixty-fourth generation Heavenly Master in Taiwan. It was purchased at Lung-hu Shan by a Hsinchu Taoist named Lin Ju-mei (see chapter 2) in 1886 and brought to Taiwan in 1888. The manual is now possessed by Master Chuang and a copy is in my microfilm collection. The book, called *Chi (Kei)-lu T'an-ch'ing Yüan-k'o*, describes the qualifications required for receiving each grade of ordination:

Grade one:	Mastery of the *Ta-tung Chen-ching*, or the *Yellow Court Canon*, and its registers.
Grades two and three:	Mastery of Ch'ing-wei Thunder Magic registers.
Grades four and five:	Mastery of the ancient Meng-wei registers of Cheng-i Heavenly Master sect Taoism.
Grades six and seven:	Mastery of the Ling-pao registers, and the ritual competency of a "Three-Five Surveyor of Merit," that is, the lowest and basic qualifications of a Taoist master.

The above list differs from the lists of Tu Kuang-t'ing, Chang Wan-fu, and the sixth-century *Wu-shang Pi-yao* only by including in second place the Thunder Magic of the Mao Shan oriented Ch'ing-wei sect.[179] Thus all Taoists, no matter what their sect or creed, were made to learn the registers of classical antiquity as well as the Sung dynasty version of Ch'ing-wei Thunder Magic in order to receive a license of ordination. The tendency to sectarianism of the Sung dynasty was thus effectively blocked with imperial sanction by the practices of the various Heavenly Masters during the Ming. Taoists were ranked according to their ability to perform orthodox ritual. A high grade as a Taoist master and the imperial sanction to teach and perform liturgy were given for following the ritual of the classical, canonical Taoist orders of the T'ang and the north-south period. The publication of an official canon during the Ming dynasty was a step toward controlling the proliferating local Taoists.

If the traditional Taoist centers sought to block the trend to diversity and local sectarianism, the popular

Taoist movements continued to multiply and spread during the Ming and the later Ch'ing and modern period. There occurred a polarization between the classical, traditional orders and the Taoists of local origin. The former orders were given the name cheng, or orthodox, and the latter were sometimes called hsieh, or heterodox, though the last term was more often applied to any Taoist or group of Taoists who practised harmful magic. Though the effort of men like Pai Yü-ch'an helped to bring the Shen-hsiao style of popular ritual into the fold of orthodoxy, local groups calling themselves Shen-hsiao continued to flourish. The Ming dynasty Heavenly Master Chang Yü-ch'u, in the canonical text *Tao-men Shih-kuei* (*Ten Norms of Religious Taoism*), decries the falsification of texts and the multiplication of local styles called Shen-hsiao devoid of both the spirit and proper practice of orthodox Taoism.[180] The local Taoist orders continue to flourish into the present and occupy much of the discussion in chapters 2 and 3 below.

The people of Taiwan, call the popular orders Redhead and the orthodox orders Blackhead.[181] One of the most popular of the local Fukien Redhead orders is the Sannai, or Three Sisters, sect, also known as the Sannai Lü Shan sect. The sect is named for three legendary ladies who practised a form of medium possession and exorcism-cure ritual, associated since T'ang times with Lü Shan in Liao-ning province in Manchuria.[182] This popular Fukienese and Taiwanese sect, however, has no known connection with Lü Shan in Liao-ning other than the name of the mountain. The sect is identified in the popular mind with the "Gate of Hell"; the term Lü Shan refers to the place in the cosmos through which the demonic forces attack the world of the living. The ritual role of the Lü Shan Taoists is to capture the demons and send them back to the world of darkness from which they attack the men and women of the community.[183] The magic of the Lü Shan Taoists, although based upon oral rather than written traditions, is respected by their

Blackhead Taoist brethren. Interestingly, however, when members of these and other local sects approach the Heavenly Master at Lung-hu Shan's southern headquarters for a license of ordination, the Redhead orders are invariably given an ordination in the Shen-hsiao style of ritual, which shows both the low opinion of the orthodox orders for the sectarian movements of the local provinces and the last place of the Shen-hsiao registers in the canonical tradition.[184]

In concluding this *Taoist oral* introduction, it must be pointed out that the esteem in which the Ming emperors held the Taoist masters did not last in to the Ch'ing dynasty. Granted high official titles by emperors of the Ming, the Taoists were stripped of all authority and all rank by the Ch'ing emperors.[185] Even harsher treatment was given the Taoists during the Japanese occupation in Taiwan. That Taoism has survived in modern Taiwan and other overseas communities, even into the modern period, indicates the important place it holds in the hearts of the Chinese people. It is significant that in present-day Honolulu, the Chinese community still maintains three Taoist priests and a number of flourishing folk temples. Far from being obliterated by the coming of technology and industrialization, Taoism has survived as the younger generation turns again to Asian roots for a sense of mystical union and festive celebration. The Chinese communities of the diaspora are witnessing a revival of traditional customs in a secular world.[186] In such circumstances the teachings of Master Chuang take on a new and timely significance.

Of course, in a brief introduction such as this, much material has had to be omitted. The great disputes between the Buddhists and the Taoists have been slighted, and many important figures have not been mentioned.[187] The selection of materials from a rich historical tradition has been made solely to give the necessary background for presenting the rituals and meditations taught by Master Chuang in contemporary Taiwan.

2. Children of Orthodoxy

Introduction

The island of Taiwan is a long, mountainous stretch of land just off the coast of southeast China. Behind its well-watered and fertile western plains are a series of high-rising mountains, which have been compared to a gigantic dragon asleep in the semitropic climate. Winds from the China mainland whistle down the straits of Taiwan and blow sand and dust into the eyes of the inhabitants. The great mountainous backdrop acts both as a watershed and a barrier to typhoons coming in from the Pacific Ocean. Chinese from southern Fukien and from the Fukien-Kwangtung border till the terraced fields of the lowlands, while Austronesian tribes dwell in the rugged mountains. Taiwan belonged first to China and was a thriving province of the Ch'ing empire during the late nineteenth century. After the Japanese war of 1895, it was forcibly appropriated by Japan and became a part of the Japanese colonial empire until 1945. With the end of the Second World War, Taiwan again became a part of China. It is the home today of sixteen million Chinese who live in a thriving, modern economy.

The Taoist master Chuang lives on the northern part of the island in the city of Hsinchu, which is seventy-two kilometers south of the capital city of Taipei on the northwest tip of Taiwan. His ancestors emigrated to Taiwan eight generations ago at the end of the eighteenth century and their descendants have lived in Hsinchu City as practicing Taoists until the present. Chuang proudly traces his teachings to monastic centers on the China mainland. From his maternal grandfather Ch'en Chieh-san he received the Meng-wei registers of an orthodox Heavenly Master sect Taoist. From the library of the eminent Lin Ju-mei, he inherited a collection of books brought back from the sixty-first generation Heavenly Master at Lung-hu Shan, Kiangsi province, on the mainland. From the family of Wu Ching-ch'un he received manuals from Mao Shan and Hua Shan, great centers of Taoist learning in central and western China. The names of the three men—Ch'en Chieh-san, Lin Ju-mei, and Wu Ching-ch'un—are well known in Hsinchu. Chuang's accounts of his Taoist antecedents can be verified from the local gazettes and the Chia-p'u family histories of the three great Taoists.

In the following pages the history of the texts in Chuang's possession and the sources of his teachings are traced from their origins on the mainland of China to the bookshelves in the second floor of the Chuang residence in Hsinchu. The story begins with the coming of Wu Ching-ch'un to Taiwan.

1. WU CHING-CH'UN AND LIN CHAN-MEI

Wu Ching-ch'un came to live in Hsinchu on Taiwan in spring 1823, the third year of the emperor Tao-kuang's reign.[1] Son of an illustrious mandarin family, Wu Ching-ch'un boasted ten ancestors in the preceding twenty-three generations who had attained the rank of Chin-shih, doctor of letters. Three other forebears had been military officials and nine had been ordained Taoist priests. When Wu Ching-ch'un's father was forty-three, the Lin clan of Hsinchu were looking for teachers for the newly founded academy of letters, the Ming-chih Hsiu-yüan,[2] a school for training the children of wealthy Hsinchu families in Confucian learning. The school's first chin-shih had been awarded in the year that Wu was hired.

Weighing the pros and cons of the life of a poor scholar in a wealthy Fukien mandarin family against a life of relative affluence in the frontier town of Hsinchu, Wu's father decided to leave the ancestral home. Packing the family belongings and taking his wife and three sons, Wu made the long journey, first by overland route to Amoy Harbor and then by boat across the straits to the port of Nanliao near Hsinchu. Wu was a man of devout piety; before sailing, he burned incense to Hsüan-t'ien Shang-ti, the Taoist god of the Pole Star, and to Matsu, the virgin patronness of sailors who crossed the Taiwan straits. Their passage was uneventful.

Hsinchu City in the year 1823 was a thriving prefectural capital, housing a Yamen magistrate with the government offices of the Tamsui district in north Taiwan. Two great families, the Lin and the Cheng clans, controlled respectively the military and the civil affairs of the city. It was not only for his learning in the Confucian classics that the Lin clan had summoned Wu Ching-ch'un and his family. The elder Wu was an accomplished Taoist, trained in the monastic traditions of his ancestors. The fourteenth, fifteenth, and sixteenth lineal ascendants of Wu Ching-ch'un had practiced Taoist ascetics atop Hua Shan in west China. A member of the clan, twenty-three generations previously, was ordained at Mao Shan in Kiangsu. Wu the elder had trained his son in the classical Taoist learning of his ancestors. The rites the younger Wu had learned from his father were a far cry from the vulgar popular rituals practiced by the Redhead Taoists of Hsinchu City. Rather than follow the practices of the professional Taoists, the younger Wu preferred to spend his days in the opulent surroundings of the Lin family villa. Daily parties, poetry reading contests, and performances of classical music were among the pastimes there. Wu Ching-ch'un was content to leave the support of the family to his father.

Unforturately, the elder Wu did not thrive in his new occupation. Though the elite patronized the Ming-chih academy and he was much sought after as a scholar in

Confucian learning, Wu soon fell ill and had to curtail his teaching. The winds from the Taiwan straits came whipping into the city and curbed the summer heat but filled the air with choking dust. The wet rice paddies around the city were breeding places for malarial mosquitoes, cholera, and dysentery. Wu died three short years after his arrival. Wu Ching-ch'un, then twenty-four years of age, was left as heir and head of the family.

Distraught and unable to support his mother and two brothers as had his scholarly father, Wu Ching-ch'un had to turn to Taoism as a means of making a living. Going to the great trunks left behind by his father, Wu broke the locks and opened the heavy lead binding. There before him were the tattered manuscripts of orthodox Heavenly Master sect Taoism. To use the meditation manuals and the prognostication techniques was a simple matter, but the complicated rituals of renewal and the lengthy ceremonies of burial could only be performed with an entourage of trained musicians and assistants. When his father had been buried and the proper time of mourning passed, when indeed the family fortunes had dwindled so that it was no longer possible to pretend affluence, Wu Ching-ch'un went to the door of the Lin family and presented his credentials.

When Wu entered the gates of the Lin family villa in autumn 1826 and displayed his legacy of Taoist legerdemain, the Lins were taken by surprise. The Lin clan was noted for its patronage of both Taoist and Buddhist ritual. But Wu Ching-ch'un's collection contained manuals never before been seen in Hsinchu. There was a complete set of the grand chiao festivals of renewal, with the documentation and the rubrical directions of mainland monastic sects. There were the dreaded Mao Shan manuals of military black magic, the so-called Tao of the Left, used in repelling an attack or winning a battle in war. Finally, there were manuals of Thunder Magic from Hua Shan in Shensi, which were powerful enough to counter the Mao Shan black magic. The presence of Wu Ching-ch'un in the city therefore offered the Lin clan a way to insure its elevation over the other political leaders in the city, as well as superiority in fighting the clan and ethnic battles that broke out every autumn and winter when the young men were not needed in the fields. The seasonal wars drained the city coffers and depleted the male population.

The Lin family of Hsinchu, one of the most influential and wealthy clans of north Taiwan, is commemorated in all the gazettes and local histories of Taiwan for its famous martial son, Lin Chan-mei.[3] He was six years old in 1826 when Wu Ching-ch'un offered his services, and the twenty-four-year-old Taoist was put in charge of training the boy in the arts of military Taoism. Lin Chan-mei, who was destined to be the great pacifier of north Taiwan, was thus brought up in the traditions of Confucian literary learning and Taoist martial arts. With the help of the military magic of Wu Ching-ch'un and the wealth of the Lin family, he was able to discipline and train a fine private army and become the great pacifier of north Taiwan. The tenure of Wu Ching-ch'un in Hsinchu was most welcome to the Lins, who patronized his styles of Taoist ritual and saw that they were adopted by the Taoists within the inner confines of Hsinchu City.

Winning acceptance for Wu Ching-ch'un's strange new ways among the resident Taoist brotherhood was a problem requiring adroit political maneuvers to solve. In the diary kept by Wu are written the simple words that he was made an apprentice in the entourage of Kuo Tao-ching, one of Hsinchu's better known Taoists. The arrangement was facilitated by a gift of money in a red envelope and both sides had reason to be satisfied with the pact. Kuo Tao-ching was evidently too old to function without an assistant and Wu Ching-ch'un had an entourage of musicians to train in the ways of orthodox ritual worship. Wu practiced under Kuo Tao-ching for ten years, sharing his unique ritual manuals with the Taoist brethren of Hsinchu City and subordinating himself in all things to the aging master. At the end of the waiting period he was given the daughter of another Taoist, the Master Wang, for his bride. With the blessing of the older Taoists, Wu then set up his own T'an or Taoist altar within the inner city. The first center for orthodox Taoist ritual in north Taiwan was established with the Lin family Westgate villa as its headquarters.

The difference of the ritual of Wu, compared with the other Taoists of the old walled city, was immediately apparent to the populace. With a little persuasion from the Lin clan, an agreement was reached that all the "little" Taoists, that is the Redhead or the Shen-hsiao heterodox orders, were not allowed to perform within the city walls.[4] Only orthodox Blackhead Taoists who performed liturgy after the manner of Wu Ching-ch'un were allowed to remain in the city. Residents who wished to hire a medium or watch the dramatic tumbling or climbing of sword-ladders typical of the popular local orders had to go outside the city walls to find a heterodox practitioner. Temples and clans within the city walls were made to patronize only the Lin supported Taoists. The prohibition of heterodox Redhead rites was maintained well into the republican period. The temples in the very center of Hsinchu still frown upon mediumistic practices, where the shrines and temples in the outskirts specialize in Redhead cults.

The scion of the house of Lin, Lin Chan-mei, was sixteen years old in 1836 when Wu Ching-ch'un began his professional career as a Taoist master. The early manhood of Lin Chan-mei was spent in schooling, in swordsmanship, and in travel. The Lin family, the gazettes say, hired a swordsman from Japan to train the youth in fighting. During the wars of pacification, he carried a sword bought in Japan, and wielded it with great efficacy. Soon the first forces were formed under Chan-mei's direction, the Fei-hu Chun or Flying Tiger troops, named after a chapter in the book of Mao Shan military magic. They quickly moved throughout north Taiwan, venturing as far south as Ta-chia and into the city of Changhua, seeking to end the savage ethnic and clan wars. With Chan-mei away, the Hsinchu gazette relates, the city feared for its life; with Chan-mei near, the city knew no enemies.[5]

Besides the wars which depleted much of the Lin family wealth and lasted almost to the end of Chan-mei's life in 1868, much of the young warrior's free time was spent in the more refined pursuits of poetry, painting, classical music, and partying. The Westgate villa echoed with the sounds of musical ensemble, dance, and song. The gazettes tell little about Chan-mei's Taoist activities. The subject is hardly mentioned by his living descendants. Yet when the great warrior posed for his family portrait, he sat with the insignia of a Taoist high priest around his shoulders. In the oral legends of his exploits his victories were attributed to powerful Mao Shan magic as well as to the strict discipline of his well-trained troops.

2. LIN JU-MEI AND CH'EN CHIEH-SAN

In its attempts to control the spiritual and temporal destiny of Hsinchu, the Lin family did not spend its money exclusively on wars. Members of the family were also devout patrons of the religious movements of the late Ch'ing era. Much of the Lin fortune was spent in building Buddhist temples outside the city as well as in supporting the orthodox Taoist fraternity within the city. The person mainly responsible for the spiritual control of the city was the fifth son of the family, Lin Ju-mei. The favorite younger brother of Chan-mei, Ju-mei was born in 1834. The Hsinchu gazettes record that the precocious child was often carried around the inner city on the shoulders of his brother, who spoiled him with endless gifts and favors.[6]

Lin Ju-mei was given the nickmane "Wu Lau-yeh," or "Big Daddy Number Five," since he followed his respected elder brother to many of the city's councils and watched the deliberations on politics and war. Lin Ju-mei soon came to be as respected as his powerful elder brother.

Where Lin Chan-mei gave lavish parties and led a flamboyant, colorful life, Ju-mei was given to study and learning. He began to train as a literatus in the Ming-chih academy and was outstanding in his study of the classics. At the same time he was encouraged by Chan-mei to study orthodox Taoism with Wu Ching-ch'un; he became a devout practitioner of inner alchemy and ritual meditation. Many of the elders of Hsinchu city who still remember the famous man of religion say that Lin Ju-mei did not have the stamina for the long and rigorous rituals of a Taoist. The difficult ascesis proved too much for him. Nevertheless it is sure that in 1851 the secrets of the Mao Shan manual of black magic (see chapter 4 below) were given to him when Ju-mei was only sixteen years old.[7]

From Taoism, Lin Ju-mei turned to join his brother Chan-mei in the wars. In that more violent adventure, he was singularly unsuccessful. Returning from a bitter conflict covered with wounds, Lin Ju-mei was long in recovering. Since the gazettes are often least clear in relating embarrassing moments of the lives of great men, the conversion of Lin Ju-mei to Buddhism is glossed over in most written accounts. His sudden penchant for Buddhist monasteries is attributed to a strange sort of "mental weakness." The expenditures of Chan-mei in war were now rivalled by Ju-mei in building and beautifying Buddhist and Taoist shrines. The Westgate villa became filled with Taoists, Buddhists, and other religious practitioners, who were beneficiaries of Lin's lavish charities. The former parties of Lin Chan-mei had filled the inner rooms of the villa with artistic scrolls and literary compositions; now the eaves and walls were covered with the religious poetry of Lin Ju-mei, done in inlaid mosaic tiles. It was his dream to make the Westgate villa a center for the spread of religious ideas, a sort of school in inner alchemy and ritual meditation.

Two events delayed the accomplishment of Lin Ju-mei's lofty ideals for another two decades. The first was the death of Wu Ching-ch'un in 1858, which left the Taoists of Hsinchu without a master. The second was the death of Lin Chan-mei in 1868, which left Lin Ju-mei in charge of the family fortunes. The demise of Wu Ching-ch'un was a serious loss for the cause of orthodox Taoist ritual within the city walls. The less orthodox ways of the Redheads began to come back as the people demanded popular rites of exorcism and entertaining drama, rather than the stately orthodox monastic rites patronized by the Lins and Wu Ching-ch'un. The elite families who came to the Westgate villa were distressed but none of them were low enough in the social scale to demean themselves by performing Taoist ritual in public. Hsinchu desperately needed a successor to Wu Ching-ch'un.

Futhermore, the energies of Lin Ju-mei now had to be devoted to replenishing the fortunes of the Lin family, totally depleted by the wars of Chan-mei. Though successful in pacifying the north, Chan-mei had not been a perfect businessman. Lin Ju-mei was forced to sell much of the family land west toward the sea and north to the dry lake districts in order to keep the family solvent. This was a full-time responsibility that diverted him from his interests in Taoism. Meanwhile, the successor to the head of the orthodox Taoist movement was born to a neighbor behind the Westgate villa.

The Ch'en clan of Hsinchu, which vied with the Lins and the other elite families for status and power in the politics and economics of the city, owned land directly behind the Westgate villa. On it lived a rather unfortunate branch of the family, not so elevated in its economic or social standing as the other branches. When a son was born to the family in 1861, the boy, Ch'en Chieh-san, was entrusted to Lin Ju-mei for his education.[8] Lin's plans for the boy were quite different from the expectations of the poor Ch'en family. Ch'en Chieh-san was first brought up in the classics and trained in the Ming-chih academy. But at the proper and tender age of ten years, he was apprenticed to a Taoist. There are still elders alive in Hsinchu today who recall the frail, intelligent Ch'en Chieh-san and regret the decision to make the boy a Taoist. The first problem was Chieh-san's health; he was plagued with and eventually died of a serious heart condition. The second was his intellectual potential. The boy would certainly have passed his Chin-shih had he been allowed to pursue his course of Confucian learning. There is no question, however, that he became an expert and accomplished Taoist. By the age of twenty Ch'en Chieh-san was the leader of the orthodox Taoist association inside Hsinchu City and the trusted associate of Lin Ju-mei in the Westgate villa. Lin Ju-mei's long-planned center for Taoist studies was now a clear possibility.

Lin Ju-mei, however, was not to be denied his desire to lead the fraternity. In 1866 he adopted into his family as a younger brother a Kuo-fang-tzu (the son of a paternal uncle) named Lin Hsiu-mei.[9] Lin Hsiu-mei was given the task of learning the meditations of inner alchemy, while Ch'en Chieh-san was accorded the more lowly duty of performing public ritual. Thus the intellectual leadership of the Taoists, and the influence of the elite clans of Hsinchu's wealthy families, was kept within the Lin household. Ch'en Chieh-san became the leader of Hsinchu's Blackhead Taoists, and Lin Hsui-mei was made the instructor in inner meditation for the elite families who came to study at the Lin family villa. It is interesting to note that neither Ch'en Chieh-san nor Lin Hsiu-mei continued in their assigned duties after the death of Lin Ju-mei. Ch'en Chieh-san, who received the great library of Wu Ching-ch'un and the books of Lin Ju-mei, went into real estate and made a fortune, while Lin Hsui-mei formed his own household and practiced meditations in private. But neither of these outcomes were foreseen by Lin Ju-mei, who went ahead with his grand plans for founding a school of orthodox Taoism. With the family fortunes replenished, Lin undertook the greatest adventure of his life, a trip to mainland China. There, at the source of orthodox Taoism, Lin hoped to gain enough knowledge and prestige to found his own school.

The Hsinchu local gazettes are agreed in reporting Lin Ju-mei's motives. They say that he was worried about the low state of Taoism in Hsinchu City. The vulgar rites of the Redheads were again invading the city proper and Taoism was no longer a socially respectable religion for the upper classes. It was to restore Taoism to pristine orthodoxy that Lin Ju-mei planned his 1886 trip to Lung-hu Shan to visit and study with the sixty-first generation Heavenly Master. The records of the Ch'eng-huang temple in Hsinchu reveal a further motivation for Lin's journey. Worried as early as 1874 about the Japanese threat to Amoy and Taiwan, Lin Ju-mei petitioned the court to make Hsinchu's city god, Tu Ch'eng-huang, protector or guardian of north Taiwan. From the sixty-first generation Heavenly Master, Lin also sought and obtained a protective talisman to defend Taiwan from foreign invasion. The journey is recorded in the gazettes, in the temple archives, and in a journal kept by Lin, which is still a part of his personal library collection.[10]

The pilgrimage left Hsinchu in the third lunar month of 1886. Lin Ju-mei took along his adopted ninth brother, Lin Hsui-mei, but left behind the brilliant young Ch'en Chieh-san, whose health evidently would not permit him the long and strenuous journey. The pilgrims set out from Nanliao harbor, at the mouth of the Hsinchu river where a narrow delta emptied into the sea, almost sixty-three years to the day after Wu Ching-ch'un set sail from Amoy harbor to Hsinchu. Unlike the uneventful voyage of the Wu family, Lin's crossing encountered storms and danger. So seasick was Lin Ju-mei that he vomited blood. The party was delayed for a month in Amoy harbor, and an oracle was consulted who determined that the cause of the illness was an evil spirit. A chiao was offered, in which the powerful Thunder Spirits were invoked to effect a cure. The small party set out again in the fifth month and finally arrived at the village of Ch'ing-chou at the base of Lung-hu Shan in Kiangsi. There a second chiao of thanksgiving was offered in the presence of the sixty-first generation Heavenly Master. The gratitude of Lin Ju-mei for his cure and safe arrival in the very center of orthodox Taoism was celebrated in a grand document that is still extant in the Lin collection. The details of the journey, the cure, and the arrival are recorded in the Shu-wen document, dated on the seventh day of the seventh lunar month, 1886. Lin had at last come to the very source of orthodoxy, and his joy was unbounded.

In all some two thousand silver taels were spent by Lin Ju-mei at Lung-hu Shan. He purchased a library of ritual and meditative manuals from the sixty-first Heavenly Master, including an ordination manual and a complete set of Thunder Magic rituals more advanced than those brought to Hsinchu by Wu Ching-ch'un in 1823. Finally a great Fu talisman of blessing was drawn by the sixty-first Heavenly Master to be hung in Hsinchu's Ch'eng-huang temple. Lin was rewarded with a high sounding Grade Two (Erh-p'in) Taoist ordination. The party returned to Hsinchu in 1888. Bringing the talisman for the Ch'eng-huang temple was the crowning point of Lin's triumphal return.[11] Now indeed the Lin family villa could be established as the center for orthodox Taoist learning in northern Taiwan. Establishing the Cheng-i Tz'u-t'an, a fraternity of orthodox Taoist priests, was Lin's first act back in Hsinchu.

When Lin Ju-mei left Lung-hu Shan, he was not accompanied by his adopted brother, Lin Hsui-mei. This quiet and contemplative man chose to stay behind and live the life of a hermit. There he outlived the sixty-first generation Heavenly Master and was ordained in two distinct orders, the Ch'ing-wei Thunder Magic sect, deriving from Hua Shan in Shensi, and the Ch'üan-chen monastic order, which had come from Pai-yun Kuan in Peking to establish a small community at Lung-hu Shan during Lin Hsiu-mei's stay. The picture of Hsiu-mei in the modern family residence shows him with the cap of a Ch'üan-chen monk.[12] When Hsiu-mei finally did return to Hsinchu in 1892, a few years before the Japanese invasion, he chose to remain quietly outside the ritual arena and did not make his influence felt in the thriving Cheng-i Tz'u-t'an. He moved out of the Lin clan villa and established a household across from the Ch'eng-huang temple on Chung-shan street, where it remains to this day.

The Cheng-i Tz'u-t'an meanwhile was flourishing under the leadership and guidance of the scholarly but frail Ch'en Chieh-san. When Lin returned to the Westgate villa, he turned over all the Lung-hu Shan manuals to Ch'en Chieh-san and appointed the young Taoist chief resident instructor in the fraternity and school of Taoist ritual. Ch'en was a quick student and soon mastered the new styles and ceremonies. Taoists came from all over Taiwan to study under Ch'en Chieh-san. Ch'en was careful to keep a list of all those who came, exacting a large fee for the privilege of learning orthodox Taoist secrets.[13] Lin Ju-mei was either unaware of the profiteering or was not concerned, since the new orthodox ways of the Cheng-i Tz'u-t'an had become famous even as far away as the Chang-chou and Ch'uanchou prefectures on the mainland—in the daily diary of Ch'en Chieh-san are the names of four Taoists who came across from Fukien to Taiwan to study.[14] Nevertheless, the joy of Lin Ju-mei in his school was premature. The seeds of destruction had been sown in the gross profit-making of the Cheng-i Tz'u-t'an members. Within a year of his death, the fraternity he had established survived in name only.

The death of Lin Ju-mei was as tragic as his life had been fortunate, and the local gazettes carried no accounts of the demise of the great spiritual leader. Worn out from the harrowing experience of crossing the straits and his later devotions, Ju-mei never quite recovered from his journey to the mountain. The depressing spectre of Japan hovered just over the horizon. After attaining the protective talisman from the Heavenly Master and the edict from the emperor making Hsinchu's Ch'eng-huang deity a king over the island temples and their spirits, he began to sense the impending failure of all his spiritual labors. The spirits of Buddhism and Taoism in ever-increasing numbers came to haunt his dreams. In a fit of depression on the eve of the Japanese invasion, Lin Ju-mei killed himself in the Westgate villa. The shock to the Cheng-i Tz'u-t'an and its profiteering members was so great that the organization did not recover. Except for a few loyal members, orthodox Taoism was dead in Hsinchu. The immediate family of Lin Ju-mei was the hardest hit by his death. The son became an alcoholic, haunted by dreams of the returning soul of his father. The eldest daughter made off with the paraphernalia, the talisman, and the Taoist implements of her father, giving them in time to her eldest son, T'ung, the artist.

After the death of Lin Ju-mei, the manuals in the possession of Ch'en Chieh-san were not returned to the Lin family. They were kept in Ch'en's own library and seldom used. Ch'en soon made his move into real estate investment. So wealthy had he become as master of the Cheng-i Tz'u-t'an that he was able to invest in land and associate with the highest of Hsinchu's elite families. Futhermore, the invading Japanese frowned on the practice of indigenous religions. The temples, that had had their social roots in local popular government, were changed into more politically stable and controllable forms of organization. Buddhism and Shintoism became the state-patronized religions, where Taoism was only tolerated at best. The Cheng-i Tz'u-t'an was dispersed and the grand collection of books and manuals distributed among its members. Only a few of the original clan members—the Chuang, Kuo, Wu, Ch'en, and Meng families—continued to practice ritual in the public forum.

3. LIN HSUI-MEI AND CHUANG TENG-YÜN

When Ch'en Chieh-san gave up the vocation of a Taoist priest for the affluence of a real estate agent, he had no intention of giving up entirely the practice of inner alchemy or the ritual meditations of orthodox Taoism. If the tasks of burying the dead, curing a child's ills, or blessing a temple were now behind him, the prestige accruing to him from his years as master of the Cheng-i Tz'u-t'an could not be easily forgotten. Futhermore, the only other possible leader of the fraternity, Lin Hsui-mei, refused to emerge from his retirement in the Chung-shan residence. Ch'en therefore decided to keep the Taoist legacy within his own family by training one of his two children as a Taoist. The older child, a girl named Ch'en A-kuei, was brilliant, strong, and diligent—the perfect choice had she been male. The second child, a boy named Ch'en A-Kung, had no inclination and was in any event too young to be instructed seriously as a Taoist. Ch'en Chieh-san therefore began training his daughter in the ways of an orthodox priest.[15] A-Kuei responded well and soon surpassed her peers, the orthodox Black-heads of Hsinchu, in ritual perfection. A-kuei's training, however, was kept within the immediate family circle, her status as a daughter of one of the elite clans of Hsinchu keeping her from performing in public.

In order to propagate the Taoist line under his own name, Ch'en Chieh-san called in a Chao-hsü husband for

A-kuei; that is, a marriage was arranged with the Taoist Chuang clan, and a contractual agreement was made with the new husband that the eldest son of A-kuei would be brought up as a Taoist in the Ch'en household. The Chuang clan in return would be privileged to share in the secrets of Ch'en's orthodox magic. Thus, at the turn of the century, Ch'en A-kuei was given in marriage and went to live in the narrow alley behind the Ch'eng-huang temple, a ten-minute walk from her father's mansion. Unfortunately Ch'en Chieh-san's always delicate heart failed and he died in 1901, a few months after his daughter's marriage and before a son was born to the hopeful union.

Ch'en A-kuei gave birth to her first son in 1911, the year of the Hsin-hai revolution. The boy, who was given the name of Chuang Teng-yün (Chuang who ascends to the clouds), inherited the brilliance of his mother and the bad temper of his father. Because of the contractual arrangements, it was expected that the young Chuang would go to the home of his maternal uncle, Ch'en A-kung, for his education. This strange man, A-kuei's younger brother and heir to their father's fortunes, was an astute businessman but a noted habitué of the city's courtesan houses. Owing to prolonged association with women of ill repute, he had contracted a social disease and could not father children. Ch'en A-kung thus welcomed the Chuang child into his residence and treated him as his own son. A double surname was given the boy; thus Chuang-ch'en Teng-yün became the official title used by Chuang to sign documents. He was to receive, besides the splendid library of Taoist books that Ch'en had inherited from the Wu and Lin libraries, the wealth of the Ch'en clan inheritance.

Chuang Teng-yün was a brilliant student and took first place in school competitions. He was also an apt pupil of Taoist ritual and was trained by his real father, the elder Chuang, in the performance of Taoist magic.

But the brand of Taoism that Chuang's father practiced was a far cry from the orthodoxy of the Lin clan. After the death of Lin Ju-mei, the heterodox practices of the Redhead Taoists had again invaded the city. The elder Chuang was, in addition, a practitioner of Mao Shan black magic. Chuang's mother was greatly alarmed at the bad training being given to her eldest son. She appealed to Lin Hsui-mei as well as to Ch'en A-kung to intervene. Nevertheless, the eclecticism of the elder Chuang had the greatest influence over Chuang Teng-yün during the years of his youth. It was not until 1926, in Chuang's fifteenth year, that a series of fateful events brought him back into the fold of orthodox Taoism.

The first of the changes in Chuang's life came when a book of his poems in classical Chinese was published by a local press. As a reward for the excellent style and calligraphy, the city government rewarded Chuang with a trip to Kyoto. After a short month's absence, Chuang returned from Kyoto to find that his uncle Ch'en A-kung had married a concubine. Not only the courtesan but now two adopted brothers and a sister were established in the household of his maternal uncle. Ch'en A-kung, out of devotion to his newly found love, had allowed the woman to adopt children of her own and make them heirs to the Ch'en family fortune. The situation was too much for the youth; Chuang Teng-yün gathered his few personal belongings and returned home to his parents.

The portrait of Ch'en A-kuei still hangs over the family altar in the Chuang residence. From a wide and honest forehead her two eyes stare down at the visitors, expressing the resolve and strength of character that undergirded her hopes and aspirations for her family. Furious with her useless and profligate brother, Ch'en A-kuei strode through the dark and narrow streets to her father's house and confronted the concubine. What right, the concubine demanded, did the married sister have to determine the inheritance of the Ch'en household?

A-kuei did not deign to speak to the woman of the streets. Her eyes flashed as in the picture over the family altar; she turned and spoke to her brother. "There was a contract made between my father and me," she said in a soft and firm voice. "According to that contract my son, Chuang-ch'en Teng-yün, was to retain the Taoist books of my father."

Terrified by the apparition of his sister and the wrath of the courtesan, Ch'en now had an easy solution to the problem. Coolies, always waiting at the street corners to make an extra piece of silver, were immediately summoned. Five cases of books and manuscripts were loaded on the sweating, bent shoulders. The whole of the Westgate populace watched as the Taoist library of Lin Ju-mei and Wu Ching-ch'un was moved from the Ch'en mansion to the poor house of Chuang behind the Ch'eng-huang temple. Good riddance, said the courtesan, as the unwanted books disappeared into the darkness. A-kuei now had her son and her father's library and was content.

Chuang was by Chinese reckoning sixteen years old in 1926 when he returned to the home of his father.[16] Delighted, the elder Chuang contracted to do a day-long ritual at the Ch'eng-huang temple, using his own son as chief cantor and assistant. To the ritual were invited many of Hsinchu's illustrious families, among them, the celebrated hermit, Lin Hsiu-mei. Reluctant as always to appear in the limelight, Lin agreed to come to the temple simply because the occasion demanded an appearance. During the ritual performed by Chuang, the elder Lin was heard to cry out in a loud voice that the ritual was not being performed in the orthodox manner. To make things worse, a sudden wind blew out the lamps. The Taoists, temple custodians, and the pious faithful were all terrified.[17] Lin strode out of the temple, followed shortly by the two Chuangs, father and son. After two days of entreaties and promises, Lin Hsiu-mei agreed to take the young Chuang Teng-yün as a disciple. The agreement was made on two conditions—that Chuang act as leader of the Cheng-i Tz'u-t'an and propagate only orthodox forms of Taoist ritual, and that each year, for nine days preceding the festival of the Pole Star on the ninth day of the ninth lunar month, Chuang and the living members of the Cheng-i Tz'u-t'an offer a chiao festival in honor of the late Lin Ju-mei.

The discipleship of Chuang lasted for two years, from his sixteenth to his eighteenth year. During that time he was instructed in the meditations of the *Yellow Court Canon* and given three annotated manuals brought by Lin Hsiu-mei from Lung-hu Shan in 1892.[18] He was also instructed in Ch'ing-wei sect Thunder Magic, to be used as a remedy against harmful Mao Shan black magic. Finally, he was taught the orthodox manner of performing the ritual of renewal, after the manner learned by Lin Hsiu-mei at Lung-hu Shan and promoted by the original Cheng-i Tz'u-t'an of Lin Ju-mei in 1888. In 1928 Chuang Teng-yün was ordained by Lin Hsiu-mei as a grade four Meng-wei Taoist, with a knowledge of the Ch'ing-wei Thunder Magic rituals. When Chuang asked the aging master why he was not given a higher grade, the prestigious grade two that Lin Hsiu-mei and Lin Ju-mei had received at Lung-hu Shan, he was told that he failed on three counts. First, he practiced the vulgar Fang-chung rites of sexual hygiene, which he had learned from his Mao Shan–oriented father. These practices were in fact forbidden by Wei Hua-ts'un in the *Chen-kao*. Second, Chuang's bad temper kept him from the higher stages of perfection; only those tested in merit and virtue could be given a grade two or three ordination. Third, the sixty-first generation Heavenly Master had predicted that Chuang would give away the secrets to foreigners. Though he would be taught the secrets, Chuang would not be allowed the rank or the insignia of the full grade two Taoist expert.

Lin Hsiu-mei died peacefully in 1928, shortly after

ordaining Chuang Teng-yün in the orthodox Lung-hu Shan manner. Except for the brief period in which he instructed Chuang, Lin never made known his Taoist secrets and practiced his ritual as well as his meditation at a private altar erected in the rear of his house. After being admitted to the orthodox ranks of Heavenly Master sect Taoism, Chuang never again performed the heterodox rites learned from his father. Instead, he practiced breath control exercises, meditations of inner alchemy, and the elite rituals that Lin Hsiu-mei had preserved in the privacy of his own apartments. Like Lin, Chuang became something of a recluse and did not often appear in public. Instead of publicizing his new ritual powers, he chose to remain hidden and practiced only in the public forum when called upon to do so. From 1928 until 1945, Chuang supported himself and his family by working as a calligrapher and secretary in the city offices. In 1945, because of the heavy American bombing, Chuang took his family to Hualien on the rugged east coast of Taiwan and remained there until the war ended. In the quiet and unhurried beauty of the mountains about Hualien, Chuang spent long hours alone, studying the manuals of Lin Hsiu-mei and preparing macrobiotic formulae and other herbal recipes from the great collection of books he had received from his spiritual ancestors.

Late in 1945 Chuang returned with his family to Hsinchu. The old household behind the Ch'eng-huang temple had suffered in fires caused by the bombing and a part of the valuable Taoist library had been burned. But Chuang had taken the most important books with him to Hualien and shortly was able to establish a Taoist center. The postwar years were difficult and jobs were scarce. There was no recourse but to turn to the ministry of public ritual in order to support his growing family. With his wife and seven children, Chuang was forced to rely on his aging mother to establish the new Cheng-i Tz'u-t'an. Ch'en A-kuei, who had dreamed for years that her son would fill the role of Lin Ju-mei in Hsinchu, now saw her hopes about to be realized. Chuang once more practiced the songs and melodies, the drumming and document writing, and began to train a fitting entourage of disciples to perform in the old orthodox ways of his fathers. The fame of the Cheng-i Tz'u-t'an began to spread and several dozen disciples came to learn orthodox Taoism.

But the joy of Ch'en A-kuei was short-lived. The new disciples were not the same sort as those from the elite families who had come to her father's house in the late Ch'ing dynasty. The new trends in education begun by the Japanese and furthered by the Nationalist government emphasized technology, progress, and industrialization—all of which worked to secularize social values. The families that had patronized Lin Ju-mei's association for Taoist meditation now were the entrepreneurs who brought factories, roads, and technology of all sorts to Taiwan. The Cheng-i Tz'u-t'an was filled with the idle, the riffraff, the lower-class laborers who were anxious to make an extra "New Taiwan" dollar moonlighting as Taoists. To perform once in a rite of burial, for instance, earned enough money for a week's living. Chuang's new disciples studied only long enough to learn the external rubrics for performing ritual and then left to set up their own Taoist altars. A religious revival was in full swing and the temples and private households throughout Taiwan were demanding the services of professional Taoists. Once again the Redheads flocked into Hsinchu City, and Chuang, in disgust, withdrew from active leadership in the fraternity of Taoist brethren.

It is interesting to note from both written and oral sources that none of the orthodox Taoists from the time of Wu Ching-ch'un to the succession of Chuang Teng-yün took up the practice of external public ritual unless forced to do so by poverty. The profession of a popular ritual master in the public forum was considered low enough by the socially elite to be undesirable for their own sons. Wu Ching-ch'un did not become an active Taoist until 1826, after the death of his father. Ch'en Chieh-san left the profession as soon as his wealth permitted. The profession of a Taoist master was passed on to his daughter's eldest son, who did not practice Taoism until financial need forced him to do so. All of these Taoists were orthodox; that is, they practiced classical, canonical liturgy and considered the meditations of inner alchemy to be an essential part of the preparation for ritual performed in the public forum. The books of Wu Ching-ch'un were copied out and put into the collection of Lin Ju-mei. These were in turn, along with the grand collection brought home from Lung-hu Shan, given to the keeping of Ch'en Chieh-san. Ch'en passed them on to his maternal grandson, Chuang(ch'en) Teng-yün. Since inheritance constitutes one of the main elements in ancestor worship, Chuang brought into his family residence the ancestor tablets of Wu, Lin, and Ch'en, and he worships the tablets of his spiritual ancestors next to those of the Chuang clan. Canonical orthodoxy was therefore considered the distinguishing feature of the ritual practiced by the leaders of the Cheng-i Tz'u-t'an tradition. The conditions for orthodoxy in the tradition were (1) texts from the Taoist Canon, (2) performance according to the classical rubrics of antiquity, and (3) preceding and accompanying meditations of inner alchemy.

The main books used by Master Chuang Teng-yün in teaching orthodox Taoism are of two kinds: those relating directly to the performance of ritual in the public forum, and those concerned with private meditation, breath control, and macrobiotics. In this book I shall present texts of the first classification, saving the second sort of meditative manual for another study. My reason is simply that the first tradition has not been written about in any western language or in Chinese aside from the published Taoist Canon. There are many works available in English concerning the techniques of breathing, yoga, and so forth, as practiced in Asian monastic traditions. There are none explaining in exact detail the application of these exercises to the performance of public ritual. In my presentation, I remain faithful to the teachings of Master Chuang, who presented the materials to me in the format outlined below.

The teachings of Master Chuang were always given with reference to one or more manuals from the collection of Lin Ju-mei or Ch'en Chieh-san.[20] Whenever possible I attended the teaching sessions with the corresponding volumes of the Taoist Canon in my own possession, to compare them with Chuang's version of orthodoxy. At first Chuang resented my audacity in questioning his orthodoxy, but he soon came to welcome the opportunity to correct the canonical texts, which were often less clear or even corrupt when compared with his own texts and the oral explanations he had learned from the aged recluse, Lin Hsiu-mei. Since Chuang was endlessly busy with the calls of his clientele, it was sometimes necessary to wait for several hours before a moment could be found for a lesson. Chuang usually expounded his doctrines on days that the almanac (T'ung-shu) considered fortunate, or on days when burial ritual was forbidden. Since burials were preceded by night-time rites, it was often necessary to come at an odd hour, hoping that Chuang would be free from the rigorous demands of burial ritual or the obligations of entertaining his many callers. The lessons always began with a period of light conversation, followed by a scolding for his sons and disciples who failed to pay enough respect to the sacred doctrines. It was often necessary to wait a long time before Chuang got to the point. Only the patient were rewarded with the revelation of orthodox esoteric secrets, when Chuang chose to speak of them.

3. The Taoist Master Chuang

A study of the teachings of the Taoist master Chuang would be incomplete without a sense of the surroundings in which Chuang lives, the effect of his magical practices on his community, and the place accorded him in society. Perhaps more important than the content of Taoist magic are the uses to which it is put in a modern Asian setting. It is most interesting from the sociological-anthropological viewpoint to ask what sort of friends Chuang has, what classes of people patronize his liturgies, and what the residents of Hsinchu City think of the Taoists in their midst. It would be a mistake to suppose that a Taoist is a popular person, a person whom one is proud to call a friend or relative. Since the ministry in which the Taoist engages is concerned with sickness, ill fortune, or death, the very mention of a Taoist's name brings memories of unpleasant events which occasioned summoning him, events which most people would rather forget.[1] Thus when funeral ritual is mentioned, one might try to recall a noted Taoist who would perform a burial service for a reasonable fee; but the family Taoist would not ordinarily be the subject of conversation at a cocktail party or a festive occasion.

It is, furthermore, most difficult to meet a Taoist master. Though the villagers are well aware that there is a local Taoist in residence, the questions of the young anthropologist or student of sinology are often put off with a shrug or a noncommittal answer. This is because the Taoist assiduously avoids all contacts either with Chinese or foreign scholars, owing to the esoteric nature of the doctrines he professes and the rituals he practices. He does not appreciate being asked about his rituals; he is not even eager to practice them unless called upon by a person in extreme need. Introductions must be arranged in advance by an acquaintance or go-between. An unwanted caller is often rejected or the introducer cursed by the reclusive master. It is of the essence of religious Taoism for the master to hide his powers behind a frugal and simple façade. "The man who claims expertise of Taoist magic is an imposter, and the man who denies knowledge is an expert," is the attitude taught to the disciples in the master's entourage. The villager's image of a Taoist is usually that of a strange man who talks to spirits, who drinks heartily, and who comes and goes as he wills. There is something sinister about his magic, his exorcism of demons, that sets him apart from the rest of his community. His friends are few and his presence is feared. Thus he is not often introduced to outsiders.

Master Chuang lives in the center of Hsinchu City in an alley behind the Ch'eng-huang Temple. On one side of the Chuang residence is a candy shop and poolhall, and on the other side is a Sento public bath built during the Japanese period. Directly opposite the Chuangs front door is the house of the wealthy Ts'ai clan, which holds itself aloof from the other, poorer families in the narrow alley. The Ts'ai family has recently constructed a three-story building with polished terrazo floors and inner courtyards for its children where they can play away from the noise and bustle of the alleyway. Next to the Ts'ai residence lives another Taoist family, the clan of Ch'en the Fat, who make a living from their proximity to the Chuang clan. Next to the Ch'en family lives a woman medium of the Lü Shan sect, the famous Mrs. Wu, who is possessed every morning at ten o'clock by the spirit of the goddess Ch'en Nai-ma.[2] Housewives on their way to and from the central market stop to chat and watch the spectacle of the possessed woman talking in the voice of the goddess. When in possession, Mrs. Wu can be made to pick up a pen and write in a strange illegible script the answers of the goddess to the questions put to her by the housewives. Redhead Taoists, called Hoat-ah by the people, are consulted to interpret her talismanic writings. Though Chuang is opposed in principle to the brand of Taoism practiced by Mrs. Wu, he and his family are on very good terms with her and exchange gifts on festive occasions.

The house of Ch'en the Fat is very poor, filled with children and grandchildren in a hot corridor that passes for their residence. So many demands are put on the services of the prestigious Chuang clan that the Ch'ens manage to survive on the flow of business that finds its way to their doorstep. The eldest son of Ch'en, himself rotund and jolly, joins in the rituals of Chuang by default whenever another Taoist cannot be found. In or near the alley also live a masseur, a family that makes cakes and cookies for wedding ceremonies and other festive occasions, a manufacturer of household Christmas tree lights, a welding and metal shop, and a home that caters to funeral banquets. With the exception of the Ts'ai clan and the manufacturer of Christmas tree lights, almost all the inhabitants of the alley depend on Chuang in some way for their customers. The musicians, disciples, and stragglers are found in the poolhall next door when they are not engaged in ritual performances. The street is always filled with children, chattering people coming and going, passing motorcycles, and the clients who come seeking Master Chuang's ritual perfection. When home, Chuang pontificates from the wicker chair in his front room, facing the street when the door is open. The scene is one of peace in a lively neighborhood.

My introduction to Chuang was originally suggested by a woodcarver named Su, who lived on a street west of the Chuang house and served as porter for the guardian gods in the Ch'eng-huang Temple's statuary. He got no further than a brusque refusal from Chuang, who had no interest in meeting a foreign student and threatened to curse Su for even mentioning his name to a foreigner. As head of the Cheng-i Tz'u-t'an, however, Chuang was the Taoist in residence of the Ch'eng-huang Temple, a hundred yards or so from the front door of his residence. It was perhaps more proper that Mr. Cheng, head of the temple committee and the man who paid Chuang's retainer, should arrange the introduction. Cheng was a descendant of the Cheng clan, which had produced a Chin-shih (doctor of letters) in 1823; he himself was a graduate of Tokyo Imperial University. He had been three times elected mayor of Hsinchu City and was spending his years in retirement as beneficiary and controller of the temple's funds. Cheng and Chuang had been friends during the Japanese period, but their relationship had become more distant after Chuang had resumed the role of a Taoist. I had the suspicion that Cheng's willingness to introduce me to the Taoist had less to do with any intended honor to me than with the opportunity to issue a reminder to Chuang, who despised the trivial pay at the temple and neglected his duties there. Yet the temple staff assured me that there was no more knowledgeable Taoist in north Taiwan—nor one more difficult to handle.

The first meeting with Chuang began with a traumatic scolding. What purpose could a foreign scholar possibly have, Chuang demanded, other than to destroy the traditions of his ancestors? Taoism was an esoteric discipline and the secrets could be revealed to none but his immediate descendants. Luckily I had brought with me a photocopy of a Taoist ritual discovered on the shelves of the British Museum.[3] When I showed the manual to Chuang, his attitude visibly changed. It was a copy of the canonical Su-ch'i rite that had somehow found its way to the British Museum in 1872; the original had been signed by a Chang-chou Taoist named Ch'en in 1734. Chuang was both startled and pleased that I should have the manual and immediately accepted me into the entourage of his followers. From the very beginning I made it clear that my purpose was not to compete with his professional ministry or his monopoly in local Taoist liturgy. Where most of the disciples in Chuang's entourage came to learn ritual and eventually set up their own business, my purposes were purely scholarly. I hoped to study and understand the texts that Chuang used in his liturgy.

Chuang, much to the dismay of those who wanted only to learn the bare minimum of ritual performance in order to set up a money-making Taoist practice, intended primarily to give instructions in Taoist philosophy, the proper understanding of the *Tao-te Ching*, the *Chuang-tzu*, and the texts of inner alchemy. To the motley crew whiling away the hours between liturgical performances in the neighboring poolroom, the lectures on breath control, exercise, macrobiotic diet, and the like were wasted. The halcyon days of the Cheng-i Tz'u-t'an when meditations were taught in the halls of Hsinchu's elite clans were gone forever. The only hope for an intellectual revival of religious Taoism lay in two of Chuang's sons, A-him and A-ga. As the latest disciple, I seemed to function as a catalyst, moving Chuang to teach his two sons more frequently and thoroughly than if I had not been there.

To each of Chuang's lessons I brought printed versions of the Taoist Canon, in order to compare them with Chuang's own manuscript collection.[4] Where the Canon was corrupt, unpunctuated, or incomplete, Chuang's texts were clear, punctuated, and completed by his own knowledge of the K'ou-chüeh, the orally transmitted esoteric rubrics. The Ming dynasty Cheng-t'ung Taoist Canon contained many more variations and schools of ritual than Chuang had thought possible. For this reason, he asked to see the Japanese studies on the subject and read the works of such noted scholars as Yoshioka,

Obuchi, and Noritada Kubo.[5] In one of Kubo's field trips to Taiwan I was able to introduce the professor to Chuang; Chuang reciprocated by performing a Tao-ch'ang ritual and the steps of the Ho-t'u dance as described in chapter 6.[6] Finally, Chuang purchased and read the work of Maspero translated into Japanese, commenting on the differences and similarities to his own grasp of Taoist history and theory. To Chuang, the maintenance of a high standard of scholarly knowledge on the state of Taoist studies was part of the orthodox tradition that he had inherited. He had withdrawn from the circle of mercenary functionalists because there was no kindred spirit with whom to communicate the results of his own study and thinking, his methods of meditative alchemy and ritual perfections. His opposition to the local Redhead orders and to many of his own disciples arose from their disinterest in intellectual matters or in the pursuit of higher stages of perfection in inner (alchemical) meditation.

Chuang did not treat all scholars who came to his door with the same trust and openness, though to all he extended a warm welcome. To each visitor he offered the hospitality of his table and the camaraderie of drink. But to most he feigned ignorance, telling outlandish tales and downing large cups of rice wine. In subsequent conversations about the proper conduct for a master of ritual, Chuang scolded me soundly for being competitive with other scholars, for showing off my knowledge of Taoist secrets, for feeling superior in any way. The first requisites for perfection in Taoist learning were peace of heart, frugality of life, and respect for all others. If the master, so much more the disciple, was required to plead ignorance and never to make display of lording it over others. This was vividly illustrated by an event that occurred at Chuang's front door during a popular religious festival.

On the fifteenth day of the tenth lunar month, the mediums of north Taiwan are accustomed to perform the rite called "Passing Through the Gates of Peril." In the dramatic liturgy a local medium is possessed by the boy god, T'ai-tzu-yeh, and twelve times leads all the children through a "Gate of Peril" constructed of paper and wood. Passing through the gate is thought to protect the children from sickness and peril for the next twelve months. A Taoist is hired to lead the procession and blow on an exorcistic cowhorn trumpet. At the end of the procession dances the medium, imitating the steps of the naughty child god. I had alerted a number of young anthropologists and visiting foreign scholars to the event which, by chance, was to take place in front of Chuang's house.[7] The medium, Mrs. Wu, was to be in trance and Ch'en the Fat in his faded vestments was to lead the procession.

At the height of the ceremony, with the foreign cameras clicking and the lady medium in the midst of her possession, a drunk man walked through the front door of Chuang's residence. On the one hand he was delighted to see foreigners, but on the other he was worried about the lack of reverence and the misunderstanding that might be occasioned by such levity in the front of the spirits; he began to scold Chuang for allowing foreigners to be present. Chuang's youngest son, A-ga, bristled with hostility and wanted to expel the drunkard violently.

"Leave him alone," said Chuang. "He is my friend."

"Is he," I asked, "or are you trying to keep A-ga from fighting?"

"He is my friend," repeated Chuang and protected the man from A-ga, who by now had clenched fists and bulging eyes like a madman. With gentleness and restraint, Chuang spoke quietly to the drunkard and led him out the door and around the corner. I followed and assisted in seeing the man off. We exchanged name cards and parted friends. To Chuang the man in trouble was the most important person in the assemblage. Although he had never seen the man before, he treated him as a comrade. More urgent than the important visiting scholars or even the fury of his own son was the distress of the man who had temporarily lost his senses. To Chuang, his role as a Taoist was fulfilled in first assisting those in need. All other duties were secondary.

Chuang was not immune from the temptation to ho-tsui or "lay one on," as an American might phrase it, but he saved his drinking for times when liturgy was not being performed. During the sacred rituals of renewal or the burial ceremonies for the dead, Chuang was sober, even if his hands shook from the long-standing effects of alcohol. His disciples might sometimes think he was in the last stages of delirium tremens, but the master always recovered by massive doses of ginseng tea and breathing exercises. The alcoholism of Chuang was a bit more than that customary in a Taoist, who is supposed to be able to hold his drink with sobriety. There were times, admittedly, when I thought it necessary to restrain Chuang from excesses. One such time was the evening of my acceptance as a disciple.[8] Chuang ordered three bottles of kao-liang wine, which he, A-ga, and I drank. When my dizziness had subsided enough for thought to return I demanded that we stop drinking and walk to the Ch'eng-huang Temple to thank the committee for our introductions. By the time we reached the temple, Chuang was sober, though A-ga and I were still reeling.

Whenever I could not show up in Chuang's front room for an evening lesson or when Chuang felt like escaping the noise of the grandchildren, the visitors, and the street in front of his residence, he would appear at our door and sit on the tatami regaling my wife and me with stories of his exploits. On one such night, we told him of the coming birth of our second child.[9] To celebrate I opened a bottle of Scotch, of which Chuang immediately drank half. The quantity was not too great, but the short span during which the whiskey was quaffed proved too much even for Chuang. I summoned a cab, but before we were halfway home, the effects began to wear off. Chuang demanded that the cab stop. There before our eyes was the great courtesan house of Hsinchu, the Moon Palace where great uncle A-kung had got his mistress.

I begged Chuang not to go in, first because scholars, especially foreign scholars, did best to keep out of such places, and second because Chuang should not really have another drop. Umbrage was taken at my last statement, and we entered. The magical effect of Chuang's appearance was a revelation to me. Still somewhat numb from the sudden dosage of Scotch, he was in a mellow and jovial mood, but the clientele who knew him disappeared in great fear.

"Bring the manager!" Chuang shouted.

A chubby man, who was obviously terrified, appeared from behind a counter.

"The manager was just taken ill and has gone home," he mumbled.

"Get us a room and two bottles of wine." Chuang headed for a booth before he could be denied entrance.

We entered and sat down, followed by a very determined and straightforward younger woman, who was certainly not a courtesan and was perhaps the owner's daughter.

"What did you want?" she asked.

"Bring us four bottles of rice wine," Chuang answered. "Two for each."

"No," I said very firmly. "That would ruin the effect of Scotch, which all experts know must not be ruined by mixing with any extraneous beverage."

"Oh," said Chuang, deeply impressed. "What should we have?"

"It is the custom to have Coca-Cola," I lied, grasping for some way to get the Taoist out of the place and home before he collapsed.

"Fine," said the young lady, "I'll bring four bottles." In no time we had four open bottles of Coca-Cola and a full glass before Chuang, who began to drink it as if it were wine.

"This is terrible!" he gasped after the first swallow.

"Let's go," I insisted. "We must get home and get up early tomorrow to study." Chuang again called for the manager, and the determined young lady reappeared. Tonight's drinks would be on the house, she assured us. There was no bill. I steered Chuang down the stairs and out the door. The hallway and entrance were bare of people except for the young lady and the weak rotund man.

"I always drink for free when I go there," Chuang said. We walked down the back streets leading to his home, skirting a puppet show in front of the temple of Eastern Peace, and finally coming to the cookie shop at the corner of Chuang's street.

"Here," Chuang stumbled; "let me buy you some cookies for Theresa and Nariko." He peered through the locked windows of the residence at a light burning in the interior. The family was still up, packing boxes of cookies and cakes for a wedding ceremony on the morrow.

"Wedding cookies?" I asked. "They are not getting married."

"They always taste better the night before," Chuang pounded on the door, "while they're still fresh."

A high school girl answered the door. Seeing Chuang with a worried foreigner, she laughed and ran to get her mother and father. The whole family came. Chuang ordered NT$500 worth of cookies for Theresa.[10]

"That is far too many," I objected. "We will never finish them."

"That's all right," said the lady. "They are free; we don't want any money for them."

"It's still too many. Just a bag will do."

Relieved, they gave me a bag full of freshly baked cookies and we arrived at last at Chuang's front door, where Mrs. Chuang, a battle-scarred and long-suffering

The Su-ch'i ritual. A-ga on the left, and A-him with back to the camera. The Taoist Kuo at the far right.

Lin Hsiu-mei.

note that the meditation room on the east dies of the villa faces the "chu-fang" or kitchen to the west; this spatial structure is observed during Taoist ritual.

Lin family villa, meditation room.

A section of the Lin family villa. Poetry commissioned by Lin Ju-mei.

Datewood thunder block of Lin Hsiu-mei.

The role of the Taoist in the Chinese community: Ming-dynasty woodblock print, *Yü-shu Ching*.

監生大神聖母
一十五種鬼
寃愆之人

woman, let us in. She put her husband on the couch in the front room where he went straight to sleep.

"Don't worry," she consoled me, for I must have looked terribly crestfallen at Chuang's condition on returning from our house, "He'll be all right shortly."

The people who knew Chuang as neighbors did not fear him as much as those did in more distant establishments who knew him only by reputation, but no one wanted to risk his possible anger. Neighbors as well as associates did anything not to offend him. That is why neither the courtesan house nor the cookie factory would accept money for his patronage.

His wrath once aroused, it was known, could mean the punishment of the "Tao of the Left," though in my estimation the fear was unfounded; Chuang's anger usually ended with shouting and did not descend to use of the terrifying powers attributed to him.

Chuang's frequent anger was not typical of those who followed the profession of a Taoist. Chuang was simply known as a man of bad temper, but in his case the temper could lead to a supernatural punishment. Among the older members of the Cheng-i Tz'u-t'an, there were none who trusted him, and none whom Chuang himself trusted. Yet there were many members to whom Chuang had a fierce loyalty and whom he would call to help at public rituals from as far away as Keelung, Taipei, Chunan, and Taichung. It seemed, in fact, that Taoists from far-away cities were more friendly to Chuang than the disciples within Hsinchu City. This state of affairs can be explained partially by professional rivalry; most of the Taoists whom Chuang had trained became his competitors if they stayed in Hsinchu but were collaborators and associates if their ritual performance territory did not impinge on Chuang's. There were, of course, exceptions to this rule. The son of Ch'en the fat, for instance, and the lesser Taoists whose mere competence was no match for Chuang's rubrical perfection were often included in Chuang's entourage of musicians, acolytes, incense bearers, and cantors. But most of these men were not loyal to Chuang and managed after a few years of training to set up their own T'an or private Taoist altar. Thus the disciples watched his ritual performances avidly, hoping to gain for their own more of the great power and ritual perfection for which he was famous.

Chuang's dealings with his confreres within Hsinchu City were thus not cordial. There was no reason on Chuang's part why cordiality should be extended to any of his competitors, since Chuang alone could transmit the secrets of Thunder Magic, the Tao of the Left, and the orthodox Meng-wei registers of a high-ranking grade four ordination. To those who did come to him, Chuang imparted a bare minimum of knowledge until he could ascertain whether the novice desired to practice meditation, the ascetic fasts of a hermit, and other forms of religious perfection, or only to learn the external rote of funeral liturgy and to memorize the tunes and rubrics of liturgies for renewal. For the latter, four to six months was sufficient.

It was advantangeous to be included as a member or acquaintance in Chuang's entourage simply to share in the great fortune accruing from his ritual practise. There were so many requests for funerals, exorcisms, and chiao rituals of renewal that Chuang's full retinue of followers, disciples, and other associates usually contained around thirty members, that is, two complete ritual teams. To Chuang himself were reserved the elite duties: in a three-day funeral service, his total performance lasted only forty-five minutes, yet that was enough to win him the highest stipend and to make the funeral the most expensive and prestigious possible. When Chuang performed the rites of renewal, the well-known Tao-ch'ang, a Su-ch'i, Morning Audience, or whatever, Taoists and laymen assembled from miles around to watch the perfection and beauty of his liturgical performance.

There were, of course, another dozen Taoists available

within Hsinchu City for the ritual needs of the people. There was Ch'en the fat, who could be obtained for half the price of Chuang and who was often seen in the smaller temples performing the P'u-tu banquet-sacrifice for freeing the orphan souls from hell or the simple day-and-a-half rite of burial used by families of lesser economic means. There was also the family of Kuo the large-toothed, and the Redhead clans of Chang and Ch'ien, both specializing in rites such as "Calming a child who suffered fright at night," or reading the simple exorcisms, prayers for blessing, and prognostications in the local temples. The Chang and Ch'ien clans were not respected, but people turned to them in doubt, since a sick child in the arms of the worried parents calls for any and all sorts of care and attention. The worried mothers of Hsinchu could be seen carrying their children to the famous pediatrician, Dr. Chou, in the early morning to receive an injection of antibiotic then to the Taoist by ten or eleven o'clock to be soothed and assured by the ringing of small ritual bells, the lighting of incense, and the casting of fortune blocks which assured the loving parents that the spirit world as well as the material world was working for their child's recovery. Others brought their children to the great Ch'eng-huang Temple, where for a fee of NT$20, the child could be given in adoption to the Ch'eng-huang deity, an efficacious way to preserve children from future harm.[11]

Perhaps Chuang's greatest rival in Hsinchu was the fellow orthodox Blackhead Taoist, Ch'en Ting-feng, or Ch'en the Thin in distinction to Ch'en the Fat. Ch'en the Thin was not related to either the Chuang-Ch'en clan or to the Ch'ens of southern Taiwan, also noted ritual experts. This man's father had come to Taiwan in the 1890s to study in the Cheng-i Tz'u-t'an. Instead of returning to Chang-chou on the mainland, he stayed behind to set up his own business and operated a busy Taoist office in the central market just south of the Ch'eng-huang temple, in the middle of the meat and poultry section of the market. Ch'en Ting-feng inherited the business from his father and turned a fine profit by reading fortunes, burying the dead, and performing at the festivals of the deities in Hsinchu's local temples. Ch'en Ting-feng was a man of slight build and cautious heart, narrow in his limits, who kept strictly to himself. In all ways the opposite of the colorful Chuang, he was a man who never lost his temper, who spoke in a quiet, mild voice, who was cold and cautious in his dealings with others. The ritual of Ch'en was well patronized, and his reputation was built on the fine quality of his liturgical performance. Ch'en was an accomplished musician, sang in a good voice, and trained his disciples in a quiet and disciplined manner. When not engaged in funeral or renewal ritual, Ch'en busily studied medicine and was a licensed Chinese herbalist as well as learned in western pharmacy. Mothers who brought their children to Ch'en found an expert not only in ritual exorcism but in curing by means of Chinese herbs and western drugs. Ch'en built a lovely two-story residence in a suburb and traveled back and forth on a Honda motorbike; he could indeed claim to live as a an urbane gentleman of learning as well as a man of devout religious piety.

Chuang and Ch'en were not on speaking terms, the drunken ways of Chuang, his violent temper, and his largesse in teaching the riffraff who came to make a living from the leavings of his table being far removed from the close and frugal demeanor of Ch'en. But the children of Chuang, A-ga and especially A-him, respected the elder Ch'en and visited him frequently. Ch'en was himself without male offspring, and so arranged to pass on his Taoist secrets to the husband of his eldest daughter, a young man named Meng who worked in the city offices. As perfect and polished in attire as his father-in-law, Meng was soon made a member of Chuang's entourage, too, a welcome change from the idlers in the poolhall who often marred the splendor of Chuang's ritual. The sons of the two warring masters became close friends. All agreed that Chuang's successor as head of the Cheng-i Tz'u-t'an was to be A-him, and the decision was made by Ch'en Ting-feng, who as the next in age to Chuang was highest in prestige and therefore by right the leader of the group after Chuang. Despite the rivalry between the two masters, Ch'en Ting-feng was wise and gentlemanly enough to see that the teachings of Chuang had been aptly learned by the elder son. A-him was in fact the most accomplished Taoist after his father, as all the other Taoists realized. Out of deference to the age and prestige of Ch'en Ting-feng, A-him frequently visited the elderly Chinese herbalist and Taoist and went with him as a son to the various meetings of the Taoist society, which his own father refused to attend. It thus was evident that, although the Cheng-i Tz'u-t'an was divided by its leaders' rivalries, it was brought together again by the gentility of the leader's son A-him and his elder rival. All that being true, however, Ch'en Ting-feng's motives for friendship with A-him may not entirely have transcended the desire to learn more about the secrets kept hidden by the wily Chuang from all his associates and revealed piecemeal to his successor.

My own dealings with Ch'en Ting-feng were at first polite but distant. Ch'en was too much a gentleman to speak against Chuang, but it was obvious that he resented my discipleship in the school of his rival. The resentment was gradually ameliorated by two sets of events, which perhaps reveal more of the personal characteristics of the two men, Chuang and Ch'en, than do my descriptions. The great English musicologist, John Levy, who had come to Taiwan searching for Taoist music to study and publish, asked both Chuang and Ch'en to record from their repertoire of ritual music. Chuang insisted on being paid for his performance, while Ch'en allowed Levy to record at no cost during a public performance. The arrangements with Ch'en were made quietly during several hours before and after the performance in his busy office in the marketplace. Ch'en cooperated to the extent of holding the microphones during the performance and was in all ways cooperative in demonstrating his various musical instruments; he seemed reluctant to get on with his daily round of sick calls and ritual business.

Chuang, on the other hand, insisted not only on being paid for his services at the rate he would charge a local customer, but demanded that his entourage have several days practice in advance and asked Levy to drive him all the way to Changhua in central Taiwan to get the proper bell and drum to be recorded in stereo. Through the forbearance and patience of the London gentleman, Chuang got his instruments, his entourage, and a recording studio for the performance. But getting him to identify the texts, write out the k'ou-chüeh, or oral secrets, which he had used, and explain his actions was like pulling wisdom teeth. All the while that the Englishman and the Taoist were together, however, Chuang was at his best, demonstrating breath-holding techniques, songs and rhythms, boasting of his magical powers, and laying on several fine banquets with the fanciest cooking of Mrs. Chuang.

The second friendly encounter with Ch'en Ting-feng, which led to a sort of understanding and incipient friendship, began with an attempt to find a missing text. Chuang, in the carelessness of his daily life and the confusion of his cabinets of ritual documents, noticed that a book was missing. The volume was not just an ordinary ritual manual used in the daily burial services but an extremely valuable rite reserved for Chuang himself to perform on the occasion of a liturgy of renewal. The manual contained the Su-ch'i, an esoteric ritual in which the *Ling-pao Five Talismans*, the bringers of good fortune, blessing, and cosmic renewal, were planted in the community.[12] That is, the bringing of the talismans into the temple would insure the spiritual renewal of the entire village. Chuang was doubly furious at the loss, since only he and Ch'en

Ting-feng, of all the Taoists within Hsinchu City, knew how to perform the rite in full. The moment was most inopportune, for I was in the process of photocopying all Chuang's documents and making a supplement to the Canon of the well-punctuated texts and commentaries in the inherited collection.

The culprit, by word of the underground, was the lowly Kuo with large teeth. Whether the theft was done with a view to a large reward for a return in time for photocopying, or whether Chuang had just imagined the loss and would find the text in a back cupboard, was hard to determine. Borrowing valued texts and not returning them was a habit among the Taoists of north Taiwan. The lesser Taoists would insure themselves a place in the great liturgies of renewal and a portion of the temple stipend by producing the only copy of a text to be used during chiao ritual. Many of the works in the original library of Lin Ju-mei, which had belonged to the Cheng-i Tz'u-t'an collection in the Westgate villa, had been dispersed throughout north Taiwan. Chuang was careful to keep the valued manuscripts with the seal of the sixty-first generation Heavenly Master locked in his cabinet on the second floor, away from the prying eyes of his many followers. But the Su-ch'i ritual was an essential part of the rites of renewal. Without it, a chiao could not be properly performed. In a joking way A-him, A-ga, and I compared Chuang to the Redhead masters, whose disciples kept copies of the manuals and never returned them. When the Redheads performed a chiao, the various disciples had to scurry from temple to temple, each performing his own version of the rituals according to the manuals stolen from the master.

The recovery of the manual was first undertaken by the violent son A-ga, who faced Kuo publicly in the central market. Kuo denied that he had the book, asserting that the guess was misplaced. He did not know how to perform the rite even if he did have it. The last statement being true enough, A-ga returned home in defeat. A-him and I carefully discussed the next step with the master Chuang. It would be possible, I reasoned, to ask Ch'en Ting-feng to intercede. If I asked Ch'en where a copy of the rite might be, he could perhaps convince Kuo at least to loan it to me to be photocopied. Chuang agreed that it was worth trying and so, with my wife, Nariko, and our daughters, Theresa and Maria (now born), as company, we rode with A-him in a taxi to the residence of Ch'en Ting-feng.

It was eight o'clock in the evening when we arrived. Ch'en had not yet returned from a funeral ritual but Mrs. Ch'en and the elder daughter welcomed us with great warmth. The conversation shifted from Japanese to Taiwanese to Mandarin, according to the generation and the person addressed. A-him was treated as a son just returned to the family. As Mrs. Ch'en served plates of candied fruit and glasses of soda water, with cooled milk for the children, Ch'en Ting-feng came in, exhausted from his daily liturgical routine. It was obvious that the elder Ch'en held A-him in high esteem. He heard the explanation of my project, finding and analyzing the Taoist manuals held by the members of the Cheng-i Tz'u-t'an, and he cooperated splendidly, opening his own trunks and showing us manuscripts that A-him had never seen. Among Ch'en's collection were two of the manuals brought back from Lung-hu Shan by Lin Ju-mei, which had been given directly to his own father and had never been a part of Chuang's collection. But he did not have a copy of the Su-ch'i. I explained as gracefully as possible that I knew where perhaps one could be obtained, if Ch'en could help us in our arduous search for it. Ch'en smiled and replied that if I could come to his office at eleven the following morning, he might have been able to locate a copy of it.

Since our family shopped each morning in the central market, it was easy enough to combine a trip to the market with another visit to Mr. Chen's tidy office. The interior had not changed since my first visit there with John Levy in 1969. The musical instruments were on the wall, the books in neat rows behind the locked windows of bookshelves. Ch'en was at work delicately writing with a Chinese brush on a sheet of yellow rice paper.

"I have the book you want," he said, looking up. "A disciple of mine, named Kuo, had it."

He took a tattered manuscript from a drawer of his desk. On the front was pasted a new strip of red paper on which was written, "From the collection of Ch'en Ting-feng." The book was indeed the Su-ch'i, but I could not tell whether it was from Chuang's collection. The personal seal of Ch'en, obviously newly printed, was to be found on every third page or so, and the signature at the end was signed with Ch'en's name.

"May I make a copy of this with my camera?" I asked. "I will be able to return it to you by this afternoon."

Ch'en readily agreed and again queried me about my business with the books of Taoist liturgy. I explained that the books held by the Taoists of Taiwan were invaluable additions to the printed Canon, since most of the Taiwanese manuals were punctuated and had commentaries and detailed rubrical explanations, while the published canonical works were bare and dry, with no sign of punctuation.

"You should have come to me earlier," said Ch'en. "Had I known what your purpose was, I would have been glad to explain to you what I know of Taoism."

I was startled and grateful for his offer, since it was difficult for any Taoist master to agree to reveal his teachings. "What can I do for you in return?" I asked. "There is so little which I have that can be of use to a master."

"I would be grateful to see some of the copies of the Canon, which you have in your library."

With the copy of the Su-ch'i tucked safely under my

arm, I returned home and photocopied the entire manual as quickly as possible. I was anxious to see what use Ch'en would make of the canonical texts that I could bring him. The Tung-hsüan section of the Canon, with the great liturgies of renewal, was the obvious choice, since it had the texts closest to those in Ch'en's own collection. I hurried back with four of the hardbound brown volumes and appeared at Ch'en's office door at one o'clock, before the first of the afternoon callers had appeared.

"Thank you for the use of your Su-ch'i," I said. "Here are some of the copies of the Canon." I waited to see what he would do with them. With restrained but obvious delight at seeing the Canon, a set of such price that he could never afford to buy it, Ch'en opened the volume carefully and located the Su-ch'i, the Morning, Noon, and Night Audiences, to compare with his own copies.

"You were quick about copying the Su-ch'i," he said, seeing my interest in what he was doing. "Have you finished with it?"

"Yes, thank you," I replied, wondering how to ask least impertinently what use the printed versions of the Canon were to him. As I hesitated, he paused and looked up, as if to answer me before I could ask in the proper manner.

"You see," he said, "the text here is the same as the Su-ch'i which you borrowed. But I am looking for the name of the spirit which the ancient author summoned to act as liaison to carry the documents to the heavens. We must study continually to know if we are indeed summoning the proper liaison official."

He continued to glance through the pages of the Canon. I promised to bring more copies from my library and he in turn promised to loan me other copies from his collection to photocopy. With the Su-ch'i on microfilm, I was able to give Chuang a printed version of the lost text, while Ch'en kept his copy of the manuscript. It was interesting, I thought, that only Chuang was sure enough of himself not to refer to the Canon for the names of the various liaison officials. Indeed, Chuang's manuscripts contained several volumes of Lu or registers containing the names, descriptions, and proper occasions for using the communicating spirits in orthodox ritual. Further, Chuang had memorized the entire text of the Su-ch'i and did not need the book during the public performance of ritual. Ch'en later admitted that only Chuang knew how to perform the rite properly. The Taoists of the Cheng-i Tz'u-t'an were waiting for A-him to become head of the fraternity, hoping to learn from him the orthodox rubrics known only to the Chuang family.

As I said above, splitting up collections of written texts and not returning a borrowed book to a master was a common practice among the Shen-hsiao Taoists of north Taiwan. The noted Master Huang, a Hakka Taoist who lives in Chung-li City to the north of Hsinchu, had an extensive collection, dispersed generously among the Redheads of Hsinchu, T'ao-yüan, and Taipei counties. It is common to see as many as fifteen Taoists traveling from village to village in the Hakka farming communities, each performing his own liturgical specialty in various village temples on a rotating schedule. Thus the fraternity of Redhead Shen-hsiao brethren protect each other in a community of economic interests, insuring that no one master will monopolize the trade in chiao liturgies of renewal.

It must not be thought that the practice of stealing, forging, or copying texts is peculiar to Taiwan or to the local Redhead Shen-hsiao orders. The early history of Mao Shan, described in Chapter 1 above, shows the literati families of the north-south period competitively struggling over possession of the prized Shang-ch'ing revelations of Wei-Hua-ts'un at Mao Shan. T'ao Hung-ching spent many years retrieving the lost books and completing the Mao Shan collection. In view of such past and present threats to the integrity of collections,

Master Chuang in modern Taiwan was rightly concerned about preserving his library. When called upon to perform a chiao liturgy of renewal, Chuang and his sons alone were accountable for the entire ritual performance. The result was a liturgy so perfectly executed as to make Chuang the most sought-after and expensive master in north Taiwan, and a minimal opportunity for attrition to the texts.

Even though social encounters with Chuang were avoided by those who did not know him and were feared even by his own disciples, there were occasions when the violent temper and shouting were subdued and the warmest expressions of camaraderie and friendship emerged. Friends from Chuang's high school days or fellow office workers from prewar times saw a different Chuang when they came to his residence. To such guests Chuang always served healthy fruit juices or drinks made from almonds and peach juice, a formula supposedly good for longevity. Chuang also made a fine millet wine flavored with the essences of black sesame and dried mushrooms, another Taoist formula for longevity. Long hours were spent talking with friends, drinking, and meditating. If it were not necessary to perform ritual for a living, Chuang said, he would spend his days in drinking and talking and his nights in alchemical meditation.

When I first met Chuang, the house was poor and untidy, the children many, and the standard of living frugal. But through the marriages of his sons and daughters, the fortunes of the family visibly improved. For the eldest son, who had chosen the career of an army officer in order to further his education, Chuang found a wife from an upper-class wealthy family. The Chuang household received a new coat of paint and fine furniture as part of the dowry. The second son married into a shoe salesman's company and moved away from his father's residence. The third son, A-him, had put aside thought of marriage until his ordination as the successor of his father, and spent his free time pursuing Taoist perfection with meditations, breath control, and physical exercise. The fourth son, A-ga, who stayed at home reluctantly to help his father in ritual, found his own bride in the farming village of Nan-liao near the birthplace of his mother. A-ga's bride was a wealthy farmer's daughter and the Chuang home received a television set, refrigerator, and automatic washing machine as part of her dowry. The daughters of Chuang likewise married well. The eldest daughter, who was trained as a medical technician, married a public official. The second daughter married the son of a paper manufacturer, and the third daughter a wealthy merchant's son. All three daughters visited home frequently, bringing their children to play in the family rooms and be spoiled by the doting grandparents. The second daughter often lived at home in order to help with writing the lengthy documents used in ritual sacrifice. Her children were dry-nursed on the breasts of their grandmother or were carried by their grandfather as he entertained guests in the front room of the busy residence. Chuang was indulgent, kind, and totally unable to discipline his grandchildren.

Only A-him was not married. Since he had been chosen to succeed in the ministry of military Taoism, that is, the ministry of exorcism, much of his energy was given to physical exercises for self-strengthening and to the techniques of fang-chung, sexual hygiene. This last practice, A-him told me, was part of the Tao of the Left and not practiced by the more orthodox Tao of the Right. The loss of semen during sexual intercourse was prevented by the techniques of fang-chung. This was only a part of A-him's rigorous training, which included running and jumping with heavy weights on each shoulder so as to be able to jump great heights when the weights were removed, strengthening the fists and the arms by hitting hard objects, and sitting in the lotus position while holding the breath for long periods of time. During the breath-holding exercises, A-him said that he could in effect breathe through the pores of his skin; he always meditated bare from the waist upward. The secrets of Chuang were gradually being revealed to him, but in such a way that no doctrine or method was ever completely revealed at one time. Chuang's greatest fear was that A-him in his youth and enthusiasm would let slip the secrets to friends and sycophants who cultivated A-him's company in order to exploit his talents. And, indeed, A-him had already a large coterie of followers to whom he taught his military exercises, his breath-control techniques, and the secrets of sexual hygiene. Whatever doubts Master Chuang had concerning his son, there was no denying that he was an excellent Taoist and had far surpassed his father in many of the feats of physical endeavor and ritual perfection. This both pleased and slightly upset the elder Chuang. Furthermore, A-him showed a kind of generosity not typical of the other members of the Cheng-i Tz'u-t'an fraternity; he refused to receive any fee from the poor and often turned down payment when he felt the donor could not afford it. There was no doubt that Chuang A-him would be a worthy successor to his father and an able leader of the Cheng-i Tz'u-t'an brethren.

My position among the disciples and children of the Chuang family was passive and unobtrusive. I took photos of the grand liturgies, a practice that proved helpful in winning friends among the Taoists, the musicians, the temple committees, and the laymen who patronized the liturgies. To all who appeared in the photos, I gave copies, which were treasured by the recipients and still hang in many of the temples and the homes of those who received them. During the great liturgies of the chiao festivals of renewal in the local temples, I also recorded the music and helped in some of the lesser roles not requiring the years of training that Chuang's sons had been through. In many of the intricate ceremonies requiring incense to be put into small holders or tiny cups of wine to be laid on the altar tables for the heavenly worthies to witness,

Chuang's hands shook too violently to accomplish the tasks. In all such instances I was given the task of acolyte, handling the incense and the wine, fetching the memorials, burning documents, and doing the other small duties which assisted the temple custodians who were unfamiliar with the intricacies of Taoist rubrics.

Finally, there were many times when the writing of documents was lagging far behind with a ritual deadline imminent, or when the need for talismans was pressing; on such occasions all hands were brought into the meditation room or the front room of the Chuang residence to assist. It was during the preparation for one grand festival that I first noticed A-him's inability to draw talismans. I asked if I might help and A-him replied with great gratitude that he would teach me how to write the talismanic charms if I would agree to sit through the process with him and follow his precise instructions. The practice of the Tao of the Left, A-him explained, had made his hands too stiff to write with the necessary flourish. He could no longer control the pen, nor did he have the talent or feeling for composing the lengthy literary documents. That was why his unwilling brother, A-ga, had been pressed into ritual service. A-ga was truly a most unwilling disciple and obeyed his father only out of filiality. But he was quick of mind and fast of hand and could use the brush to compose memorials, rescripts, documents, and other ritual compositions faster than any other member of the family. To A-him fell the duty of executing the sacred dance steps, turning exorcistic somersaults in midair, fighting the demons with sword, spear, halberd, and axe, and summoning the proper spirits into the talismanic charms drawn by others.

I followed A-him's instructions and, using the models in Chuang's manuals for rubrical composition, drew the five Ling-pao talismans, the twenty-eight stellar talismans, and the Pole Star charms. When done, A-him lit incense and, chanting in a voice loud enough to fill the whole house, called down the proper spirits into the charms, sealing each in a large folded paper container. We then both left the front room, while Chuang slept on the couch, to have an evening tien-hsin snack in the temple concession. A-him's favorite stall was noted for a sausage made of glutinous rice, seasoning, and smoked pork, a delicacy that was indeed proper for the cold winter evening. With a bottle of beer to add cheer to the occasion, A-him spoke of his frustrations, his hopes, and his future plans for the Cheng-i Tz'u-t'an.

"A-ga does not want to be a Taoist," he said. "He is terribly jealous of the literary secrets my father has revealed to him, yet does not truly believe in the spirits he has been taught to summon."

"Yes, but A-ga is filial," I replied. "He knows that the Cheng-i Tz'u-t'an needs both of you in order to make your father's work a success."

"It may seem that way to you because whenever you are here he listens closely and seems to study. But did you know that A-ga once ran away?"

I did know that A-ga had gone to the port of Keelung and taken a job as a radioman on a merchant vessel. Chuang had gone after him, creating a grand scene on the dock, demanding that the master of the shipping company allow his son to return. Chastized by the verbal abuse, A-ga returned reluctantly to his father's household and continued the role of a Taoist, but with no heart for the rituals.

"It is because my father's hands shake that A-ga is necessary to him. Only A-ga can write the memorials and rescripts in a hand fast enough to keep up with the demands on my father's and my own ritual performance."

I told A-him how important I thought it was that his father reveal all of his secrets: "He has kept so many to himself that if he chooses to reveal some to you and some to A-ga, at least we are sure that more of what he knows will be passed on to future generations." I said that I hoped A-him's resentment of his recalcitrant brother would not prevent him from seeing the necessity of having Chuang pass down for posterity what had been taught to him by his three Taoist masters.

"You are right in fearing that much of what my father knows may be buried with him," A-him agreed. "The secrets of the meditations are simple. I have learned them as well as the dance steps, the mantras, talismans, and mudras. But what my father keeps from us is the most essential part of our instructions."

"And what is that?" I was thinking that I might be able to find in the Canon the secrets that Chuang kept from his sons.

"What do you think it was that the Taoist Ch'en wanted when he asked to see your copies of the Canon?" Warmed by the beer and sausage, A-him grew bolder.

"He wanted to know the name of the proper liaison official to be sent off during certain rituals."

"More important, he wanted to know the description of the spirit; without knowing what the spirit looks like, how can he summon him?"

"Has your father told you the descriptions of the various spirits?"

"Only for some," A-him answered. "He has told you some, and others to A-ga. But the main spirits, those for the Su-ch'i, the Morning, Noon, and Night Audiences, he keeps to himself."

"What else has he not yet revealed?"

"The dance of the *Ho-t'u*," he answered. "You will see him do it soon."[13]

"But surely the rubrics must be written somewhere in one of his manuals. You should be able to figure out which spirits are summoned according to the rubrics of the yüeh-chien method and the other techniques that he teaches."

"True, but without the k'ou-chüeh (the oral transmission), it is difficult to fathom."

The hour was already late, and we returned to the front room of Chuang's house to complete the preparations for the chiao festival. Chuang had already left the room to attend to some details in the temple. A-him described the spirits that he could summon and I in turn promised to find what I could in the volumes of the Canon in my own room. The dance of the ho-t'u for which A-him had such admiration was soon to be used by Chuang in a manner that well justified the son's respect for the rite and his desire to learn it.

Having spoken something of Chuang's relationships with the ordinary people of Hsinchu, with his friends, and with his own family, I must say something about how Chuang behaved towards the spirits and other Taoists when summoning his magical powers from the heavens. If his magic was more powerful than others', it was likely that the practitioners of the Tao of the Left would be reluctant to pit themselves against his method. That this was indeed the case can be seen in the following instances observed and recorded during my stay with Chuang in Hsinchu. Since it was often necessary to corroborate Chuang's stories by interviewing villagers who witnessed the events, I have included an account of the impressions of the witnesses who saw Chuang's performance.

The first case involved the use of Mao Shan black magic, in which the Six Chia spirits were invoked to harm a fellow Taoist.[14] One day while I was sitting in the front room of the Chuang residence, a man from the Hakka district near Chupei, ten kilometers north of Hsinchu, entered in a state of great agitation and begged to see Chuang. Turning his head as if bothered by an intruder, Chuang asked what had occurred.

"My brother, a Taoist whom you know, is being attacked by Mao Shan magic," the man said, holding his farmer's hat in both hands and bowing his head in supplication. Chuang sat up suddenly as if an electric shock had run through him.

"Mao Shan?" he glowered. When Chuang is angry, his eyes open very wide, an expression he assumed when exorcising evil demons as well as when scolding his subordinates. "Where are you from?"

Upon hearing the location, Chuang immediately put on his grey overcoat and walked out the door, telling his wife he would soon be back. He motioned A-him and me to stay where we were and took a taxi to the distant farming area. In about two hours he was back, very drunk and pleased with his prowess.

Upon arriving at the farmhouse, Chuang had found the afflicted man, a minor Taoist, gasping in bed with a high fever. The family insisted that another Taoist was using black magic against him. Chuang computed the chia spirit of the day and then summoned the spirit of the Pole Star, p'o-chun or the kang spirit of Thunder Magic, to subdue it. He then paced the steps of the *ho-t'u* a total of twelve times, as described in chapter 6, sealing off the room from the attack of the Mao Shan Taoist.[15] He finally commanded the chia spirit to return and attack the Mao Shan Taoist who had caused the trouble. Satisfied that the attacker would be punished and the sick man relieved, Chuang declared the ritual ended. The man soon arose, feeling much better, and served Chuang a bottle of warm rice wine and other refreshments. Chuang finished off the bottle of wine on the spot and took the taxi back to Hsinchu.

Within a few moments of Chuang's return, while he was still boasting proudly to us of his success, a stranger entered the front door. Obviously shaken, the man announced himself as the practitioner of the Left Tao whom Chuang had just overcome by his Thunder Magic. With abject apologies, he promised never to use the evil magic again and backed out the door, disappearing hastily down the alley too rapidly for me to question him about his state of mind. Before long the farming family appeared, bringing a catered feast of various soups, noodles, and sashimi (raw fish with green mustard). The word of Chuang's victory soon spread around the neighborhood. A-him told me privately that the previous year another such battle had taken place in which another Taoist had died after attempting to oppose the Mao Shan Taoist's black magic. Whatever the explanation for Chuang's success and the previous exorcist's failure, it was certain that the man who had just apologized and fled was visibly shaken. The reputation of Chuang as a powerful master was confirmed in the neighborhood by the event, and Ch'en the Fat came from across the alley to ask about being instructed in Thunder Magic.

The second event concerned the exorcism of a man whose possession occurred during the performance of one of Chuang's solemn liturgies of renewal.[16] The incident took place during the festival of renewal for the temple of the goddess Matsu in Chung-kang ward of Chunan City, south of Hsinchu. Chuang was in the process of performing a Su-ch'i ritual, and I was able to record the entire event on tape and on film, with the mudras and mantras used by Chuang in the expulsion. The Su-ch'i ritual, according to the earliest rubrics in the Canon, is supposed to begin between 11 P.M. and 1 A.M., the time to correspond to the symbolic renewal effected by planting the Five Talismans. But Chuang, despite the rubrics and his own prognostications indicating that the later hour was more propitious, decided to perform the rite between 8 and 10 P.M. One reason was to accommodate the village elders, all of whom wished to witness the beautiful event and were reluctant to wait up until midnight. The second reason alleged was the need to begin the rite called Morning Audience at 3 A.M.[17] By putting the Su-ch'i earlier in the evening, we could all be assured of a few hours rest before the strenuous rite of the Morning Audience. But Chuang's real motive was his own physical condition. After the first full day of ritual, he was exhausted and his hands were shaking from the effects of the fast and abstention from alcohol. The only people in the temple who knew that the rite was beginning at the wrong moment were A-him and I, and although I attempted briefly to suggest we sleep earlier and perform the rite at the proper time, Chuang was adamant.

A violent wind was blowing from the Taiwan straits as the rite began, echoing through the temple and distorting the sounds on the recording. By the time of the fa-lu mandala building, the wind had subsided and the interior of the temple was peaceful, presaging good fortune. Suddenly, during a particularly lyric moment in the ritual, the whole gathering was disturbed by the obvious possession of the local medium, right in the center of the temple. The man had stripped to the waist and taken on the strange features of the possessing god, whose name everyone breathed forth in unanimous recognition.

"T'ai-tzu-yeh!" the temple custodian whispered into my ear. The village elders and the other Taoists seemed pleased that such a propitious deity had come into the temple, but Chuang was angered. He continued to perform the rite as if nothing was happening. But then the demon seemed to become enraged and followed Chuang, imitating his every motion. As if to add insult to injury, the medium began to speak in the boy god's weirdly high and piercing voice. To the horror of the entire entourage he was saying: "The rite was begun at the wrong hour! The rite was begun at the wrong hour!" Chuang turned and faced the possessed man, his eyes wide with rage. Taking the posture of the Pole Star mudra, he breathed deeply and used the Thunder Magic rubric to expel the deity.[18] In a moment, the possessed man left the temple, collapsed, and came out of his trance.

Chuang then declared his own right to determine the hour when ritual was to be initiated.

When the rite had ended, the temple committee came to ask Chuang if indeed the ritual had begun at the wrong hour. Voices were raised, but Chuang insisted on his own privilege to decide when the various liturgies should begin. Neither A-him nor I said anything, and the medium, of course, could remember nothing of his possession or what he had said during the trance. The matter was dropped, but the head of the temple committee, a large man who was a devout Buddhist, begrudgingly admitted to me later that the power of Chuang was indeed great to have expelled the spirit so easily. The remainder of the chiao festival was a great success and no bad effects were seen to come from the wrong timing, proving Chuang's power over the heavenly spirits to be indeed effective.

Many other anecdotes could be told to convey the impression Chuang made on the community around him, his relationships with his friends and neighbors, and his attitude towards the spirits. For instance, whenever I came for a lesson in ritual Taoism, Chuang always began by worshiping his ancestors, burning incense to the two tablets on his main family altar. One of the tablets honored his own forebears, the Chuang clan, and the other contained the tablets of all the Taoists from whom he had inherited his manuals. There were memorial scripts for the Wu, the Ch'en, and the Huang clans, as well as the memory in Chuang's own mind of the powerful Lin brothers, Ju-mei and Hsiu-mei, who had contributed so much to his own perfection. He also had a deep and abiding devotion to the Taoist spirits on his altar, especially to the eight-armed four-headed statue of Tou-mu, the mother goddess of the Pole Star, patron of his variety of Taoism.[19]

Chuang's approach to his spirits was one of complete devotion and strict observance of propriety and rubrical perfection. Where other Taoists allowed their disciples to do things such as eat from the sacrificial offerings or drink the sacrificial wine, Chuang would not allow any talking or whispering during his ritual and looked neither to the left or right when engaged in public prayer. He was ferociously loyal to the men who worked for him, forgiving their weaknesses, even their cheating him on innumerable occasions. Ch'en the Fat, for instance, had taken many ritual objects from Chuang's home, even from his altar, and never returned them. Many of his closest disciples had broken away to form businesses of their own. It was essential to Chuang's character to make nothing of any of his possessions, his reputation or his knowledge, hiding his talents from all but the closest disciples and his own sons, living in a carefree manner. Chuang was, in all ways, a Taoist and took joy in his ritual profession.

The relationship of Chuang to the belief of the common man, that is, to what many social scientists call "folk religion" or "Chinese religion" was basic. This institution, which is very hard to delineate, is not an organized religion but a belief shared by the Han (Chinese) people with myriads of local variations; it can be defined basically as the religion of the cosmological theory of yin-yang and the five elements. That is to say, the yin-yang five-element theory, when euhemerized or personified as a system of spirits and demons who rule the invisible world, is the basic tenet of the system called Chinese religion. A Taoist as such is a firm believer in Chinese religion and participates in all the local cults, ancestor worship, and whatever else is considered to be of faith by the people whom he serves. Thus Chuang believed in the spirits that the citizens of Hsinchu City believed in. He offered religious sacrifice on the birthday or feast day of a popular local deity, he freed the hungry souls from hell in the P'u-tu ritual of general amnesty for the deceased, and he performed funeral ritual in which the spirit of the deceased was led through the labyrinthian tortures of hell's bureaucracy to the heavenly realms of the immortals. These practices were basic to Chinese religion in Taiwan's cities and villages; and to all the underlying beliefs, Chuang ascribed with a deep and convinced devotion.

At the same time Chuang was externally a man of the world, one educated by the Japanese and in the mandarin literati traditions of his forebears. To the agnostic, Chuang said nothing of his Taoism, and to the common man, everything of the theology of folk religion. But for himself and his sons he kept the esoteric doctrines of monastic Taoism, the techniques of breath control, inner alchemy, refinement of the spirits, and meditation. In the following pages I shall describe a minute part of Chuang's beliefs and practices, but a part nevertheless basic and not well known either in the west among scholars or in China. The secrets of religious Taoism, even those contained in the printed Canon, must depend upon men like Chuang for preservation and proper explanation.

PART II
The Teachings of Master Chuang

4. The Tao of the Left

Introduction

When Chuang began to give lessons in Taoism to his sons, A-him and A-ga, he did not begin with the esoteric "Tao of the Left" or the elite meditations of inner alchemy, but with the practical first steps of drum playing, ritual dance, and song.[1] To A-him, the elder of his sons destined for the profession of ritual Taoism, Chuang taught the military exorcisms, the handling of sword and spear, tumbling, and the art of self-defense.[2] To the younger son A-ga, Chuang taught the arts of literary Taoism, the composition of official ritual documents, brush stroke, and song.[3] The older son was a much better student than the younger and learned his own role and that of his brother to perfection. A-ga, on the other hand, was embarrassed to perform ritual in public and wanted a more acceptable, modern profession. My introduction to Chuang and acceptance as a disciple had a beneficial effect on A-ga, who suddenly realized the value of his studies in the eyes of a foreign scholar. Much to the delight of the elderly Chuang, his two sons, and more especially A-ga, attended the instructions given for my benefit. Because of my presence and my questions concerning the sources of Chuang's teachings, A-ga tried to outdo his brother A-him in the esoteric knowledge of meditative Taoism and became proud of his role as ritual expert in the public forum. My presence at public ritual lent much prestige to A-ga's performance and led him to study Taoism in a scholarly manner.

Chuang's selection of the Tao of the Left as the first manual to use in my instruction was at first puzzling.

The manual was both extremely elite and difficult to master. Chuang insisted that he had learned the manual first from his own father, but further questioning made clear that he had not yet taught the method to his own sons. Nowhere else in his documents was there such a clear explanation of how the spirits were to be commanded and summoned at the Taoist's discretion. The book was the most detailed in Chuang's library in explaining the method of forming mudras, reciting mantras, and performing the accompanying meditations.[4] I was quite surprised one day when we were summoned to the second floor of the Chuang residence to watch as Chuang paged through the valuable old manuscripts in the Taoist trunks and book cases.

1. MAO SHAN MAGIC: THE TAO OF THE LEFT

"Today I shall speak of the Tao of the Left," Chuang said. He told A-ga to bring the manual called *Ch'i-men Tun-chia*[5] from the shelves in his bedroom. The manual was wrapped in white cloth, and consisted of four chüan or paperbound texts, each with forty or so handwritten folio pages. We passed the four books around, examining the rice-paper pages. The text had been copied out in 1851, the first year of the Emperor Hsien-feng's reign. At the end of each section was written the date and the name of the copyist, a teacher of Lin Ju-mei who had been hired to copy out the text in Lin Ju-mei's name.

"The book comes from Mao Shan," said Chuang. "It was brought to Taiwan by Wu Ching-ch'un in 1823, and came originally from Wu's grandfather, twenty-three times removed." He brought forth an ancient and tattered manual with the title *The Family History of the Wu Clan* (*Wu-shih Chia-p'u*) written on it.[6] On the first pages of the family history could be seen the account of how the first Taoist in the Wu clan had gone to Mao Shan and been ordained a high-ranking monastic priest.

"The manual was acquired by the Wu clan at Mao Shan, but in fact it must be classified as a sort of military magic that originated at the famous Wu-tang Shan, a Taoist center in Hupei province noted for its military ritual." Chuang told again the story that we had heard many times, of the origins of the Wu-tang Shan military sect, of the supposed founding of the order by Chu-ko Liang during the wars of the Three Kingdoms, and the emphasis of the order on military arts, T'ai-chi ch'uan, and battling with the sword. Since most of Chuang's stories were hagiographic, that is, pious folk stories rather than historically accurate accounts, I challenged his description, using the preface of the *Ch'i-men Tun-chia* manual as proof.[7]

"Surely the manual here has no relationship either to Mao Shan and the famous Shang-ch'ing sect or to the *Yellow Court Canon*, the basic text of the order. It is difficult to see how it relates either to Mao Shan, where Wu's ancestor is said to have acquired it, or to the Wu-tang Shan military tradition, since the manual mentions nothing of either mountain."

"You are not wrong in supposing that the manual does not belong to the Mao Shan Shang-ch'ing sect, which is wholly orthodox and historically from a tradition quite different in content from the text we have here." As he spoke, Chuang opened the first volume of the manual and quoted from the preface.

"The manual was copied out at the beginning of the Ming dynasty, and was entitled *Ch'i-men Tun-chia*, a marvelous method for hiding the Six Chia spirits in the microcosm, and calling them forth to do battle. The early Mao Shan sect was concerned with inner alchemy and attaining longevity by ritual meditation. Like all other Taoists, Mao Shan monks later began to bury the dead and perform rituals of renewal. The present manual, therefore, is called Mao Shan Magic only because it was propagated there many centuries later, during the Sung period (960–1278). I say that it must originally have come from Wu-tang Shan because of the preface. Here we see that the method explained in the manual is attributed to Chu-ko Liang, the famous general of the Three Kingdoms period (221–263). Methods of military magic are traditionally said to have come from Wu-tang Shan in Hupei, the place where Chu-ko Liang practiced his battle tactics and developed the *Pa-chen T'u*, the Battle Chart of the Eight Trigrams." Chuang opened the first manual to the pages where the battle chart was explained.[8]

"Then the manual cannot be a *Ch'i-men Tun-chia* like the popular pamplets that can be bought next door at the Ch'eng-huang temple."[9] I showed Chuang the pamphlet I had just purchased, with the same title as the manual in his collection. He took the book, peered at the first few pages, and returned it with a chuckle.

"This sort of manual is very late, and cannot be traced back earlier than the Sung. The only similarity in the two volumes is the title. In fact, these four volumes, which I have just taken out of my collection, are a Lu or register of the spirits' names and appearances, and the secret charms and talismans for bringing them under the Taoist's power. They are only called *Ch'i-men Tun-Chia* to offset the idle and curious who might chance upon the book in my library. In fact the book of military magic is very dangerous and must not be lightly shown to the outsider, who may put it to evil use. Because it is Tso-tao, the Tao of the Left, officialdom has condemned the book and punished those who practiced it throughout Chinese history. Orthodox Taoists have the manual only in order to combat those evil Taoists who practice black magic to harm the men and women under their spiritual care. I explain it to you only so you may use it to help men, and never to harm them by its powers."

Chuang settled back into a more comfortable position before beginning his lesson. A-him, the elder brother, sat straight and alert. A-ga, the younger, looked for some avenue of escape. Chuang began to repeat his injunctions about preserving the secrets he was going to reveal and never using the feared Tao of the Left except to help one's fellow man. Orthodox Taoists like himself and his sons were never permitted to use such techniques except in the most extreme conditions.

A-him often complained about his father's long introductory discourses, which were designed to make us restless and unwilling to wait for the truly important revelations. Today's lesson was not like the others. In a brief few sentences, Chuang got to the point. There were three preliminary warnings, he said. The heart must first be made to control the impulses and the phantasms which entered the mind. Before such a dangerous doctrine was imparted to the disciples, the master must assure himself that their hearts were pure and their motives simple. Anyone learning these secrets who intended to use them for gross profit or for harming others needlessly would be punished drastically by the spirits. The second warning had to do with self-discipline. The spirits will only obey those who are upright and who have practiced the rubrics so thoroughly that not the slightest detail is missing. The third point concerned the method of bringing the power of the spirits into one's own body. The mind had to be emptied of all cares and worries and the body purified in all respects before the power could be brought into the microcosm of the body.

Paraphrasing the text, Chuang chanted:

The heart and the mind must be as one,
Purified from any sullied desires.
Only the pure of mind can touch the heavens
Only the upright of heart can assemble spirits.
Nature obeys the upright and (Cheng) orthodox.[10]

A hundred days before beginning the rite for enfoeffing the spirits, the disciple must begin by regulating his mind and senses. The exercise of breath control and meditation on the purest of the heavenly spirits must be practiced daily upon arising and before going to bed. The Taoist must envision the three principles of life in the center of the microcosm, the Yellow Court within his own body, and see himself contemplating before the eternal, transcendant Tao. When the Three Principles of Life—Primordial Heavenly Worthy, Ling-pao Heavenly Worthy, and Tao-te Heavenly Worthy—are present, then mystic contemplation on the eternal Tao is possible. As the time for beginning the ritual approaches, the Taoist must abstain from meat and practice celibacy. He must be particularly careful to give good example to his neighbors, by acts of benevolence and mercy towards the poor, loyalty to his friends, and filiality to his parents. Only then will it be possible to perform the Tun-chia rites; if at any time during the period of preparation or of ritual enfeoffment the Taoist fails to act virtuously, the spirits will immediately refuse to obey him.

Though ritual perfection is demanded in every detail, the vestments worn by the Taoist during the ceremonies may be of his own choice. He may wear the white robe with square hat of the southern monastic orders, the black robe with the fish hat of the Ch'üan-chen sect, or the bright red embroidered robes with the gold crown of the Cheng-i Taoist. The clothes are not important, as long as the rubrics are performed with ritual perfection. Quite unlike the literary Tao of the Right, there are no musical instruments, percussion pieces, or other paraphernalia used (see chapter 5 below). The ritual objects, the sacrificial offerings, and the meditations are described in section 2 below. They are listed as they occur in the Tun-chia manual, with Master Chuang's oral explanations.

2. Preparing for the Ritual

1. *Selecting a site for the Taoist altar.*[11]
Choose a site where a river flows between two mountains.

It must be an area where gentle breezes blow and the air is fresh and unpolluted. There, draw on the ground a "Battle Chart of the Eight Trigrams" (Pa-chen T'u, as in figure 1 below). The battle chart is drawn by pacing off sixty-four steps in a circle, one for each trigram in the *Book of Changes*. Next, go to the very center of the circle and set up an altar in honor of the Pole Star (Tz'u-wei T'an). One table is needed for an altar, and there should be a second table, such as a bench used for a chariot rest, on which to lay the incense and other ritual objects. On the main altar are to be laid out the sacrificial objects. Enclose the whole area in a tent made of blue-green cloth. The area is thus protected from the elements and casual onlookers.

On the table in the center of the sacred area are to be arranged the following items:

1. A stone rubbing block for making ink.
2. Two earthenware candle holders.
3. Two stone flower vases.
4. Two rubbing blocks for making ink, one of red and one of black rubbing compound.
5. Two bowls of pure spring water.
6. The special seal carved from datewood as described in part 4 of this section.
7. The talismans of the six Chia spirits as described in part 5 of this section.

One tall flag pole eighteen feet in height and twenty-eight smaller poles six feet in height are arranged around the sacred area according to the plan shown in figure 9 below. Next, the Taoist must prepare the following sacrificial offerings:

1. Dried deer meat.
2. The meat of an owl.
3. A rabbit's foot.
4. A fox's liver.

5. Lamb's blood.
6. Pure white rice wine.
7. Deep breathing incense.
8. Cedarwood incense.
9. An unlacquered wooden basket.
10. An antique ritual sword.
11. A yellow mulberry candle.
12. Paper for drawing talismans in five colors.
13. An oil lamp blue-green in color.
14. Red dates.
15. Roasted chestnuts.
16. A purple crab.
17. A white chicken.

The care of the master's vestments and the bringing of his food must be entrusted to two youths who have not yet reached puberty. The idle, the riffraff, and the impure must not be allowed to enter the sacred area. No one may approach the central altar but the Taoist and the two acolytes.

The rite for enfeoffing the Six Chia spirits must begin on a chia-tzu day and end on a keng-hai day, that is, it must cover a full sixty-day cycle. The Taoist must perform the ritual every day for sixty days, calling down one spirit each day, except on the fourth day when two spirits are enfeoffed, one in the morning and one in the afternoon. Thus the six spirits are summoned every five days. Each spirit, over a period of sixty days, is summoned a total of twelve times. By the end of the period, the Taoist will have completely familiarized himself with the ritual, so that he may perform it at will without referring to the manuals or forgetting any of the minute details.

2. *Constructing the Battle Chart of the Eight Trigrams.*[12] First, go to a spot by the river which is not frequented and select sixty-four clean stones. These will be used to set up

a battle chart of the eight trigrams around the interior of the sacred area. Next, go into the sacred area and locate the northeast direction, which is called the "Gate of Life" in the battle chart, or the trigram Ken in the eight trigrams. This is the most important of the eight gates, around which the ritual of enfeoffment revolves. Do not let anyone see how the arrangement is done, or the method of setting up the trigrams. The eight trigrams are given the following names:

1. The trigram K'an in the north is called Hsiu, or rest.
2. The trigram Ken in the northeast is called Sheng, or life.
3. The trigram Chen in the east is called Shang, or injury.
4. The trigram Hsün in the southeast is called Tu, or blockade.
5. The trigram Li in the south is called Ching, or vantage point.
6. The trigram K'un in the southwest is called Szu, or death.
7. The trigram Tui in the west is called Ching, or alarm.
8. The trigram Ch'ien in the northwest is called K'ai, or opening.

Four of the clean stones taken out of the river are to be laid out in a straight line behind each of these gates, and four stones in a line at a point halfway between the gates, so that there are a total of sixteen lines of stones stretching out, four to a line, around the circle. The manner of arranging the stones is seen in figure 1.

The Battle Chart of the Eight Trigrams in figure 1 relates directly to the Pa Kua, or the prognostic chart of the eight trigrams. The significance of the illustration is, however, wholly military. Behind each of the "gates" lies hidden an attacking army of demons. By the marvelous Tun-chia method explained here in the manual, the Taoist

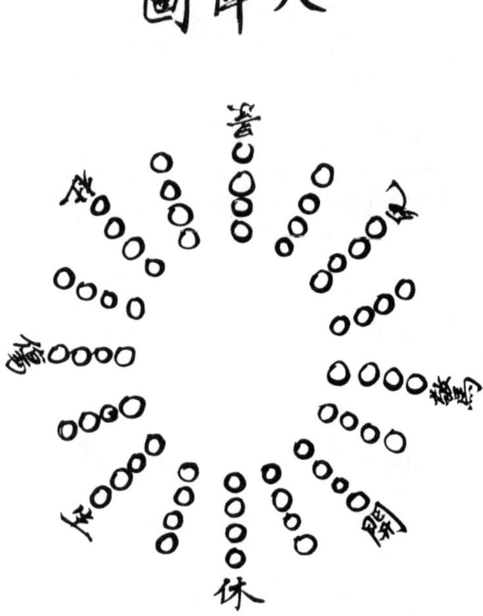

Figure 1. The Battle Chart of the Eight Trigrams, showing how the sixty-four stones are laid out in sixteen rows, four stones to each row, around the sacred area.

learns how to envision the harmful demon and render him or her subservient to his commands. In the method to be taught below, the Taoist will learn how to envision each of the spirits and how to form the proper mudra and mantra to enfeoff or bring the spirits under his power. To do this he must have memorized the battle chart and its relationship to the eight trigrams, as illustrated in figure 2. The Taoist can thereupon summon the spirits at any time by constructing the battle chart, either by dancing the magic "steps of Yü" (illustrated in figure 3) or by tracing the chart in the left hand (figure 4).

Figure 2. The eight trigrams arranged in the order of the Posterior Heavens—that is, with the trigram li in the south, or top of the chart, and the trigram k'an in the north, at the bottom of the chart. The Taoist envisions the chart on the floor of the sacred area.

The Taoist paces or dances around the battle chart according to the footsteps enumerated in figure 3. That is, he starts in the north, the trigram K'an (figure 2), and dances through the various positions until he reaches the trigram Li in the south. It must be noted that the numbers in figure 3 are in fact the mystic enumeration of the magic square. No matter in which direction the numbers are added—vertically, horizontally, or diagonally—a row of

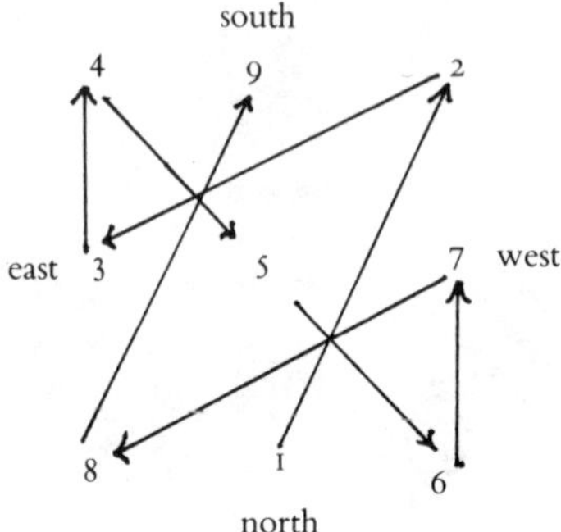

Figure 3. The sacred steps of Yü arranged as a "magic square" in ritual dance.

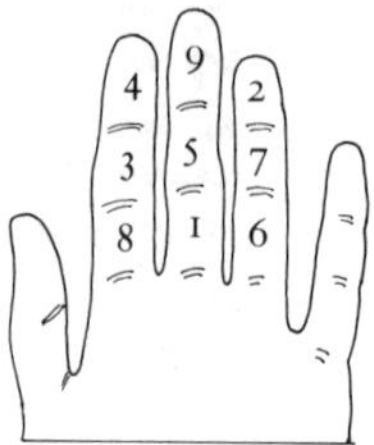

Figure 4. The magic square envisioned on the left hand of the Taoist.

three numbers will always add up to fifteen. As the Taoist paces around the sacred area according to the enumeration of the magic square, he summons, commands, or envisions the demonic spirits at the various gates. It must also be noted that the magic square can also be depicted on the left hand and the same sequence traced out by pressing the tip of the thumb to the proper joints (figure 4). The system is used not only in a sacred dance step but as a key to understanding the structure of the heavens. The spirits whom the Taoist calls under his command are thought to reside in the Pole Star (the seven stars of Ursa Major) plus two other stars in the northern heavens. In the next step, the disciples learn the magic square as it is found in the heavens.

3. *The Position of the Nine Stars in the Heavens.*[13]

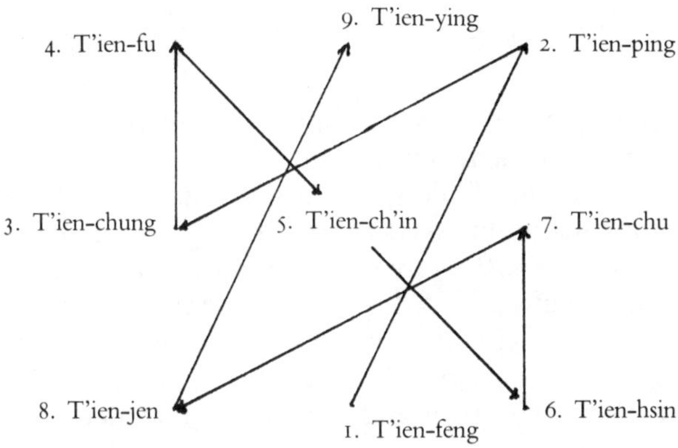

Figure 5. The nine stars in the heavens, seen as a magic square.

Each of the nine stars has a secret style name and corresponds to one of the trigrams in figure 2. Furthermore, the Taoist must learn which of the five cosmic elements —wood, fire, metal, water, or earth—the star is subordinate to, in order to marshal all possible spiritual forces to the task of subordinating the power of the spirit to his command:

STAR	SECRET NAME	TRIGRAM	POSITION	ELEMENT
T'ien-feng	Tzu-ch'in	k'an	1	water
T'ien-jen	Tzu-ch'ang	ken	8	earth
T'ien-chung	Tzu-ch'iao	chen	3	wood
T'ien-fu	Tzu-hsiang	hsün	4	wood

STAR	SECRET NAME	TRIGRAM	POSITION	ELEMENT
T'ien-ying	Tzu-ch'eng	li	9	fire
T'ien-ping	Tzu-hsü	k'un	2	earth
T'ien-chu	Tzu-chung	tui	7	metal
T'ien-hsin	Tzu-Hsiang	ch'ien	6	metal
T'ien-ch'in	Tzu-chin	k'un (bis)	5	earth

Each of the nine stars has a special talismanic charm and a mantric spell, which will be given in part 7 below. The nature of the Six Chia spirits is such that only the most powerful magic invoked by the Taoist will make them obey his orders; the power of the nine stars is necessary to bring them under the Taoist's control. But before accomplishing any of the commands, the Taoist must first see to the carving of a special seal, which is used to stamp all the talismans and documents intended to summon the spirits.

4. *Making the Special Ritual Seal.*[14]
Select a piece of fragrant datewood without flaw. Cut from this a 2.8-inch block, a perfect cube. On a propitious day, begin woodcarving by meditating and building the mandala (as described in chapter 4); that is, command the pure spirits to guard the doors and windows of the room in which the carving is to take place. One must circulate the breath after the Thunder Method (described in chapter 6) and then begin to carve the seal. First draw the outline of the seal on the bottom of the woodblock, and then carve out the figures according to the illustration in figure 6. When done, the talismans of the nine stars (described in part 5 below) are drawn on a piece of yellow paper, which in turn is used to wrap the seal. The seal, wrapped in yellow paper, is then enclosed in a stone case.

Figure 6. The Ch'i-i Tsung seal.

The stone case is then sealed with wax and cannot be opened until the Taoist is ready to use it for summoning the Six Chia spirits. The special wooden seal is thus guarded by the spirits of the polar stars, and is always kept in a stone case when not in use. It is strictly forbidden to let it be seen by menstruating women or by the ritually impure. Ink for the seal is made from pure spring water and red powder mixed in such a way that the seal prints clearly and legibly. The seal may never be used negligently. When putting it back into the case after use, always recite the following incantation:

The command of the Heavenly Emperor!
Who dares to wait for a moment!
The Emperor's seal.
Quickly, quickly, obey his will!

When using the seal one is not allowed to talk, least of all to laugh or act frivolously. If used without due respect and seriousness, it will lose its power and the Yin-ping spirits of the netherworld will lose their trust in it.[15]

5. *Learning to draw the talismans of the Six Chia spirits.*[16] The next step in learning to summon and command the Six Chia spirits is most difficult for the novice to accomplish since it requires a smooth and rhythmic flow of the writing brush. Each of the Six Chia spirits has its own talismanic charm, which must be committed to memory in every detail. The Taoist may not carry along his prompt book or have recourse to a library when called upon to exorcise a demon or turn away some evil force that is threatening the community. The charms of the Six Chia spirits are particularly difficult to execute, making it all the more obligatory that the disciples who would learn the method commit the talismans to memory at this point. The talismans are shown in figure 7.

Each of the talismans is drawn on a seperate piece of yellow paper in black ink. When completed, the talisman is stamped with the special Ch'i-i Tsung seal and burned in order to summon the spirit.

6. *The talismans and mantras of the nine stars.*[17] As mentioned in part 3 above, the nine stars of the northern heavens must be especially invoked in order to win power over the Six Chia spirits. That is to say, each of the Six Chia spirits is a general leading an army of spiritual soldiers. All are ready to leap forth at the summons and call of the Taoist, provided that he has gained power over them by a knowledge of the talismanic charms and mantric incantations of the nine polar stars, i.e., the seven stars of ursa major plus two hidden stars. The next step in mastering the Tun-chia method is therefore to memorize and master

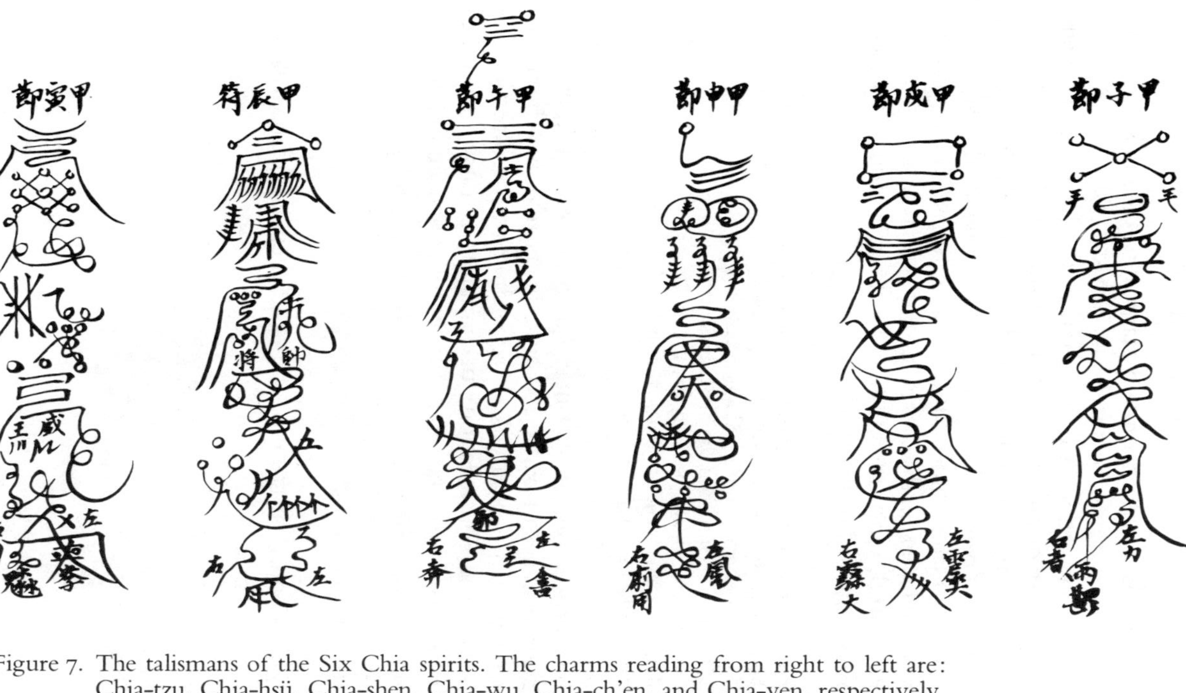

Figure 7. The talismans of the Six Chia spirits. The charms reading from right to left are: Chia-tzu, Chia-hsü, Chia-shen, Chia-wu, Chia-ch'en, and Chia-yen, respectively.

the use of the talismans and mantras of the nine stars. The manner of using the star spirits is this.

First, determine the direction in the heavens in which the handle or tail of the constellation Ursa Major is pointing. The method will be more completely described in chapter 6 below. Next, draw whichever of the Six Chia talismans one wishes to use as a summons on a piece of yellow paper, and seal it with the special seal.

Second, when the talisman has been drawn and sealed, recite the following spell:

Honor to the heavens. Let the Tao be followed.
Succor to the nation, peace to the people!
The spirits have bequeathed a heavenly book,
Used now to summon the Six Chia spirits!
Come forward, and hear my commands!
The talisman is sent off, burned in the fire!
Chi-chi Ju Lü-ling!!

Third, when the talisman has been burned, then take another piece of paper and quickly write down the name of the star to be invoked, according to the direction in which the constellation (ursa major) points. Draw the talisman for the star, stamp it with the seal, and recite the following: "In the _____ year, _____ month, _____ day, _____ hour, I (*Taoist title*) affix the seal. Carry out my orders, Chi-chi Ju Lü-ling."

The mantras of the nine stars and their talismans follow.

Figure 8. The talismans of the nine stars.

SPELL OF THE T'IEN-FENG STAR

Deep and dark, black and murky,
Armored hero of the mystic north,
Broad and vast, leave no traces,
Riding on the violent winds.

Great thy strife, power for sorrow,
Rout the enemy in deep confusion.
Join your army to my forces,
All pervading demon vapors!
Chi-chi Ju Lü-ling!

SPELL OF THE T'IEN-HSIN STAR

Out of chaos came the first gestation.
Floating above, pure and clean.
Yang, like a diamond, moved and created.
Yüan-hsiang Li-chen! (The trigram Ch'ien)
The four seasons were put in order,
The myriad creatures brought forth
by transformation!

Six dragons await your majesties!
Used to transport precious gems!
Beautiful, resplendent, awesome, dreadful!
Generals leading a multitude of the
realized immortals
In front of and behind the Six Chia spirits,
A hundred million fighting troops!
I do here and now command you,
Together assemble, in purity and quiet.
Chi-chi Ju Lü-ling!

SPELL OF THE T'IEN-JEN STAR

T'ien-jen

High mountains piled up,
Reaching to Mount K'un-lun,
Precipitous, steep, dangerous, lofty,
Clouds of vapor to the horizon's limit.
Mountain gullies hide the immortals;
Birds and beasts learn from them.
Grass and trees flourish and grow.
Shen-ch'a and Yü-luei,
Elves' and goblins' heroic essences,
Cause stones to fly and boulders to walk,
Spew forth fog and move the clouds,
Bind and fetter heaven and earth.
Chi-chi Ju Lü-ling!

SPELL OF THE T'IEN-PING STAR

Most heavily sullied of the spirits,
Thou whose ability to bear suffering
 is limitless,
Rivers from thy depths are carved and
 mountains born,
The myriad nations' boundaries cut.
The breadth and length is measured out,
Soil piled up and mountain ranges shaped.
The five elements exhaust the infinite
 visible forms;
Fire smolders, wood grows stronger,
Water held in lakes and rivers,
Metal treasures buried,
Stretching in space across nations, and
 downward in time
Through generations.
Here to this military camp in the wilds,
Within the eight trigrams and nine squares,
Which are indeed but tiny boundaries,
I command you, now today,
Crowd in about me, all ye spirits!
Chi-chi Ju Lü-ling!

T'ien-ping

SPELL OF THE T'IEN-YING STAR

T'ien-ying

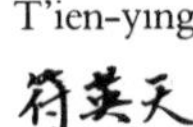

Essence of the fiery star Ying Huo,
Green-faced great spirit,
Fiercely, mightily, your anger flares.
Parching red searing light!
Scorch the heavens, dry the seas,
Burning rocks and melting metal.
The skies fall and the earth collapses!
All due to thee (Hsing) star.
Splendid, brilliant, shining, glittering,
Your light breaks the gathering dusk.
With your great drum you control the winds,
Burn up what has been hoarded and amassed.
The Chi, Pi, Yi, and Ch'en stars,
All are famed for their power over fire.
Today I call you under my command,
Bright-spirited striding soldiers.
Chi-chi Ju Lü-ling!

SPELL OF THE T'IEN-FU STAR

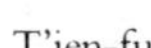

T'ien-fu

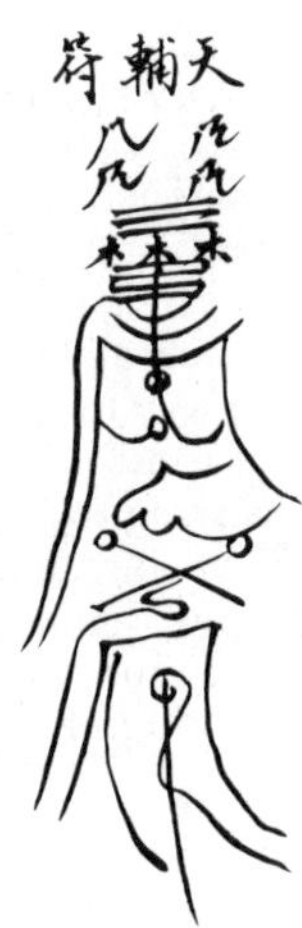

A deep mist, hovering, threatening;
Heaven and earth exhale, inhale.
East is turbid, west is murky.
The four seasons' strength exhausted,
The power to give life used to depletion.
The heavens shake, the earth trembles,
Waves dash up and touch the skies.
Blowing sands blind the vision!
Fire, with your overwhelming majesty,
With your overflowing power,
Help me carry out the role of master!
Bring your flags, your drums, your standards.
Here today I now command thee!
Bring to me your awesome power!
Chi-chi Ju Lü-ling!

SPELL OF THE T'IEN-CHUNG STAR

T'ien-chung

Ch'ung-ch'ung, the sound of thunder!
The nine heavens assemble together;
From the trigram Ch'ien going forth,
They enter by the trigram Chen.
A sudden shower, followed by a rainbow,
A single thunder clap!
From the depths arises a rain dragon,
Evil forces' courage buried,
Demonic spirits' traces obliterated!
Thunder shakes a hundred Li!
A shattering fist, crushing, booming.
With your sound of thunder crashing,
Help me, send a fearsome wind,
Here and now I command thee, assemble,
Drumming, dancing hordes attend!
Chi-chi Ju Lü-ling!

SPELL OF THE T'IEN-CHU STAR

T'ien-chu

Awesome, baleful, hard as steel,
Cold, sharp, glistening, gleaming,
Points and edges sheathed in cloth.
Spears and halberds numerous as clouds,
Touching the heavens and dragged in the earth,
Majestically gushing forth like a spring.
No way to prevent its forward progress.
His name is famous, his power inherited,
Assisting the White Emperor of the West.
Fire comes quickly obeying his commands.
I, now, summon thee to assemble,
Awesome, courageous, in rank after rank.
Chi-chi Ju Lü-ling!

SPELL OF THE T'IEN-CH'IN STAR

Oh thou god who rules in the center,
Sitting, you govern the eight directions.
The Yellow Emperor has a command:
Let the four quarters praise you!
The Ch'i-men magic gates respond to you;
Your going forth is from the gate of earth.
Dwelling in the center you rule the outer,
Helping the weak, controlling the strong.
Proclaim the magic words *Om-na-t'a*!
Left and right, strike and scatter.
Those who lose him wither,
Those who would grasp him die.
With fire he purges the deceitful!
The eight trigrams acclaim him!
I now summon thee hither.
Thou who in simplicity are good and wise.*
Chi-chi Ju Lü-ling!

T'ien-ch'in

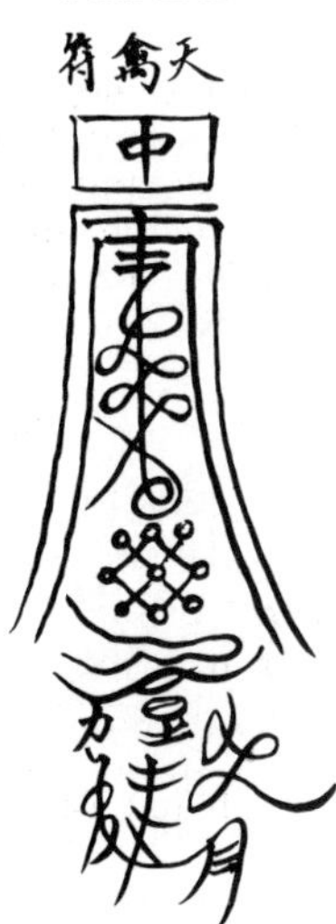

The nine talismans with their accompanying mantric spells must all be memorized before the next step in the instructions for summoning the Six Chia spirits. The day on which a particular charm or spell is used must be determined by looking at the almanac which the Taoist master keeps in his own possession. Thus, the nine stars are arranged as in figure 5, in such a fashion that the eight points of the compass and the center each receives one of the stars. The direction in which the handle of ursa major points in the northern heavens indicates the mudra and mantra that the Taoist is to use at any given time during the day or night. The method is explained in chapter 6, and can be seen illustrated in figure 21. The Six Chia spirits and the nine talismans are therefore used according to the month, day, and hour, the cycle of summoning the spirits changing with the rotation of the heavens. Rather

*variant readings: thou who choose goodness and wisdom.
choosing (only) the good and the wise.

than refer continually to the almanac, the Taoist master usually memorizes the chart. Thus the spirits become effective and are put into use as the Pole Star points in their direction. Since it is impossible to know or guess this direction during the day or on a cloudy evening, the Taoist has a chart worked out to which he can refer as needed.

7. *How to make the standards of the twenty-eight constellations.*[18]

Twenty-eight standards are to be set up inside the sacred area in a great circle. The flags are made of silk and the poles to which they are attached must be six feet tall. The silk called for in the rubrics is to be of the five basic colors of the elements—green, red, yellow, white, and black. But in fact the flags for the twenty-eight standards are made of seven colors; there are two shades of red in the south and two shades of black in the north. Thus there are four flags in each of seven colors—twenty-eight flags, one for each of the twenty-eight constellations. The flags must be woven of silk with the warp and woof both colored with the same dye. The constellation is drawn in the upper corner of each flag, and the symbolic animal is drawn in the center. The standards may be listed in the following groups.

1. The constellations subservient to wood, which are to be drawn on standards of blue-green silk:
   The Chiao constellation with a Chiao rain dragon.
   The Tou constellation with the Hsieh unicorn.
   The K'uei constellation with the wolf.
   The Ching constellation with the An (Han) wild dog.

2. The constellations subservient to metal, which are to be drawn on standards of white silk:

The K'ang constellation with a dragon.
The Niu constellation with an ox.
The Lou constellation with a domesticated dog.
The Kuei constellation with a sheep (goat).

3. The constellations subservient to earth, which are to be drawn on standards of yellow silk:
The Ti constellation with a badger.
The Nü constellation with a bat.
The Wei constellation with a ring-necked pheasant.
The Liu constellation with a roebuck.

4. The constellations subservient to the sun, which are to be drawn on standards of red (hung) silk:
The Fang constellation with a rabbit.
The Hsü constellation with a rat.
The Mao constellation with a cock.
The Hsing constellation with a horse.

5. The constellations subservient to the moon, which are to be drawn on standards of azure (deep blue) silk:
The Hsin constellation with a fox.
The Wei constellation with a swallow.
The Pi constellation with a crow.
The Chang constellation with a stag.

6. The constellations subservient to fire, which are to be drawn on standards of crimson (ch'ih) silk:
The Wei constellation with a tiger.
The Shih constellation with a pig.
The Tsui constellation with a monkey.
The Yi constellation with a snake.

7. The constellations subservient to water, which are to be drawn on standards of black silk:

The Chi constellation with a leopard.
The Pi constellation with a snail.
The Shen constellation with an ape.
The Chen constellation with an earthworm.

For all of the standards, use hand-rubbed ink made on the stone rubbing block, as in the directions in part 1 above. When the pole and pennant are completed, insert a pheasant's feather in the head of each standard, being sure that the pole itself is six feet tall. Each flag staff with standard and feather must then be set up, as can be seen in figure 9.

8. *Summoning the spirits to the center of the sacred area.* The Six Chia spirits are summoned from behind a standard according to the time of the year, month, day, and hour, as computed in the method shown in chapter 6, figure 21. Each of the spirits has his or her own post, unit, and garrison name, as will be explained below. In the middle of the circle of twenty-eight standards is to be placed the great standard, which acts as coordinating general for all of the spirits summoned. Thus the spirit soldiers will not dare to leave until they hear their unit called. They can be commanded to go forth to overpower the enemy when summoned by the mudras formed on the Taoist's left hand, combined with the recitation of the mantric spells and the drawing of the talismanic charms. The standard for the large pole in the center is to be made of yellow silk, in the center of which is written, "Lien Chen-ping Ta Yüan-shuai" (Commander General for Drilling the Spirit Soldiers).[19]

The incense table and the altar of sacrifice are set at the base of the great standard in the center. The pole is to be twelve feet high. The writing and sending off of talismans, the use of the special seal, and the rite for swearing in the spirit generals are all to be done at the foot of the great standard. On the very top of the pole is affixed a wooden

Figure 9. Arranging the standards of the twenty-eight constellations.

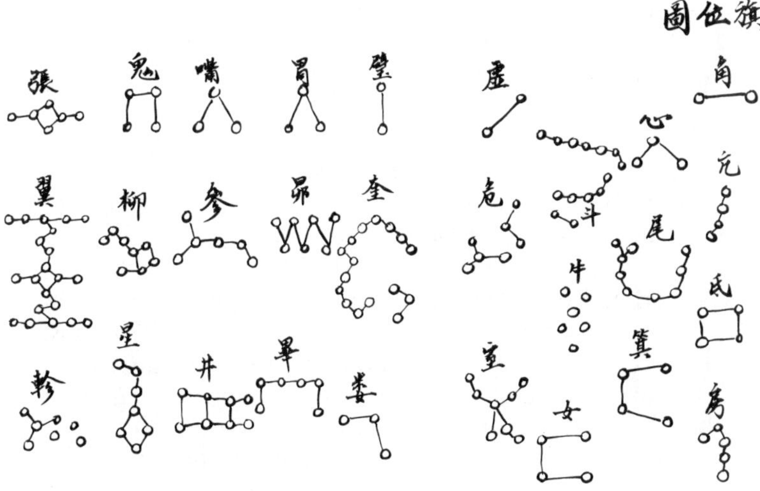

Figure 10. The twenty-eight constellations.

block or tablet on which the following warnings are inscribed in gold: on the front side, "Chin shu" (Imperial Decree); on the back side, "Shang-ti T'e Ling Tzu Yang" (By special decree of the Heavenly Emperor, Talismanic writing!).

The twenty-eight standards and the central pole are set up inside the Battle Chart of the Eight Trigrams, which was described in part 2 above. Each of the poles must be set up in the proper place with reference to the eight trigrams, that is, the eight gates of the battle chart. At each of the gates, the "jade girl" spirits are to be appointed as guards of the entrance, according to the method for building the mandala described in chapter 5 below. The Six Chia spirit generals can now be "refined," or brought under the Taoist's control. It is necessary to envision the appearance of each spirit, and to execute the mantric summons, mudra, and talisman, to enfeoff them under the Taoist's power. Once completed, the ritual can be repeated at will. The spirits will be always ready to obey the Taoist's wish and order.

9. *How to set up the t'an sacred area.*
Set up the altar so that its back is to the north. That is to say, when the Taoist faces the altar he should be looking north, while the altar faces south. The t'an or sacred area should be twenty-four feet square and eighteen feet high. There are four entrances, the four "gates" of the trigrams. Do not let anyone approach the area or look down from the surrounding mountain tops. No impure thing must be allowed near. If the rite is to be effective and the Taoist to gain power over the spirits, only the morally and ritually pure can be allowed near the area. Youths who have not yet reached puberty should be used as acolytes, and all implements brought within the sacred area should be new and clean. When leaving the sacred area upon the com-

pletion of each rite, straighten up the mats, realign the stones, and see that the poles are all in order. The Taoist must determine ahead of time the direction from which the particular spirit is to be summoned. Thus the three directions which the Taoist faces during the rites are either k'ai (the Gate of Heaven, or the trigram ch'ien); hsiu (the north, or the trigram k'an); and sheng (the northeast, or the trigram ken). Only when the altar has been set up with every detail accounted for should the ritual begin. Whenever sleeping, eating, or drinking, always leave the sacred area. The Taoist should choose the ground directly to the north of the t'an altar for his own resting place. It is forbidden to eat the five grains or the three noxious meats (dog, eel, and goose) during the sixty days of the ritual. One must also bathe before entering, and see that every rubrical detail is perfectly fulfilled.

10. *The time of day and direction for enfeoffing the Chia spirits.*

The rite is to begin on the Chia-tzu day closest to the summer solstice, and should be carried out in the following order:

1. On the chia-tzu day, at the mao hour (6 A.M.) face the trigram chen (the east) and close the entrances to the sacred area. The spirit chia-tzu is then refined according to the rubrics described below.
2. On the i-ch'iu day (second day) ... [missing from the text].
3. On the ping-yen day (third day) at the mao hour, face the trigram ch'ien, and from the gate called sheng summon forth the chia-shen spirit.
4. On the ting-mao day (the fourth day) ... [missing from the text].
5. On the ting-mao day (two spirits are enfeoffed on

the fourth day) at the shen hour (3–5 P.M.) enfeoff the chia-ch'en spirit from the gate called sheng, using the proper talisman and rubrics.

6. On the wu-ch'en day (fifth day) at the mao hour face the trigram k'an and from the gate called sheng enfeoff the chia-yen spirit, using the proper talisman and observing all the rubrics.

The chia-hsü spirit, who is enfeoffed on the second day, and the chia-wu spirit, who is refined in the morning of the fourth day, are not included in the list here, but are included in the rubrics written below. Thus the Six Chia spirits are brought under the Taoist's power over a period of five days, two spirits always being enfeoffed on the fourth day, thus making six spirits each five days. The rite is repeated twelve times over a period of sixty days, until the Taoist is thoroughly familiar with the process.

11. *The esoteric ritual names of the Six Chia spirits.* During the performance of the various rites which summon and "swear in" the different Six Chia generals, the spirits are addressed according to their secret Taoist names. The following list gives the ritual name, the tzu or style name, and the hao or title by which the spirits are summoned. It is necessary to remember the names of the spirits in order to understand the text of the ritual in the next section.

1. The chia-tzu spirit's ritual name is Yüan-te; his style name is Ch'ing-kung; his title is General Huang-chen.
2. The chia-hsü spirit's ritual name is Ling-yi; his style name is Lin-chi; his title is General Chung-chih.
3. The chia-shen spirit's ritual name is Shen-ch'üan; her style name is Chieh-lüeh; her title is General Kang-hsien.
4. The chia-wu spirit's ritual name is Ch'an-jen; her

style name is Tzu-ch'ing; her title is General Hsiao-lieh.

5. The chia-ch'en spirit's ritual name is T'ung-yüan; his style name is Jang-ch'ang; his title is General Tang-ti.
6. The chia-yen spirit's ritual name is Hua-shih; his style name is Tzu-fei; his title is General Chi-sha.

12. *A description of the appearance of the six spirits.* The most jealously guarded secret of the Taoist master is the "register" or lists of the spirits' names, titles, and appearances, without which the performance of liturgy is a hollow shell, a weak imitation of the orthodox, classical tradition passed down from antiquity. The most critical part of a Taoist master's instructions is the description of the esoteric spirits' countenances, clothes, weapons, or other accouterments, which the Taoist novice who presents himself for a grade at ordination must account for. Disciples wait years at a master's feet to learn the secret names and the descriptions such as those here revealed in the text of the Mao Shan manual of military magic. The text reveals the heavenly stem, and therefore the element (direction) to which the spirit is subservient, the appearance of his or her face, clothes, weapons, and supernatural powers. A learned master can draw a picture of the spirit from memory, so well are the following passages kept in mind.

1. The Chia-tzu spirit's heavenly stem is Wu. He is twelve feet tall, with two horns on his head, the face of a rat, and the body of a man. His mouth is tapered and pointed like a knife. He has a yellow beard and yellow hair, and his eyes protrude. He wears the Yüan-p'ao imperial robe, with a gold belt around the waist. In his hands he carries a Chiang-muo staff for controlling demons. From his belt hang a long bow, a sword, and a beaded pearl shield. The mantric cry which is used to

summon him and his troops is "Hsi-t'a!" His lieutenant general is the Ting-mao spirit, and he leads an army of a hundred thousand soldiers. Such is his power that he can move mountains and plug up the sea, make the ground shrink or stretch, cause rocks to move and sand to fly. His spiritual strength is great indeed, and he always works barefoot.

2. The Chia-hsü spirit's heavenly stem is Chi. He is nine feet tall, with the face of a man and the body of a snake. His countenance is purple, and on his head he has a golden crown. He wears a yellow robe with a golden belt, from which hangs a golden shield. Around his shoulders is coiled a snake, and in his hands he grasps a spear made of eight snakes. Hanging from his belt is a gold sack filled with stones and arrows without feathers. His mantric summons is "Tsu-chung!" Under his command is the lieutenant general Ting-ch'iu, and a hundred thousand spirit soldiers. Such is his power that by drawing a line on the ground he causes a river to appear; by forming a small mound of earth with the hands, he can change it into a massive cliff; with his power one can drill a well, fill up trenches, attack and invade a city, hurl stones and scatter sands. The god is violent and merciless. There is nothing that he fears.

3. The Chia-shen spirit's heavenly stem is Keng. She is ten feet tall, with the face of an ugly woman, yellow hair, and large protruding white teeth. On her head is a crown made of pearls. She wears a purple robe fastened with a jade belt, with scarlet sandals on her feet. In her hands she grasps a huge sword capable of splitting mountains. Over her breasts she wears chain-mail armor. Her mantric summons is "Cheng-jan!" Under her command is the lieutenant general Ting-hai and a hundred thousand spirit troops. By her power one can make swords fly and knives shoot out, break the enemy's ranks with self-propelling spears. Those who approach the camp (Battle Chart of the Eight Trigrams) will be cut down like

blades of mown grass. Mounted cavalry troops or bandits, there are none that do not bow and fear her orders. By nature she loves to kill, and no one who meets her lives to tell.

4. The Chia-wu spirit's heavenly stem is Hsin. She is eight feet tall, and her face is white and clear complexioned, with pretty features and delicate eyes. Her hair is done up on top of her head in a bun, and her robe is made of silver armor with a silver belt. She rides an excellent horse with red spots, and in each of her hands she carries a double-edged sword. Her mantric summons is "Ch'ing-hsiang!" which is intoned like singing a song. Under her command are the lieutenant general Ting-yu and a hundred thousand spirit troops. By her power, one can summon a fog and make clouds arise, befuddling the enemy so they lose their way. She can also cause gold and silver to come into one's hands, but only for the sake of good, or for helping the cause of the Tao. When the enemy approaches the camp, whistle, and she will send forth flying spears. By performing her rite, her unbounded courage will be turned against the enemy who will flee in terror. It cannot be determined ahead of time whether or not she will sally forth riding her red horse.

5. The Chia-ch'en spirit's heavenly stem is Jen. He is twelve feet tall with an ugly, frightful face like a Vajra (Kongo) spirit, with a three-peaked crown on his head. On his body he wears golden armor and in his right hand he carries a halberd, while standing atop a black dragon. His mantric summons is "P'o-lieh!" The Ting-wei spirit is his subordinate, with a hundred thousand spirit troops under his command. With his power one can dry the rivers and empty out the sea, walk on water as if it were earth, level city walls, wipe out the enemy, and ride on mists and clouds. By blowing on paper cutouts, one can change them into an army, and call a legion of soldiers out of the skies to destroy the enemy. The Chia-ch'en spirit's character is sharp and hard as steel.

6. The Chia-yen spirit's heavenly stem is Kuei. His face is the color of black millet, and his head is shaped like a leopard's. Around his forehead is wrapped a red cloth, and around his waist is belted armor. On his feet are high boots, and in his hands, a whip made of steel. His mantric cry is "K'ung!" Under his command is the lieutenant general Ting-yi, with a hundred thousand troops. By his power one can summon a great wind, shake mountains, burn fields, cut down enemy soldiers, uproot trees, cause sand to fly, and make men lose their senses. By invoking him, one can create the image of false forests and conceal one's body so that attackers can do no harm. The Chia-yen spirit's temperament is dark and foreboding.

13. *On the sacrificial offerings to be laid out during the ritual.*[20]

A table for holding the offerings must be set up at the Gate of Life, or at the base of the standard used during the ritual. The altar is always set up so that it faces the south, that is, the Taoist faces the north when standing in front of the altar. The offerings are laid out in the following order: in the first row, put the cups of wine; in the second row, the dried fruit; in the third row, the uncooked meat; in the fourth row, the cooked meat; and in the fifth row, the candles, vases, and so forth. The layout of the altar and the position of the Taoist with his acolytes are shown in figure 11.

With the above prescriptions, the first instruction of Master Chuang regarding the enfeoffment of the Six Chia spirits came to an end, with the assignment that each of us was to read the manual of instructions and come to the following day's lesson ready to draw the talismans and form the mudras as illustrated in the following pages. Since the description is meticulous and dry, it is recommended to read only one spirit's ritual at a time. The

English text is complete and can be used as described in the text.

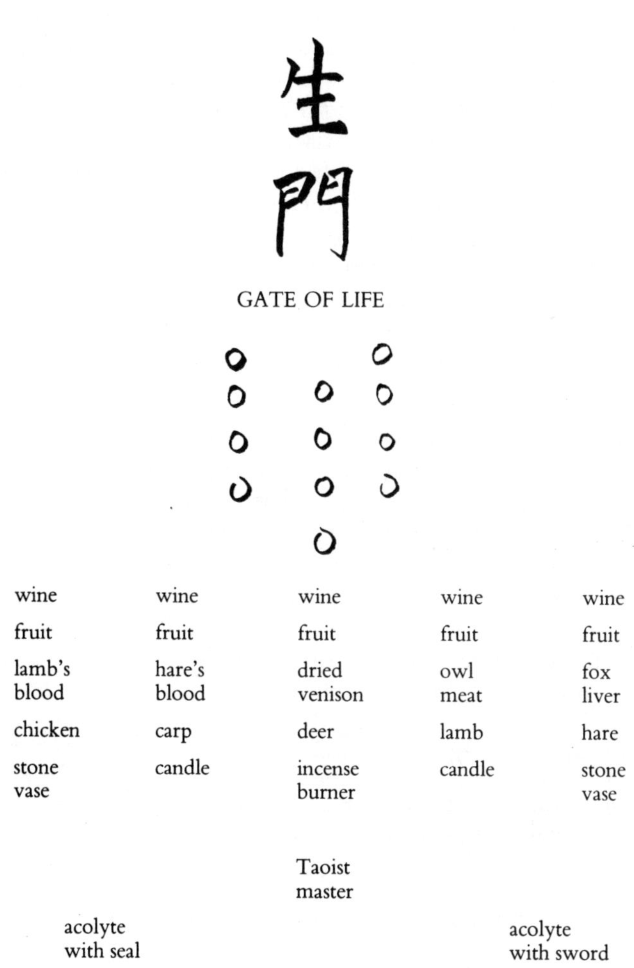

Figure 11. The arrangement of the altar for sacrifice.

3. PERFORMING THE TUN-CHIA RITUALS

With the sacred area now ready, and the seal, talismans, and other implements prepared, the Taoist master may now begin to refine, or bring under control, the Six Chia spirits. At the proper time indicated for each ritual, the Taoist goes to the incense table at the foot of the central pole and there draws the talismans to be used for the day, sealing each one with the special seal. He then goes to the gate in the Battle Chart of the Eight Trigrams, indicated as the proper gate for the ritual, and there lays out the sacrificial offerings. The ritual of enfoeffment takes place at the gate, facing the direction indicated in the rubrics. The various mantric spells are then recited, the mudras formed, and the Ts'ui talismans drawn in the air, according to the directions written below.[21]

1. *The ritual for refining the Chia-tzu spirit.*

On the Chia-tzu day, at the Ting-mao hour (6 A.M.) the Taoist master goes first to the central flagpole and there performs obeisance. He draws the proper talismans for the day and stamps them with the seal. When done, he proceeds to the position on the battle chart marked K'ai, the Gate of Opening, where he faces the east. There, he lays out again the sacrificial offerings, lights incense, and bows in worship, while reciting:

To the central, flowery land of China,
The gods have given a heavenly book.
The substance of heaven, the path to the Tao!
Now drill and enfoeff the spirit armies;
Honor to thee, General—.

The Taoist master then recites the conjuration:

Shang-ti has given his command!
Hold on high the talismans, grasp the seal,
Command and enfoeff the Six Chia spirits.

Uphold the orthodox, dispel the heterodox,
Protect the nation, bring peace to the people.
Totally eradicate all falsities and lies.
Grant the petition we make with this offering.
Let us successfully carry out the ritual,
To master the marvelous Tun-chia method.
Bearing the Chia-tzu talisman,
I stand at the T'ien-chung position;
Here I pitch my camp, delighting
To be at this marvelous gate;
From afar I summon the spirits,
None dare delay to fulfill my commands,
Once seeing the power of the talisman I hold.
Wind and fire come at my summons!

At this point the Taoist stands still, bows, and then performs the nine-step dance of Yü as shown in figure 4. While performing the dance he recites the T'ien-chung mantric spell (as in section 2, part 7 above) and burns the T'ien-chung talisman. When the conjuration is finished, the Taoist stands very still, closes his eyes, and meditates, envisioning the spirit as described above. The meditation lasts for a half hour. When done, he takes the sword, looks upward toward the sky, and draws in the air the "appearing" talisman (Ts'ui fu, as in figure 12) with a single stroke. Thereupon he forms the Huang-chen mudra (figure 12) and recites the Huang-chen mantric spell below.

Figure 12. The Huang-chen talisman and left-handed mudra.

The Huang-chen mudra is performed by first opening the left hand so that the nails of the index finger and the ring finger are stretched out parallel to each other, with the middle finger stretched slightly above. Next, bend the middle finger down and press the index finger and the ring finger over the nail of the middle finger, so that the nail cannot be seen. Finally, press the little finger and the thumb over the nails of all three fingers. Use the sleeve to cover the mudra so that it cannot be seen. The talisman for making the Huang-chen spirit appear must be practised by the Taoist in the air many times before he actually uses it ritually, so that it can be completed smoothly and perfectly without faltering, or cutting off the action before completion.

The following is the mantric spell for summoning the Huang-chen spirit:

O thou commander of heaven and earth,
General Huang-chen!
Yellow beard and yellow hair,
Rat face and man's body,
Yüan robe and golden belt,
Staff of steel and engraven fan,
With your lieutenant general Wen-pa [Ting-mao],
Red-faced, towering in stature.
From Hsü and Wei and the Pole Star
Call forth your heroic troops!
Level mountains and shrink the earth!
Stones fly and dust fills the air.

Thereupon the Taoist recites the mantra of Shang-ti:

Ka! Ch'a! Kon! Om!
Quickly come and assemble here!
Receive my commands, carry them out!
Chi-chi Ju Lü-ling!

When finished chanting the mantra, the Taoist closes his eyes and meditates, holding his breath until he hears a humming in his ears. Then he takes the great sword again and repeats the talisman for making the spirit appear, drawing it quickly in a single stroke. Then forming the mudra on his left hand, he repeats the above mantric spell, this time substituting two new lines for the original beginning:

You alone are the purest of lords,
General Huang-chen!
Yellow beard and yellow hair . . .

When he reaches the ending, "Receive my commands, carry them out," he adds the magic words in a scolding voice:

Khat-chhit is thy name!
Chi-chi Ju Lü-ling!

With the mudra still formed on the left hand, he closes his eyes and meditates again until he perceives just above his forehead, that is, directly above the eyes, a red light and then a yellow light. He immediately takes the sword again and draws the appearing talisman in the air for a third time. The mantric spell is repeated a third time, substituting for the first two lines:

The Wu ritual for summoning Yüan-te
General Huang-chen
Yellow beard and yellow hair . . .

Reaching the next to last line ". . . carry them out," he adds:

No terror that you cannot suppress,
Appearing in a wraith of fire,
Quickly, upon seeing our needs,
Send down lightning and thunder!
Chi-chi Ju-Lü-ling!

When the Taoist has finished the mudra and mantra a third time, he again closes his eyes and meditates until he sees a red light in a purple fog before him, like the coming of an army all in dark uniforms. When he hears the angry sound of a violent wind and the clapping of a thunderbolt, then the spirit has arrived. Taking the seal in his left hand and the sword in his right he cries out:

Now you may hide!
Five days hence come back again,
And show your true form!

Having finished the rite, he returns to the altar by the central pole, bows for a moment in worship, and retires from the area.

2. *The ritual for refining the Chia-hsü spirit.*
On an I-ch'iu day (the second day), likewise at the Mao hour (6 A.M.), the Taoist master goes to the main standard and lights incense, performing obeisance, and writing the talismans for the day as before, stamping them with the seal. When he has finished, he goes to the gate marked Sheng in the Battle Chart of the Eight Trigrams (the northeast) and faces east. There again he arranges the sacrificial items and offers worship at the standard marking the gate, bowing with lighted incense in his hands. He then begins the incantation as follows:

To the central flowery kingdom of China,
The gods have given a heavenly book.
The substance of heaven, the path of the Tao!
I now summon and enfoeff the spirit armies.
Honor to thee, General———.

The Taoist master then begins to recite the following conjuration:

Shang-ti has given his secret command.
Hold up the talisman, grasp the seal!
Command and enfoeff the Six Chia spirits!
Stand by the orthodox, dispel all evil,
Protect the nation, bring peace to the people.
Completely eradicate all cunning deceits.
Help us successfully to carry out the rites,
For investing and commanding the Chia spirits.
On this day, at this hour,
I take the Chia-hsü spirit's true talisman,
And stand at the T'ien-jen position.
Here I establish my residence,
Delighting to be at the gate of life!
From afar answer my summons.
Do not for a moment wait to come.
Once having known the power of the talisman,
Wind and fire come at my command.

The Taoist then paces the sacred dance steps (Steps of Yü) while reciting the T'ien-jen mantra and burning the T'ien-jen talisman. When done he stands very still and erect, closes his eyes, and meditates for a period, envisioning the spirit of Chia-hsü. He then takes the great sword and in the air draws the Ts'ui talisman for making the spirit appear. When the talisman has been drawn, he forms the mudra on his left hand and recites the mantric spell, as below.

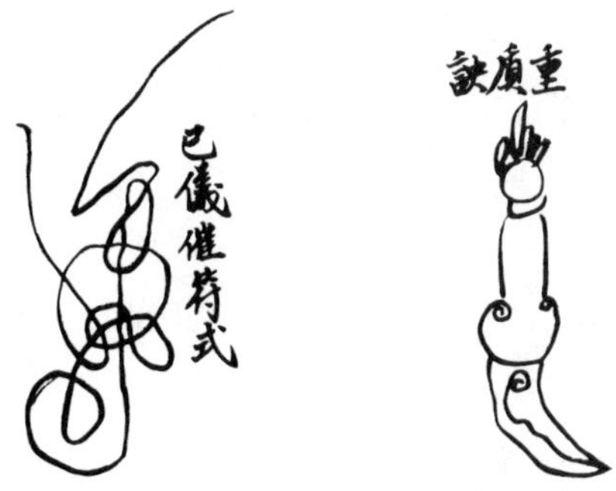

Figure 13. The talisman and mudra of the Chia-hsü spirit.

To form the mudra, use the left hand, bend the thumb, and bring down the index, ring, and little fingers so that the nails are parallel with the top of the thumbnail. Stretch the middle finger straight upward. The mudra must be covered with the sleeve so that no one can see how it is formed. The talisman must be practiced until it is perfectly mastered. One should try to write it as if drawing on a piece of paper held in mid-air. There must not be the slightest deviation or faking on the part of the Taoist. Only when the form is perfected can it be used in the ritual.

When the talisman has been drawn in the air, the Taoist forms the mudra and recites the following mantric spell of the Chia-hsü spirit Chung-chih:

Come down from your position in the Lou star,
O thou spirit Chung-chih!
Giant body, coarse and ugly,
Man's face and serpent's body,
Clothed in the yellow color of center,
Armor and helmet made of gold,
Snake spear eight feet in length (eight-pronged
snake spear)
Serpents coiled around your body.
In your satchel arrows and stones,
Innumerable your magical changes.
With your lieutenant Ting-ch'iu,
Holding an axe and ringing a bell,
Under your control a hundred thousand soldiers,
Like a forest of wolves and tigers.
Cause a river to gush forth!
Seal the mountain passes! Level cliffs,
Scatter sand, make rocks fly,
Piling up to become a mountain!

To this is added the secret mantra of Shang-ti:

Om! Gu! Hsi! Ken!
I command thee approach the Hsü position!
Hear my orders, carry them out!
Chi-chi Ju Lü-ling!

When finished with the mudra and the mantra, the Taoist closes his eyes and concentrates until he senses a wind blowing from behind on his ears. He then takes the sword and draws the appearing talisman in the air for a second time, being sure to complete the character without once breaking the smooth flow of the stroke. The talisman is drawn in the air twice, without pause. He then repeats the mantric spell and the mudra, changing the first two lines to read:

All hail to thee! With ranks of soldiers,
Numerous as a forest, General Chung-chih . . .

After the words "Hear my orders, carry them out" in the next to last line, he adds:

Has my second summons reached you,
As I shout out your name?
Chi-chi Ju Lü-ling!

When the mantra and the mudra have been repeated for a second time, the Taoist again closes his eyes and concentrates for a short time. When he sees a yellow mist arising before his eyes, he then takes the sword and writes the appearing talisman in the air a third time. The talisman must now be drawn in the air a total of three continuous times, after which the mudra is again formed and the mantric spell recited. The first line of the mantra is changed to read:

God of the Chi rite, hidden spirit,
O thou General Chung-chih . . .

Again at the next to last line the words are added:

Carry out my commands, do not hide yourself,
From afar come and show your true form.
Put your perverse obstinacy to use,
Mercilessly wield your cruel sword.
Chi-chi Ju Lü-ling!

Having finished the mantra, the Taoist again closes his eyes and concentrates, envisioning a yellow light directly before him, like a wall cutting off everything that is in front. Then the sound of a bell ringing in the ears will be heard. This is the sign that the god is coming. Immediately as the god comes, take the sword in the right hand and sing in a loud voice:

Now go back whence you came,
To come again five days hence,
Showing your true appeance.

With the spirit sent back, the ritual is completed. The Taoist master then returns to the central standard and replaces the seal and the sword on the table. He bows deeply in obeisance and leaves the ritual area.

3. *The ritual for refining the Chia-shen spirit.*
On a Ping-yen day (the third day) at the Ting-mao hour (6 A.M.), the Taoist master goes to the central standard, lights incense, and bows in obeisance. He then draws the talismans proper for the day and signs them with the special seal. He goes to the gate marked Sheng in the Battle Chart of the Eight Trigrams (Gate of Life, same position as on the preceding day) and faces the northwest. The sacrificial objects are laid out on a mat in front of the gate and the Taoist lights incense, bowing in obeisance. He thereupon recites the incantation:

The secret orders of Shang-ti!
Hold on high the talismans, grasp the seal!
Command and drill the Six Chia spirits.
Support the orthodox, suppress the false.
Protect the nation, bring peace to the people.
Put an end to all evil deceits.
Help us successfully to complete the Tun-chia rites.
On this day, at this hour,
I take the Chia-shen spirit's true talisman,

And stand at the T'ien-hsin position.
Here I establish my residence,
Delighting to be at the Gate of Life.
From afar answer my summons,
Do not for a moment wait to come.
By using your talisman as proof,
Wind and fire obey my command.

The Taoist then bows in worship, rises, and performs the steps of Yü, as before. While dancing the sacred dance steps, he chants the mantric spell of the T'ien-hsin star and burns the T'ien-hsin talisman. When finished, he closes his eyes and meditates for a time. When done, he takes the sword in his right hand and draws the appearing talisman in the air with a single stroke, while forming the mudra on his left hand, and recites the mantric spell.

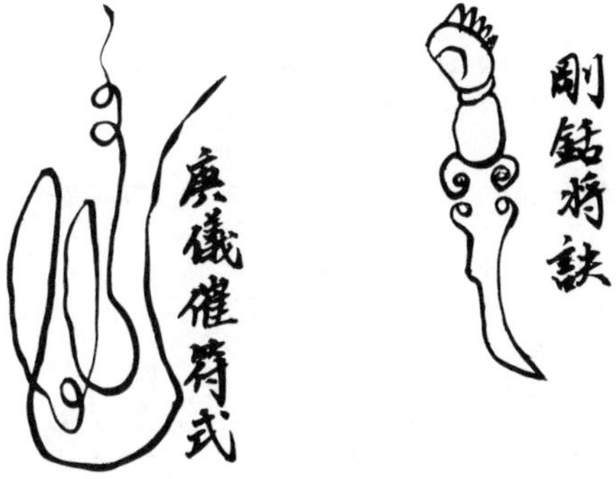

Figure 14. The talisman and mudra of the Chia-shen spirit.

When drawing the talisman in the air, it must be remembered that the Taoist is to use strength on the downward movements and on the curves. The final stroke is made from left to right across the base of the character, then rises swiftly on the right side, finishing with a final flourish off to the right. As with all of the

Ts'ui or "appearing" talismans, the Taoist must practice the stroke until it is perfect and smooth, finished in a single flowing motion. In the mudra pictured in figure 14, press the nails of the index, fourth, and fifth fingers into the palm of the left hand. Meanwhile, use the tip of the nail of the middle finger to press hard against the bent thumb, so that the tip of the finger touches the line where the nail and the cuticle meet on the thumb. The following is the mantric spell of Kang-hsien, the Chia-shen spirit:

Thou fierce general,
Suppress and bind heaven's changes!
White teeth and gold hair,
Steel armor and woven pearl helmet,
Embroidered robe and jade belt,
Steel axe and carved bow,
With your lieutenant general Ting-hai.
Black-faced, covered with wrinkles,
With your spirit troops of a hundred thousand soldiers;
Your flying sword tossed into the air,
Slay the enemy! A mountain of corpses!

To this is added the secret mantra of Shang-ti:

Shan! Shuo! Hung! P'ing!
I command thee, approach the Battle Chart!
I summon your awesome wind,
To come and obey my battle orders.
Put on display your mighty power! (military merits.)
Chi-chi Ju Lü-ling.

When done, the Taoist master closes his eyes and meditates until he hears in his ears the sound of a hollow shell. He then immediately takes the sword and draws the talisman in the air twice, followed by the talisman used by the preceding Chia-hsü rite, which is also drawn twice. The mantric spell is repeated with the first two lines changed to read:

O Kang-hsien, ferocious general,
Chieh-lieh thy style name,
White teeth and golden hair . . .

Immediately after the next to last line, "Put on display your mighty power," the following lines are added:

If at once you do not come,
I shall shout aloud your name,
Chi-chi Ju Lü-ling!

When the mudra has been formed and the mantric spell recited a second time, the Taoist closes his eyes and meditates again for a moment, until he sees a white vapor stretching up into the heavens to the Milky Way. Then he immediately takes the sword and draws the talisman in the air three times. The talisman of the Chia-hsü spirit is also drawn three times, following which the mantra is read a third time saying:

O spirit of the Keng rite, the Shen-ch'üan,
Thou here, Kang-hsien,
White teeth and golden hair . . .

After the next to last line, "Put on display your mighty power," the Taoist adds the conclusion:

It is not allowed to delay for a moment;
Come at once to the battle chart's center!
The seal and the sword have cut away our sins,
Preventing and covering all lack of respect!
Chi-chi Ju Lü-ling!

When finished, the Taoist closes his eyes and meditates until he hears the sounds of swords and spears assembling on both sides. This is the sign that the god has arrived. The Taoist then takes the sword in the right hand and the seal in the left and shouts in a loud voice:

We pray thee, be indulgent,
Return whence thou hast come;
Come again five days hence,
Showing thy true form!

The Taoist then returns to the base of the central standard, replaces the seal and the sword and, after offering incense and bowing in obeisance, retires from the sacred area.

4. *The ritual for refining the Chia-wu spirit.*
On a Ting-mao day (the fourth day) at the Kuei-mao hour (6 A.M.), the master dons his sacred vestments and goes first to the ritual table at the base of the central standard. There he offers incense and bows in obeisance three times. He then draws the talismans to be used for the ritual of the Hsin spirit, Chia-wu, and signs them with the seal. He thereupon proceeds to the gate marked Sheng in the Battle Chart of the Eight Trigrams, and faces the northeast. There he lays out the sacrificial offerings, offers incense before the Gate of Life (the gate marked Sheng), and bows three times. The conjuration is then recited:

To the central, flowery land of China,
The gods have given a heavenly book.
The substance of heaven, the path to the Tao.
I hereby command and enfoeff the spirit soldiers.
Hail to thee General———.

The Taoist then recites the following conjuration:

The secret orders of Shang-ti!
Hold high the talismans, grasp the seal!
Command and drill the Six Chia spirits.
Uphold the orthodox, suppress all evil,
Protect the nation, bring peace to the people,
Put an end to all deceitful lies.

Help us successfully complete the Tun-chia rites.
On this day, at this hour,
I take the Chia-wu spirit's true talisman,
And stand at the T'ien-fu star's position.
Here I establish my dwelling,
Delighting to reside at the Gate of Life.
From afar answer my summons,
Do not for a moment wait to come.
By using the power of your talisman as proof,
Wind and fire come at my command!

The Taoist then bows in worship, rises, and dances the sacred steps of Yü. During the ritual dance he recites the T'ien-fu mantric spell and burns the T'ien-fu talisman. When the dance is completed, the Taoist slumps back on the ground, sitting with closed eyes. Before his eyes he

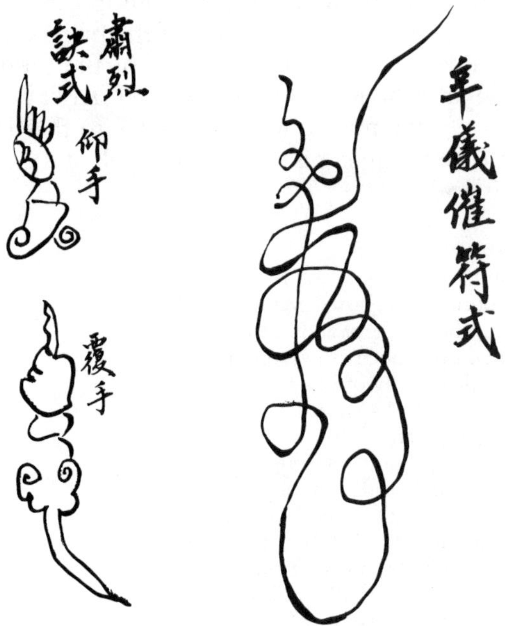

Figure 15. The talisman and mudra of the Chia-wu spirit.

sees a thick blue vapor, quiet and dense. He immediately arises and paces (the steps of Yü) to the south position. Taking the sword, he then traces in the air the appearing talisman of the Chia-wu spirit, General Hsiao-lieh, while forming the mudra on the left hand and reciting the mantric spell.

For drawing the talisman, first grasp the sword firmly in both hands and use force to form the first four loops. Then, in the second series of loops and curves, release the left hand and use the right hand only to form the strokes. Finally in the third stage, raise the sword and in a single stroke, rising outward to the right, finish off the tail of the talisman. It is necessary to practice the character until fluent. For forming the mudra, first press the nails of the middle, ring, and little fingers against the upper part of the bent thumb. Press the thumb down into the palm of the hand, so that the tips of the fingers touch the palm, while the nails touch the top of the thumb. The index finger is pointed straight upward. Always remember to cover the mudra with the sleeve so that it cannot be seen. The following is the mantric spell of the Chia-wu spirit Hsiao-lieh:

O thou spirit Chia-wu,
Commander Hsiao-lieh!
Lovely countenance, powdered face,
Delicate eyebrows, light and lustrous.
Hair bound up, golden crown on the head,
Armor made entirely of silver,
Mounted on a heron-winged horse,
Again sallying forth on foot,
With a pair of precious swords,
Joyfully singing ballads and songs.
With your lieutenant general Ting-yu,
Of the pearl crown called Te-jen,
Leading a hundred thousand troops,
Summon the rain and call up the clouds!
Cause sun and moon to disappear!
Move them as you wish, up or down,
Enemy lances totally beaten,
Their courage deadened, their spirits lost.

To this is added the secret mantra of Shang-ti:

Chü! Cho! Ling! Ting!
From afar I summon thee to come!
When you hear my command, come at once,
Chi-chi Ju Lü-ling!

When finished, the Taoist closes his eyes and meditates for a while, until he hears approaching the sound of beautiful music being plucked on strings. Thereupon he takes the sword and draws the appearing talisman in the air twice, following which he also draws the talisman of the preceding Chia-shen spirit twice. The mantric spell is then repeated a second time, changing the first two lines to read:

O thou General Hsiao-lieh,
Clever, nimble, quick and bright,
Lovely countenance . . .

The next to last line is also changed to read:

If I call again and you do not come,
Punishment will be thy lot!
Chi-chi Ju Lü-ling!

When done, the Taoist closes his eyes firmly and meditates until he senses before him an auspicious cloud with a wondrous fragrance. Thereupon he takes the sword and draws the talisman three times and repeats the mantric spell, changing the first two lines to read:

O spirit of the Hsin ritual, Ch'an-jen!
General Hsiao-lieh . . .

Upon reaching the next to last line, "When you hear my command, come at once," he adds:

I fear that my prayer is late,
Commanding the sword to make your form take shape!
Chi-chi Ju Lü-ling!

When finished he closes his eyes for a time, until in front of the eyes can be seen a light made of five colors and in the ears can be heard the sound of ballads being sung. This is the signal that she has come. On the first time that she appears before the Taoist, be warned that she is frivolous and fickle and must not be abruptly ordered about. On the very first encounter, her attitude is often one of flirtatious laughter. In such a case, address her with a stern countenance, saying:

I command thee to go back whence thou came!
Five days hence come once again.
Bring your troops with disciplined control!
Come here to my altar and hear my commands!

If the Taoist does not actually see her face, he must add the following harsh order:

Five days hence come again,
Showing your true form!

In a few moments the light will disappear completely. Then, very slowly, retreat to the original position in front of the standard in the center of the area, replace the seal and the sword, bow in obeisance, and leave the area.

5. *The ritual for refining the Chia-ch'en* spirit.
On the Ting-mao day (also the fourth day) at the Chia-hsü hour (gloss: read between the Shen and Hsü hour, or 6 P.M.), the Taoist master dons his sacred vestments and goes to the central standard to burn incense and bow in obeisance. There he draws the talismans for the Chia-sh'en rite and stamps them with the seal. When completed, he proceeds to the position in the battle chart marked Sheng, that is, the Gate of Life, as in the preceding ritual meditations. At the Gate of Life he faces the south and lays out

the sacrificial offerings. He thereupon lights incense, bows three times, and begins the recital of the conjuration:

To the central, flowery land of China,
The gods have given a heavenly book.
The substance of heaven, the path to the Tao;
With it I command and enfoeff the spirit soldiers.
Hail to thee General———.

The Taoist then goes on to recite the following:

Shang-ti gives an order (secret order),
Hold high the talisman, grasp the seal!
Command and drill the Six Chia spirits.
Uphold the orthodox, suppress all evil.
Protect the nation, bring peace to the people,
Put an end to all deceitful lies.
Help us successfully to complete the Tun-chia rites.
On this day, at this hour,
I take the Chia-ch'en spirit's true talisman,
And stand at the T'ien-ying position.
Here I establish my dwelling,
Delighting to dwell at the Gate of Life.
From afar answer my summons,
Do not for a moment wait to come.
By using your efficacious talisman,
Wind and fire come at my command.

When done, he bows in obeisance. Then rising, he dances the sacred steps of Yü. During the sacred dance, he recites the T'ien-ying mantric spell and burns the T'ien-ying talisman. When done, he stands still, closes his eyes, and concentrates on seeing the spirit. He meditates until he hears in his ears the sound of violent waves crashing. He immediately takes the sword and with violent strokes cuts the appearing talisman in the air. Though very complicated, the talisman must be drawn in a single stroke. While drawing the strokes, he forms the Tang-ti mudra on his left hand and recites the Tang-ti mantric spell.

Figure 16. The talisman and mudra of the Chia-ch'en spirit.

For drawing the talisman in the air, begin by holding the sword straight up and let it fall in a downward stroke. Then lift the blade in the various convolutions, putting strength on each of the curves, and slashing downward in quick motions. The last stroke moves outward and upward to the right, then slashes downward, curving slightly outward. Be sure to coordinate the reciting of the mantra with the forming of the talisman. The mudra is formed in three stages. First, press the middle finger and the ring finger together firmly, then press them down to touch the print of the thumb. The pressure is then released, the thumb bent further downward, and the nails of the middle and fourth fingers are then pressed against the nail of the thumb. In the third step, the little finger is also bent downward and pushes the middle and ring fingers off the nail, so that the nails of all three fingers now touch the top of the thumb, the little finger itself resting on the thumbnail. The index finger is pointed straight upward, and the hand turned so that the palm faces outward. The following is the mantric spell:

O thou spirit Chia-ch'en,
General Tang-ti,
Highest leader of the heavenly forces!
Protector of the stars of the northern skies!
Prepared to destroy all wily deceivers!
Crab-faced, hideous, repulsive, ugly,
All thy apparel made of scaly armor,
Halberd sending forth rays of light,
Riding on a black dragon!
You come floating on a turbulent mist!
With your lieutenant general Ting-wei,
T'u-tui her secret name,
Leading a hundred thousand spirit soldiers.
Mists arise and clouds assemble,
Mountains rise up and seas tumble.
Demons wail and spirits tremble.
Riding through the skies on spirit tigers,
Vapor turns into teeming soldiers!

To this is added the secret mantra of Shang-ti:

Hou! Ho! Meng! Ming!
I call thy name! O come quickly!
Hear my commands! Carry them out!
Chi-chi Ju Lü-ling!

When finished, the Taoist meditates for awhile with closed eyes. He sees before his eyes a black vapor seething and curling. Then he takes up the sword and draws the appearing talisman in the air twice, and adds to it the talisman of the preceding Chia-wu spirit which is also drawn twice. He then recites the mantric spell a second time, changing the first two lines to read:

O thou General Tang-ti,
Do I hear the sound of brawling?

The next to last line is also changed to read:

A second time I call you, but you do not come!
With a loud shout I call your name!
Chi-chi Ju Lü-ling!

When the mantra has been recited and the mudra formed a second time, the Taoist again closes his eyes and meditates. When he hears in his ears the sounds of whistling, brawling, and swaggering as in a military camp, he again takes the sword and draws the appearing talisman in the air, this time repeating the strokes three times. Following this the talisman of the preceding Chia-wu spirit is also drawn three times. The mantra is repeated with the first two lines changed to read:

O thou who penetrates to the primordial northern heavens!
General Tang-ti . . .

The last two lines are also changed to read:

If you still refuse to obey my commands,
You will be punished by the strictest rules!
Chi-chi Ju Lü-ling!

When the mudra has been formed and the mantric spell recited, the Taoist meditates a third time with closed eyes. He sees a black vapor arise like a protective wall. In his ears he hears the sounds of a myriad horses prancing and snorting, with spirited neighing. This is the sign that the spirit has come. Immediately he takes the seal in the left hand and the sword in the right and sings out in a loud voice:

Hear thee, go back whence thou came!
Come again five days hence,
Showing your true form!

When finished with the recitation, the Taoist returns to the standard in the center of the sacred area, replaces the seal and the sword and, after performing the usual obeisance, retires.

6. *The ritual for refining the Chia-yen spirit*

On a Wu-ch'en day (the fifth day) at the Yi-mao hour (6 A.M.) the Taoist master dons his ritual vestments and goes to the standard in the center of the sacred area. There he lights incense and bows in obeisance three times. He then writes out the talismans to be used in the ritual for enfeoffing the Chia-yen spirit and stamps them with the seal. When done, he proceeds to the Gate of Life in the Battle Chart of the Eight Trigrams and faces the north. There he lays out the sacrificial offerings, lights the incense, and bows in obeisance. The following conjuration is recited:

To the central, flowery land of China,
The gods have given a heavenly book,
The substance of heaven, the path of the Tao.
With it I drill and enfoeff spirit soldiers.
Hail to thee great General———.

The Taoist then continues with the following recitation:

Shang-ti has given a (secret) order!
Hold high the talisman, grasp the seal,
Command and drill the Six Chia spirits.
Uphold the orthodox, suppress all evil.
Protect the nation, bring peace to the people.
Put an end to all deceitful lies.
Help us successfully to complete the Tun-chia rites,
On this day, at this hour,
I take the Chia-yen spirit's true talisman,
And stand at the T'ien-p'ing position.
Here I make my dwelling,
Delighting to live at the Gate of Life.
From afar, answer my summons,
Do not for a moment wait to come.
By the efficacious use of your talismans,
Wind and fire come at my command.

When done, the Taoist bows, rises, and performs the sacred steps of Yü. During the dance, he recites the T'ien-p'eng star's mantric spell and burns the T'ien-p'eng talisman. When the dance and recitation are finished, he stands still, closes his eyes, and meditates, concentrating on seeing the spirit. When he hears in his ears a sound as of a mosquito humming, he immediately grasps the sword and draws the appearing talisman of the Chia-yen spirit in the air with a single stroke. During the writing of the talisman, he forms the mudra on his left hand and recites the mantric spell of Chi-sha.

Figure 17. The talisman and mudra of the Chia-yen spirit.

To draw the above talisman in the air, hold the sword by the handle and raise the sword forward and upward. Use force to form the first stroke downward, slanting crosswise and then upward. In the next stroke, the sword is turned to form the four circular figures, as illustrated, Finally, the sword is lifted and the four slanting strokes formed with great power, moving backward and forward in an upward motion, applying pressure at the points. A forward and upward stroke, forming the tail of the figure, brings the talisman to a conclusion. To form the mudra, bend down the index finger of the left hand so that it touches the nail of the little finger. Then press the thumb against the nail of the little finger with some pressure, holding all three fingers down close to the palm. Then extend the middle finger and the ring finger straight upward, pressed against each other with the nails parallel. Cover the entire mudra with the left sleeve so that it cannot be seen. The following mantric spell is recited:

Chi-sha, Chi-sha!
Black killer from the Niu and Nü stars,
Leopard's face and tiger's whiskers!
Hat of red and face of black!
In your hands a whip of steel,
Violent, oppressing, killing, punishing.
With your subordinate general P'ing-nan (Ting-yi)
Hideous teeth, beard of red,
Leading a hundred thousand spirit soldiers,
Like a pack of bears or wild dogs!
Secretly hiding your oppressive form!
When an enemy approaches, shoot out spears,
Summon forth a violent wind!
Shake down the mountains, level forests,
A sheet of flame crosses the heavens!
Spears fall like clouds, killing all!

To this is added the secret mantra of Shang-ti:

Ts'u-hu! Hung-p'a-ha!
From afar I summon thee to come.
Hear my orders, commanding the troops!
Chi-chi Ju Lü-ling!

When the master has finished, he closes his eyes and meditates, standing very still for some time. All will be quiet and still, as if there were no results. Then the Taoist takes the sword again and draws the appearing talisman twice without pause while reciting the mantric spell. The first two lines are changed to read:

O thou General Tzu-fei,
I pronounce thy secret name Chi-sha!

The last two lines are also changed to read:

If called again thou dost not come
I'll call in thy stead the spirit Hsi-t'a!
Chi-chi Ju Lü-ling!

When the mantra is completed a second time, close the eyes and meditate until in front of the eyes a thin fog is envisioned. Then immediately take the sword and draw the talisman in the air three times, while reciting the mantric spell and forming the mudra with the left hand. The first two lines of the spell are changed to read:

By performing thy rite, rocks are melted;
With thy soldiers in ranks, Chi-sha!

The last two lines are also changed to read:

Dallying stubbornly more and more!
Hold the weapons to the fore!
Courage flashing like bolts of lightning!
Chi-chi Ju Lü-ling!

When finished, the Taoist must close his eyes and meditate again, until before his eyes there appears a strange sort of pure, clear mist. Since the spirit is by nature deep and foreboding, it is not easy to arouse or envision him. If this is the case, repeat the talisman, mudra, and mantra again three times, thus bringing the repetitions to a total of six. After the sixth time, wait until there appears a light, like a ray of fire in front of the eyes, and in the ears there is an angry roar. When this happens, take the seal in the left hand and the sword in the right and shout in a loud voice:

Never again dare to dally in coming!
Now you may go back whence you have come!
Five days hence come back again,
Showing your true form!

The Taoist then returns to the table at the central standard, replaces the seal and the sword, and bows in obeisance. With this he retires, having completed the first cycle of five days in refining the method for summoning and hiding the Six Chia spirits.

On the second series of five days, the Taoist repeats the meditations, continuing to summon the Six Chia spirits according to the directions given above. The spirits are each summoned twelve times over a period of sixty days. During the total time of the ritual, the Taoist must always keep the sword and the seal near to himself, replacing them in their respective cases after each use and putting them under his pillow when he sleeps at night. At the end of the sixty-day period, all the temporary items used in the rites—the flag poles, standards, wooden tablets, and the like—are to be destroyed by burning. The Taoist digs a hole, builds a fire inside, and, after burning all of the materials, covers the ashes with rock and the rock with dirt so that no trace is left. The spirit generals, once brought under the Taoist's command, will come at his summons to obey whatever orders he may give them. The following books of the manual (parts three and four of the Tun-chia manual) list sixty or more uses to which the spirits can be put. Though the spirits are mainly used to combat one's enemies in battle, they can also be used to cure illness, exorcise, and protect the Taoist from black magic used against him by a rival practitioner.

Whether from the very beginning the practice of esoteric Taoist ritual was made extremely complicated simply to preserve its proper use for the truly devoted follower, or whether the progress of time increased the exacerbating details necessary to perform the rituals properly, is difficult to determine, especially in the instance of a text such as *Ch'i-men Tun-chia*, the military manual from Mao Shan quoted above. The text is only partially canonical, in that the Six Chia spirits are summoned and used in many orthodox rituals. The rite for enfoeffing the spirits is not found in such detail in the Canon, nor are the terrifying uses to which it is supposed to be put, such as slaying one's enemies, moving mountains, or causing a shower of spears to fall from the heavens. These are not in any sense a part of orthodox, state-approved, and acceptable ritual. Two K'ou-chüeh or oral secrets are transmitted with the text of the Tun-chia rites, which identify the Taoist who knows the method and can be seen in use among the more knowledgeable masters of Taiwan. The Six Chia spirits are truly terrifying demons and their control is not a matter for the weak-hearted or the pretender among the Taoists. This is especially true of two of the spirits, the Chia-wu spirit of the fourth day and the Chia-yen spirit of the sixth day. To control these two demons, and any other spirit who refuses at first to obey the Taoist's commands, a special series of techniques must be used, ones that have become a part of the orthodox Taoist's repertoire.

In the case of the Chia-wu spirit, who appears as a beautiful woman but who is in fact a demon fond of killing, the Taoist must be immensely cautious. For the Chia-yen spirit, who is a brawler and a very recalcitrant servant, the Taoist must learn to use the following rubrics. If the spirit comes in a terrifying shape, eighty feet in height or in the form of a monstrous demon, so hideous that the Taoist is tempted to run in terror (or "hide himself in the earth" as the text puts it), it is absolutely necessary to show no sign of alarm, but to open the eyes wide so that they bulge and look straight at the misshapen demon. He then must say:

I have here thy registers, O general,
How dare you use a false shape!
Hiding your true appearance!
Now be sworn in by my feudal treaty![22]

The Taoist then takes a mirror, which was made of polished metal in earlier times but now can be a simple looking glass, and draws on both sides. On the reverse side, the Taoist writes all the esoteric names of the spirit, names not usually written out. The writing is done with red ink so that it can be rubbed out easily. On the front side is then drawn the appearing talisman—again, a form usually never drawn except in the air so that the ordinary human and spirit may not see how it is written. The reverse side of the mirror is held up facing the demon, while the Taoist is writing the talisman. When the talisman is finished, the mirror is then turned and held straight towards the demon so that the talisman can be clearly seen. The spirit will then very clearly say the words:

My master summons me here.
What wishes do you have for me to carry out?

With a serious voice and a stern countenance the Taoist answers:

By the secret orders of Shang-ti,
An order has come down commanding thee,
——— of the Six Chia spirits,
Perform the rites of the eight trigrams chart,
Exhaust all manner of magical changes,
Bring aid to the nation, peace to the people,
Fulfill the heavenly Tao!
Respectfully respond to your taboo names!
Cautiously follow heaven's will!

The mirror is then turned so that the taboo names face the spirit. The Taoist must then see the spirit fall to its knees in respect and say to the Taoist:

I swear to be under your command.
Whatever your orders, I will obey.

The Taoist master then answers:

I mutually promise, with thy taboo talisman,
To live up to the duties incumbent on your vows.

The Taoist then goes with elation to the standard in the center of the sacred area and, after bowing in obeisance, announces to heaven:

By imperial decree we have fulfilled and accomplished.
The enfoeffment of the spirit ———.
(repeat all of the taboo names.)
Together let us carry out the heavenly law!
I swear there will never be any deceit between us!

When the recital is finished, the Taoist takes a white cock, cuts the comb with the sword, and lets some of the blood fall into a bowl. Taking the bowl in his hands, he first presses it to his own mouth, tasting the blood. Thereupon he offers it to the spirit. The spirit, too, imbibes of the blood. The Taoist then proceeds to the table and takes the talisman of the spirit, which was previously written of a piece of yellow paper, and holds up the talisman in the air. Then while holding the talisman in the left hand and the sword in the right, he cuts down the center of the talisman so that it is cut into two pieces. The left half is kept for the Taoist himself and the right half is given to the spirit by burning. Finally, the Taoist recites the mantric spell commanding the spirit to return, reminding him or her, meanwhile, to come back again in five days, as in the directions above.[23]

The ceremony of cutting the cock's comb and swearing in the spirit general must be performed at least once for each of the Six Chia spirits. If the spirit appears regularly on the second summoning—that is, during the second period of five days—it is performed on that occasion. Otherwise the Taoist must go through the above special rite to make the spirit appear in its true shape and then continue the swearing-in ceremony. Although the rite of cutting a cock's comb is very ancient and is accepted as a part of the orthodox Taoist's repertoire of ritual activities, it is very different from the stately classical liturgies of the Tao of the Right to be discussed in the next chapter. The violent, military rituals of the Tao of the Left are indeed suspect of being tainted with sectarianism, though the greatest effort is made by the Taoist to remain pure and virtuous and to use the rites only "for the good of the nation, and peaceful life of the people." There is no doubt however, that the magic of the Six Chia spirits has been used to man's detriment, and the "Left Tao" from very early times came to mean a kind of black magic that was punishable as an offense against the imperial authority.[24] Practitioners of the Tao of the Left were considered to be sectarian and punished throughout different periods of Chinese history. The manual itself, therefore, warns that the method is only to be used to help a Chinese emperor restore the throne, or to come to the aid of a person who is being attacked by black magic. The Taoist who practices this method is thought to use his own vital forces to exhaustion and to die young, because of the great effort required to command and control the terrifying Chia demons. Though a good master will learn the method, he will seldom put it to use and then only to come to the aid of a man or woman in distress. Chuang's use of the method, described in chapter 3 above, was confined to exorcistic retaliation.

Whatever the power ascribed to the strange Tun-chia rites, there is no question that the style of liturgy must be categorized as heterodox, or at least outside the accepted orthodox style of meditation. The classical Thunder magic of chapter 6 is invoked to counteract its harmful effects. It is possible that Lin Chan-mei invoked Tun-chia magic in his battles to pacify north Taiwan. The manual was at least in the Lin family library by the first lunar month of 1851 and was used by the Taoists of Hsinchu as late as 1970 (chapter 3 above). The difference in heterodox Mao Shan magic and the classical, stately Tao of the Right will become evident as we consider Chuang's teachings in the next chapter. The spirits of orthodox Taoism are bearers of peace, blessing, and contemplation, the ultimate effect of which is meditation in the presence of the eternal Tao of Transcendance. The Tao of the Left is, indeed, a polar opposite of its classical orthodox counterpart.

5. Orthodox Ritual: The Tao of the Right

Introduction

Orthodox Taoist ritual has traditionally been distinguished from the popular local rites of village magicians by a form of liturgical meditation leading to union with the Tao. The purpose of classical, orthodox ritual is threefold. For the adept, it leads to mystical union and immortality. For the men and women of the villages, it brings blessing and renewal. For the souls of the departed in the underworld, it brings salvation and release from the punishments of hell. Though innumerable local variations and styles of Taoist practices have evolved through the historic forces that wrought change in China, the basic format and purpose of orthodox ritual have remained constant to the present day. After a brief meditative hymn and entrance rite, the Taoist still begins orthodox ritual with a meditation called fa-lu for exteriorizing the spirits from his body. Next, the meditation of ritual union is conducted, during which the Taoist master ascends to the heavens and presents a memorial or grand written document before the throne of the eternal Tao. Finally, the ritual concludes with the fu-lu, or the restoration of the spirits to their places inside the microcosm. The orthodox Taoist master bases his meditation on a notion taken from the first seven chapters of the *Chuang-tzu*, where the ancient sage proposes, "The Tao dwells in the void." By "fasting in the heart" (hsin-chai) and emptying the microcosm, union with the eternal transcendent Tao is effected.[1]

1. Kinds of Orthodox Ritual.

The earliest passages in the Canon which treat of Taoist

ritual in a systematic manner divide the liturgies of union into various types and styles according to the purpose for which the particular rite is offered. Thus in the sixth-century *Wu-shang Pi-yao*, liturgies are directed to the Three Realms—heaven, earth, and the underworld—to win blessings, help men and women, and free the souls in hell.[2] Gold Register (Chin-lu) rituals of renewal and Yellow Register (Huang-lu) liturgies of burial are frequently mentioned.[3] A ritual which no longer occurs, for casting dust and ashes on the heads of penitents, is described.[4] The word "chai," taken from the court ritual of the feudal period and the Han, was commonly used to name the meditative rituals of early Taoism. Chai meant, according to the early Shuo-wen dictionary, a period of fasting and purification preceding a sacrifice. The term "hsin-chai," or fasting of the heart described by Chuang-tzu, became a form of explicit Taoist meditation and is listed in T'ang dynasty sources as a commonly known Taoist practice.[5]

The word "chiao" was also used interchangeably with chai to describe Taoist ritual. Whereas in the Taoist Canon chai appears more frequently in the sixth-century *Wu-shang Pi-yao*, the word chiao, or sacrifice, is found in the dynastic histories to describe the rituals offered by Taoists at the court of the emperor.[6] During the T'ang period, the two words, chiao, which meant literally the pouring out of wine and the offering of incense and tea in sacrifice, and chai, seem to have been used synonymously. In the Sung dynasty and later canonical sources, a clear distinction is made between ritual offered for the living, which came exclusively to be called Gold Register chiao (Chin-lu chiao), and rituals for the dead, called Yellow Register Chai (Huang-lu chai). This latter classification is ordinarily used by Master Chuang, and the other Taoists of Taiwan. By the Sung dynasty, the grand festivals of village renewal had been developed into a set formula, whose general plan is still evident in Taiwan.[7]

Following the custom established in the Sung dynasty,[8] when a Taoist master is hired to perform his ritual in modern Taiwan, the people of the village ordinarily call the entire festival a chiao, that is, a pure sacrifice. But concurrently with the chiao, a chai or set of ceremonies for freeing all the souls from hell is also celebrated. Thus the modern village festivals include both a chiao and a chai. Like a great symphony in which two melodic themes are developed, the Taoist performs a set of rituals whose purpose is to win blessing from heaven and union with the transcendent Tao, and at the same time celebrates another set of ceremonies whose purpose is to free the souls from hell. In the first set of rituals, which are properly called chiao, the meditations of union are performed. These meditations invariably begin with the fa-lu rite for emptying the microcosm and end with the fu-lu for restoring the spirits to their proper place. In these rituals, wine, incense, and tea are offered to the heavenly spirits, hence the word chiao used to describe them.[9] In the second set of rituals, the Taoist reads lengthy canons of merit and litanies of repentance, in a formula which does not make use of the classical fa-lu rite of emptying.[10] The chai ceremonies for freeing the souls end with a great sacrifice called the p'u-tu in which raw meat is used to offer to feed the souls in hell.[11] The word chai is now used to describe these latter ceremonies, a change from the more general sense in which the word was used in the past.[12]

2. RITUAL MEDITATION LEADING TO UNION WITH THE TAO.

According to the teachings of Master Chuang, orthodox chiao ritual is solidly based on the yin-yang five element theory of the cosmos. In a strictly religious interpretation of chapter 42 of the *Lao-tzu*, the Taoist reverses the process whereby the "Tao gave birth to the One; the One gave birth to the Two; the Two gave birth to the Three; the Three gave birth to the myriad creatures."[13] By orthodox ritual, the Taoist "returns to the roots," that is, he "refines" or "returns" the microcosm to the state of primordial simplicity, hun-tun, in order to be united with the eternal, transcendent Tao of the Wu-wei.[14]

The Tao is a nameless, unmoved first mover, as described in the first chapters of the *Lao-tzu*. The Tao gives birth to the One, which is interpreted to be the Tao of immanence, that is, the moved first mover, also called t'ai-chi (Great Principle) or hun-tun (primordial chaos). Primordial chaos, or t'ai-chi, is personified by religious Taoism as the first of a Taoist trinity, Yüan-shih T'ien-tsun, or Primordial Heavenly Worthy. Within the microcosm of man he stands as symbol for primordial breath, the basic life-giving substance within the body. His dwelling place is within the head of man, where he resides in an esoteric place called the Ni-wan.[15] When called forth from within the microcosm, he always appears in a blue-green mist. In the macrocosm, he is the ruler of the highest heavens.

"The One gives birth to the Two," the next line in chapter 42 of the *Lao-tzu*, is also personified as a spirit by the religious Taoists. The second spirit, Ling-pao Heavenly Worthy, stands for the liaison spirit between heaven and earth. Thus the term "ling" refers to the half of a talisman kept in the heavens, and the "pao" to the precious half buried in the earth.[16] Ling-pao Heavenly Worthy is the symbol for the spirit or shen in man. His rule is in the center part of the body and, when summoned forth, he appears in a yellow light.

"The Two gives birth to the Three," the next line from the verse, refers to the third of the Taoist trinity, Tao-te T'ien-tsun, who is taken to be a mystical personification of *Lao-tzu*. Tao-te Heavenly Worthy is symbolic of vital essence within man, which resides in the lower abdomen.

When called forth, the "vital essence" spirit always appears in a bright white light.

Thus the Tao is seen to give birth in turn to three principles—breath, spirit, and vital essence. These three principles are in the philosophic order expressed by the notions t'ai-chi, yang, and yin. In the religious order they become three Heavenly Worthies, the "Three Pure Ones" (San-ch'ing). From the Three Pure Ones are generated the five movers or the five elements: wood, fire, earth, metal, and water; and from the five movers come the myriad things of nature.[17]

The complicated process of refinement from the many to the one, which the Taoist attempts to perform through ritual, is difficult to describe in a brief lesson. Years of instruction from a master are required to perfect the method. If the purpose of orthodox ritual can be stated in a single sentence, it is perhaps this: the Taoist, by his or her ritual, attempts to progress from the myriad creatures, back through the process of gestation, to an audience with the eternal, transcendent Tao.[18] In a series of ritual meditations, the Taoist adept empties out the myriad spirits, until he or she stands in the state of hun-tun, or primordial emptiness. At that moment, the Tao of transcendence, wu-wei chih Tao, comes of itself to dwell in the emptied center of man. This process is called hsin-chai, or fasting (voiding) the heart. Orthodox ritual is thus defined by ritual purpose. Taoists who perform their liturgies for the purpose of union are called orthodox. Taoists who perform their liturgies for the sake of making a living, curing a cold, or simple exorcism, are not. The distinction is strictly observed, and the rank given to a Taoist at the time of ordination is determined by his or her ability to perform the various meditations of union.[19]

The teachings of Master Chuang are explicit in deciding the official title given a Taoist. The criteria for ranking a Taoist are found in the ordination manual of the Heavenly

Master, a copy of which was purchased in 1886 by Lin Ju-mei and is at present in the possession of Master Chuang. The criteria are:[20]

Grade one	knowledge of the *Yellow Court Canon*, the meditative manual of the Mao Shan *Shang-ch'ing* sect.
Grade two and three	knowledge of the Ch'ing-wei sect style of Thunder Magic (see chapter 6).
Grade four and five	knowledge of the Meng-wei registers of the Heavenly Master (discussed in this chapter).
Grade six and seven	knowledge of the Ling-pao registers of the San-wu Tu-kung (Three-five Surveyor of Merits).[21]

Thus the interpretation of Taoist ritual emphasizing the meditative aspects of union with the Tao is considered "orthodox" because it derives from the classical orders of the north-south period and the first Taoist Canon. To the original list of orthodox rituals are added those of the Sung dynasty Ch'ing-wei sect; the reason for the inclusion of Ch'ing-wei Thunder Magic will be studied in the next chapter. Its association with Mao Shan and the meditative tradition will be seen to be a strong factor in ranking it as one of the highest forms of Taoist ritual meditation. Yü tao ho yi, the meditation in which the Taoist "joins himself as one with the Tao," continues to be the decisive factor in ranking the expertise of a master.[22]

The disciples of Master Chuang were, therefore, ranked according to their ability to perform interior meditation. There were three kinds of disciples who flocked to Chuang's ritual performances and listened to his discourses in the front room of the busy Hsinchu residence. The first group were the retainers and the musicians, who came simply to earn a few extra Taiwanese dollars as drummers, flutists, violinists, and cymbal players. These men were minor Taoists in their own right and could on occasion fill in as acolyte or even read one of the lengthy canons of merit and repentance. But they were never ordained and were not given the secrets of ritual meditation. The second group of disciples were the Taoists who belonged by family descent to the Cheng-i Tz'u-t'an, the fraternity of Taoist brethren of Hsinchu City and other parts of north Taiwan. Descendants of the famous Taoists who had flocked to Lin ju-mei's center for studies in the late Ch'ing period, these men were professional Blackhead or orthodox Taoists ordained to the lowest San-wu Tu-kung, the grade six "Surveyor of Merits." They knew and followed the meditations outlined below by Master Chuang.

The last and highest circle of Chuang's disciples were his sons, A-him and A-ga, who were destined to become masters after the retirement of their father. To this elite circle I was sometimes admitted, not as a rival in the profession of public ritual but as a scholar interested in sources of Chuang's teachings. My questions, as related in chapter 3, provoked A-him and A-ga to deeper study, a result that made Chuang quite happy. Many of the esoteric doctrines, which Chuang had hidden even from his sons, were found in my borrowed copy of the printed Taoist Canon. This made my attendance at the lessons appreciated by both A-him and A-ga. It was clear, however, that we were given only a fraction of the total knowledge of Master Chuang. It was required of the older son, A-him, to study some twenty years, from his eleventh to his thirtieth birthday, before even being considered for ordination. For this event, mastery of the meditations of union with the Tao were required.[23]

3. TEACHINGS CONCERNING THE MEDITATIONS OF UNION. (The *Ling-pao Five Talismans.*)

The discourses of Chuang on the Tao of the Right always

began with a lengthy lesson on "basic doctrines," the so-called Pen-wen.[24] These evening sessions were very long and boring and my first reaction was to try to escape them. Since there was no way of avoiding the lecture if I was to obtain the esoteric oral teachings that always came at the very end, I soon learned to take copious notes of Chuang's discourses. My efforts were rewarded when I realized, by comparing the notes with canonical texts, that Chuang's long monologues paralleled passages in the early Taoist Canon. I soon learned that canonical passages could be substituted for Chuang's lessons and brought the Canon for him to read instead. According to the teachings of Master Chuang, the progress from the many spirits of the cosmos to the meditation of union with the Tao went according to well-ordered stages. Thus one began with the ritual called "Inviting the spirits," when all of the benevolent rulers of the cosmos were summoned. From the initial ritual, the adept passed through a gradual refinement, reducing the number to nine, five, and three spirits, until finally only one spirit was present in the microcosm. On the evening set aside to speak of the five spirits who rule the five elements, Chuang commented on the following canonical passages: ***(in Chuang's words)***

Primordial Heavenly Worthy spoke,
To the five elder emperors,
The crowd of great holy ones of the ten heavens,
All of the assembled lords of the transcendent ultimate (Wu-chi),
With their wives, who were gathered together,
In the realm of red brightness,
Sitting in a fragrant garden,
Under a fragrant mulberry tree.[25]

The cosmos was described in Chuang's meditation as being in darkness, that is, generation was not yet accomplished. In the period before Lung-han (before primordial gestation), the *Ling-pao Five Talismans* (the same given to Yü the Great to control the floods), were described as initiating the process of light, life, and generation:

A bright five-colored light penetrated the abyss,
In the five directions.
Suddenly in the heavens there appeared writings,
In the shape of characters, each ten feet square.
They appeared quite naturally,
Generated by the Tao,
Above the mysterious void.
In the very center of the five rays of light
Were carved wen writings.
These sparkled and glittered in a dazzling manner,
Their light penetrated outwards in the eight directions;
A subtle, vital light, spreading out like the spokes of a wheel.
The light was so bright that one could not look directly at it.
The mind was befuddled by the light.[26]

In the canonical text, the *Ling-pao Five Talismans* are described as a wheel of five lights, the source of primordial breath, hub of the eight trigrams and the eight directions.[27] They resonate through nature with a harmonious melody: ***(in Chuang's words)***

The heavenly writings, jade characters,
Flew off and disappeared into the primordial breath
Of the mysterious void,
Where they congealed and became Ling-wen,
"Writings which bear spirit and life" (ling-pao chen-wen).
Joined to the eight trigrams, they became harmonious tones.
Joined to the five talismans, they became chang charms.
From possessing them, the primordial state
Called Lung-han was formed.[28]
The visible world was generated.
The workings of water and fire,
Life and death,
The myriad kalpas, and
The light of primordial yang were initiated.
The two principles, yin and yang
Used them to carve out the three realms.
The holy sages mounted them,
To attain to union with the transcendent.
The five sacred peaks hold them,
And are thereby filled with spiritual power.
All things by possessing them have life breath (ch'i).
The nation which possesses them is at peace.
The Ling-pao five writs
Are the middle way of generation,[29]

The root of heaven and the way of earth,
Deriving from the (Tao) of Wu-wei.
He who holds them will not die.
He who honors them will have eternal life.
He who holds them in feudal oath[30]
Will see the realized immortals descend.
They who practise and perfect them
Become immortal spirits;
Passing over the struggle of death, they
Enter into eternal life.

The five writs are also called "great Sanskrit secret mudras," a term used since the early sixth century alluding to the fact that the five talismans were drawn in "bird-like" esoteric symbols which resembled the foreign Sanskrit words coming from India.[31] The *Ling-pao Five Talismans*, therefore, are seen as five lights issuing from the eternal transcendent Tao before the gestation of Primordial Heavenly Worthy; that is, they helped to form the immanent Tao, or Hun-tun, the stage of primordial chaos which was the beginning of cosmic gestation.[32] The five writs order all of nature (li tzu-jan) and are the source of life breath (ch'i).[33] They allow the Taoist adept to cross over from the state of a mortal man into immortality or hsien-hood. They assist the dead to cross over from the realm of stygian darkness into eternal life. In a passage from the sixth-century Canon, intoned by Master Chuang from my borrowed manual, the *Ling-pao Five Talismans* are described in their present-day role in Taoist ritual:[34] ***(in Chuang's words)***

The Ling-pao true writs
Were generated before Primordial Heavenly Worthy,
In the center of the void abyss,
Before heaven and earth's roots.
Before sun and moon gave off their light,
In the dark and murky transcendent ancester (Tao),
They produced Hun-tun, yin and yang.
Because of them the great yang, the sun was made;
Because of them the spirit chart (*Ho-t'u*) was formed.[35]

The primordial originator alchemically refined them
In the abyss of the yang palace;
Formed them in the palace of flowing fire.
As they were formed, they sent off rays of red light.
Thus they were called ch'ih-wen, bright red writs;
Again they were called Ch'ih-shu Ling-t'u
The red script spirit chart.[36]
Thus the myriad emperors were able to have audience with the Tao,
To fly up and stride in the void of emptiness,
To travel in the heavenly realms,
While burning incense and scattering flowers,
They chanted the sacred spirit writs.
It was at this time that the heavens sent down the
Twelve mysterious regulators (twelve stems),
And the earth responded with the twenty-four rules.[37]

The heavens hold the five writs as feudal treasures,
And thereby rule all that is above.
The earth guards them as a secret,
Thereby causing peace to reign.
The five ancient emperors hold them in their hands,
Thus causing stability and proper order in nature.
The three sources (sun, moon, and stars) are sustained by them,
Thus maintaining celestial light.
The highest holy ones worship them,
And are thereby realized.[38]
The five sacred peaks obey them,
Thereby attaining spiritual power.
The emperor (son of heaven) holds them,
And thereby rules the nation.
The nation that possesses them attains the Great Peace (T'ai-ping).[39]

4. PREPARATIONS FOR ORTHODOX RITUAL MEDITATION. It was evident from the lessons of Master Chuang that he expected his sons and disciples to be familiar with the doctrines of the *Lao-tzu* and the *Chuang-tzu*, and to meditate upon and familiarize themselves with the process of gestation and the functioning of the cosmos described in these works. The process of instruction was carefully planned, and I was scolded for trying to accelerate matters to the heart of Chuang's esoteric magic ritual. The order

of instruction, Chuang told me, would take more than ten years and could not be accelerated without doing harm both to the disciple and to the doctrines.[40] The following is the traditional order of transmitting the doctrines of orthodox Taoism:

1. Profession of the ten rules or vows of the Taoist novice.
2. Reception and mastery of the *Lao-tzu Tao-te Ching.*
3. Meditation and ritual of the Three Pure Ones (San-ch'ing).[41]
4. Meditation and ritual of the Five Talismans (*Ling-pao Wu-fu*).
5. Reception and mastery of the *Yellow Court Canon.*[42]

Only after receiving the above manuals and listening to the instructions of Master Chuang concerning the process of gestation from the Tao of transcendence, and only after understanding the workings of yin and yang, the production of the five elements, and the other myriad details of the yin-yang five element cosmology, was mention made of the esoteric rubrics of religious Taoism.[43]

The process of receiving the rules or vows of the Taoist novice and putting them into practice was a matter of great concern for Chuang and a source of scolding for myself as well as for his sons. I was continually reprimanded for haste, for competitiveness with my colleagues, and for attempting to introduce Chuang to other foreign scholars. The vows of esoteric transmission were binding on the master and on the disciple, and the response of the Taoist towards all outside inquirers was inevitably one of ignorance.[44] When passing on the vows or rules of religious Taoism, Chuang sat facing the west, composed himself, and addressed us only after we had settled down to listen in quiet composure. The following are the first ten rules given to the novice:[45] *(in Chuang's words)*

1. Banish all hatred from the heart. Hatred, anger,

and brooding cause the powers of yin to devour the inner man.
2. Be benevolent and merciful to all living things.
3. Do good to all and avoid acts which harm others.
4. Purity of heart and mind include banishing impure thoughts.[46]
5. Both in interior thoughts and exterior acts be loyal to friends. Never speak badly of others, especially of a fellow Taoist.
6. The breath of life must be regulated; nothing should be taken in excess. Wine may not be drunk during ritual.
7. Do not try to win over others, but always yield and take the last place.
8. Do not argue or dispute, but behave always as if in the presence of spirits.
9. Put self-interest last, and never be critical of others. Life breath is injured by seeking praise or resenting blame.
10. Use the whole heart and mind to achieve equality, union, and peace.

For each of the books or rituals revealed by the master, there is a set of rules, or chieh, which the disciple must follow in order to "walk in the way of the Tao."[47] Thus, before receiving the *Ling-pao Five Talismans* the following set of rules is proposed for the disciple:[48]

1. Do not kill, but respect all living things.
2. Do not lust after another man's wife, or any woman.
3. Do not steal or take any recompense unjustly.
4. Do not use deceit, to win one's own way.
5. Do not get drunk, and at all times act with sobriety.[49]
6. Love all relatives, with respect and harmony. Treat all men as relatives.
7. See the good points in all men, and help their hearts to be joyful.

8. If a person is sad, help him or her to be happy and blessed.
9. Treat all others as if their desires were one's own. Never seek vengence.
10. Work that all may attain the Tao.

The chieh or rules of the Ling-pao talismans thus teach the young disciple the attitude necessary to have in order to perform ritual for the benefit of the men and women of the community. One of the greatest fears of the masters of esoteric ritual is that the terrifying magical powers given to the novice may be used to harm and not to help men. Thus the disciple is carefully watched and tested before the secrets of esoteric ritual are revealed.[50] The rules are summarized in the simple "three commandments" given before the meditation of union.[51]

1. Don't forget the roots to seek the branches.
2. Don't benefit the self to the harm of others.
3. Don't get involved in things and lose the Tao.

In his final words before entrance is granted to the sacred ritual area, the master tells the disciple, "When one performs the pure chai ritual, there is no need to go to the mountains. For it is not in the mountains but within the empty center of man that the Tao is found." The purpose of the chai, therefore, is union with the eternal Tao.[52]

5. THE CHIAO RITES OF UNION.

As the final days before the performance of a chiao festival of renewal approaches, the Taoist master's household is filled with the bustle of preparation. Typically, the household of Master Chuang is totally mobilized for the occasion. Both the men and women of the family are asked to write the many documents to be sent off to the heavens by burning. In long night sessions, Master Chuang gives final briefings to his sons and his closest disciples. The Taoists who will assist with the esoteric rituals of renewal and union are chosen, the footsteps rehearsed, the melodies sung, and the stage rubrics practiced. The disciples are reminded of the seriousness of the event, of the need to look neither left nor right when performing the ceremonies, to remain at all times filled with the sacredness of ritual meditation:[53] ***(in Chuang's words)***

Man's body (microcosm) is noble.
Therefore the Tao opened a path,
Bequeathing chieh rules, ching canons, and wen scripts,
Whereby the bodily state could be transcended,
By a higher state of union with the Tao.
By preserving life essences,
Through performing the rituals,
And promising to fulfill the moral commandments,
The heart is quiet and contemplates darkness (yin);
The will (chih) is fixed on undivided brightness (yang);
All thought is reduced to the one (hun-tun).
The six fu administrative centers of the microcosm[54]
By centering (in the Yellow Court) are without sensation,
Inside and outside, pure and empty,
Joined as one with all of nature.
Then one offers incense, and pronounces the vows,
Causing the heart to ascend to the heavens,
And all the heavenly spirits to come down to earth,
To hear the music of the sacred liturgy, and
To answer the prayers of all men,
According to how they have kept the moral precepts,
And followed the way of the eternal Tao.

The occasions for performing a chiao festival are many. The village and city temples of Taiwan each perform a chiao of renewal once every certain number of years on the occasion of temple remodeling. Some villages perform the chiao of renewal once every sixty years at the beginning of a chia-tzu cycle.[55] Other villages perform a chiao every twelve, five, or three years to free the souls from hell or to exorcise the evil spirits that cause sickness and misfortune.[56] On special occasions, such as the ordination of a new Taoist priest or the commemoration of a Taoist divinity, the Taoist masters perform a private chiao of devotion. Such a chiao is performed annually by the Cheng-i Tz'u-t'an of Hsinchu City on the birthday of the mother goddess of the Pole Star.[57] In bygone days on the mainland of China, the great Taoist monasteries celebrated continuous chiao which lasted as long as 72, 81, or 108 days. On all such occasions, the format of the chiao is basically the same. A minimum of 3 or 5 days are required to perform the rites of meditative union.[58]

The chiao liturgies are clearly divided into three distinct kinds: (1) the exterior rites of offering, performed in the open forum for whole community to see; (2) the lengthy canons of merit and repentance, recited inside the temple to effect release of the souls in hell; and (3) the k'o-i rites of meditative union. The k'o-i rituals, as I have said, are easily identified by their format. Classical k'o-i ritual always begins with the fa-lu meditation for exteriorizing the spirits from the microcosm and ends with the fu-lu which restores the spirits to their original places. A complete list of all the rituals offered at a chiao festival will indicate to the reader the complexity of the modern (Sung dynasty) liturgy of renewal and union, and at the same time illustrate the place of the k'o-i rituals in the overall chiao.[59] In the following list, the k'o-i rituals of union are in italics. The public rituals are indicated with an asterisk. The rites oriented to the freeing of the souls from hell are left unmarked.[60]

The Chiao Festival

FIRST DAY	CHINESE TERM
1. Lighting the temple lamps*	Pai-shen Teng
2. Sending off the memorial*	Fa-tsou, Fa-piao
3. "Opening the Eyes"*	K'ai-kuang

4. Inviting the spirits*	Ch'ing-shen, Chu-sheng
5. Purifying the sacred area*	Chin-t'an
6. Jade Pivot Canon	Yü-shu Ching
7. Noon offering*	Wu-hsien, Wu-hung
8. Litanies of repentance (10 vols.)	Ch'ao-t'ien Pao-ch'an
9. Lighting lamps to the Three Pure Ones.	Fen-teng[61] Chüan-lien, Ming-chung
10. *Ritual of the Ling-pao Five Talismans.*	Su-ch'i

SECOND DAY

11. Reinvite the spirits	Ch'ung-pai[62]
12. *Morning Audience*	Tsao-ch'ao
13. Three Officials Canon	San-kuan Ching
14. Three Officials Litany of Repentance (3 vols.)	San-kuan Pao-ch'an
15. *Noon Audience*	Wu-ch'ao
16. East Pole Star Canon	Tung-tou Ching
17. South Pole Star Canon	Nan-tou Ching
18. West Pole Star Canon	Hsi-tou Ching
19. North Pole Star Canon	Pei-tou Ching
20. Central Pole Star Canon	Chung-tou Ching
21. Pole Star Litanies of Repentance (5 vols.)	Wu-tou Pao-ch'an[63]
22. Jade Emperor Canon (3 vols.)	Yü-huang Pen-hsing Ching[64]
23. Jade Emperor Litany of Repentance	Yü-huang Pao-ch'an
24. *Night Audience*	Wan-ch'ao
25. Floating the Lanterns*	Fang shui teng

THIRD DAY

26. Reinvite the spirits*	Ch'ung-pai

27. Sending off the Grand Memorial*	Teng-t'ai Chin-piao
28. Nine Hells Litany of Repentance (10 vols.)	Chiu-yü Pao-ch'an
29. *Audience of Union*	Tao-ch'ang, Cheng-chiao[65]
30. Feeding the hungry spirits (2 vols.)	P'u-tu
31. Thanking and seeing off the spirits	Hsieh shen, Sung shen

The above thirty-one ceremonies are augmented by a number of dramatic rituals of local origin, which do not belong to the orthodox or canonical tradition and often are part of an oral tradition. That is, they are usually memorized and not found in written form. The "noon offering" occurs each day of the chiao festival, and other popular dramatic rites, such as the climbing of the thirty-six sword ladder,[66] the summoning of the Jade Emperor, expelling the demon king[67] and the like, are performed at the will of the Taoist Master or by demand of the local populace.[68] Thus there are variations found between north and south Taiwan and even between village and nearby village in north Taiwan. The basic structure of the chiao is not affected by these colorful local variations. Furthermore, the order of performing the rituals themselves is often changed by local Taoists and by certain orthodox sects of Sung dynasty origin.[69] The rituals used in the chiao festival are therefore determined by the training of the Taoist master and the sect to which he owes allegiance.

Thus many local Taoists of north Taiwan and of overseas Chinese communities, such as in modern Honolulu, perform a simplified version of the chiao in which the aspects of renewal and blessings are emphasized and the rites of union are not performed. In a simple one- or two-day chiao, the Taoists commonly perform the following rituals:[70]

1. Fa-tsou, sending off the memorial.
2. Chu-sheng, inviting the spirits to be present.
3. Reading the various canons of merit, such as the *Pole Star Canon*, *Three Officials Canon*, etc.
4. Reading the litanies of repentance, the various Pao-ch'an manuals.
5. Feeding the hungry souls, in the P'u-tu or P'u-shih.
6. Concluding rite for seeing off the spirits.

The blessings from such a liturgy derive from the canonical readings and from the grand P'u-tu banquet for freeing the souls from hell,[71] rather than from the classical k'o-i meditations of union.

The distinction between the classical orders who call themselves "orthodox" and the popular local orders is, therefore, clearly seen in the manner in which the Taoists perform the chiao. Only the orthodox Taoist masters of a grade six (Three-five Surveyor of Merits) or higher ordination use the classical k'o-i rituals of union in performing a three- or five-day chiao.[72] These rituals, as underlined in the above list, are:

1. The Su-ch'i: the meditation on the *Ling-pao Five Talismans.*
2. The Tsao-ch'ao: the meditation on the first of the Three Pure Ones, Primordial Heavenly Worthy, symbol of primordial breath.
3. The Wu-ch'ao: the meditation on the second of the Three Pure Ones, Ling-pao Heavenly Worthy, the symbol of spirit.

4. The Wan-ch'ao: the meditation on the third of the Three Pure Ones, Tao-te Heavenly Worthy, symbol of vital essence.
5. The Tao-ch'ang: more commonly called Cheng-chiao, the meditation of union with the transcendent Tao.

The meditations are taught by Master Chuang as a sort of ritual alchemy, progressing from the first rite of the five talismans to the final meditation of union. An ordered series of meditations leads from the many, that is, the myriad creatures of the macrocosm, through a series of refining stages, to the eternal Tao of simplicity. Thus in a first meditation, the myriad spirits are reduced to the five prime movers (the five elements). The five are reduced to the Three Pure Ones, or the three principles of life. Finally, the three are reduced to the state of simplicity, or Hun-tun. In this last state, the Taoist master attains union with the Tao. The term "hsin-chai," therefore, as applied to religious Taoism and its interpretation of the *Chuang-tzu*, refers to the above series of ritual meditatons. The Tao comes to dwell in the heart which is emptied of the myriad spirits.

My own problem, after hearing the explanation of Master Chuang concerning the esoteric meditations of union, was a crucial one. If only a few of the higher Taoist masters knew the meditations called hsin-chai, how efficacious were the many rituals and festivals celebrated by the deprived local Taoists who did not know the elite meditations? That is, if the meditations were essential to chiao ritual, most of the chiao celebrated throughout Taiwan by the lower Redhead Taoists of the various Shen-hsiao, Lü Shan, or Ling-pao orders were ineffective. Furthermore, not only were the shorter one- and two-day chiao totally lacking in the esoteric k'o-i rite of union, even the orthodox masters of a lowly grade six rank might perform the externals of a Su-ch'i or a Tao-ch'ang without knowing the higher stages of meditative union.

The answer, Master Chuang assured me, lay in the proper understanding of Taoist ritual. The efficacy of the rite was in the exact execution of the rubrical directions, the summoning of the spirits, the sending off of the heavenly document, and the various mudras and mantras accompanying the Taoist's petitions. Even within the ranks of orthodox Taoism there were grades of esoteric teachings and spiritual perfection. The efficacy of the ritual depended on rubrical perfection, ex opere operato, but was vastly enhanced and elevated by the spiritual life of the master, ex opere operantis.[73] Thus in the two levels of esoteric teachings, the rituals could first be seen as a summoning of spirits, each in its proper attire and with the classical color or vapor accompanying the vision. Each of the esoteric rites had a secret liaison official, the envisioning of whom made the rite efficacious. For each ritual a document was prepared and the proper liason official summoned to carry it to the throne of the heavenly worthies. The appearance of the liaison officials, the mudras and mantras necessary to command them, and the proper spirit to whom the document is addressed, were among the most important secrets required to make the rituals effective. The following are the spirits addressed for the various rituals, with their messengers:[74]

1. Su-ch'i: Primordial breath prior heavens T'ai-yi heavenly worthy, with the lightning bureau Heavenly Lord Chang and the messengers of the Shu-wen, and the piao documents.
2. Tsao-ch'ao: Heavenly Marshal Hsieh, with the green tz'u document official T'ung-tzu.
3. Wu-ch'ao: Official of earth, T'ai-sui deity with the Heavenly Marshal Yin, the im-

	mortal bearer of the shu-wen document.
4. Wan-ch'ao:	Official from beneath the earth, the military spirit Marshal Wen, with the immortal bearers of the shu-wen and piao documents.
5. Tao-ch'ang:	The heavenly lord of eternal life; with the official bearers of the shu-wen document.

Each of the k'o-i meditations thus has a special liaison official and a specific heavenly deity to whom the rite is addressed. By addressing the documents to the proper deity, in the specified formula, and with the liaison messenger appointed for the day, the ritual is effectively performed. The chiao can be interpreted on a lower, less esoteric plane as a sending off of documents to the various deities who control the forces of nature. By the ritual perfection of the Taoist, the spirits of the cosmos are prevailed upon to grant heavenly blessing, give abundance on earth, and free the souls from hell. But on a higher, meditative plane, the chiao is interpreted as a ritual for bringing about union with the Tao. That is to say, the Taoist first unites himself to the Tao of transcendence, and then carries the petitions of the men and women of the community before the thrones of the heavenly worthies. Thus in the final definition, the highest form of esoteric Taoism is seen to be based upon the premise that the master first unites himself with the Tao and then uses his supernatural powers to save others. From his position of esoteric union, he coaxes and cajoles the spirits of the three realms (heaven, earth, and underworld) to give man blessing. All his marvelous powers come to him by reason of union with the Tao.

The higher esoteric plan of the k'o-i rituals are therefore seen to lead to a state of mystic union. The Su-ch'i ritual begins the alchemical process of refining the spirits of the microcosm by establishing a feudal union with the five primordial rulers of the five elements. The ritual itself enacts the ancient ceremony for enfeoffing a vassel by a feudal lord. The Taoist, who plays the role of hun-tun or t'ai-chi, takes five talismanic contracts, the *Ling-pao Five Talismans*, described in the opening pages of this chapter. These true writs, the same used by Yü the Great to control the floods, the same brought by a dragon-horse to Yao and Shun to confirm their rule over the cosmos and later buried in the spirit-cave atop Mao Shan, are now used by the Taoist to renew the life-giving power of the five elements in the cosmos. The talismans of the east, south, center, west and north one by one are used to establish a feudal contract. The talismans are ritually burned and their vapors visualized in the Taoist's meditation. The Ling half of the talisman ascends to the heavens and the Pao is buried inside the microcosm. The table below shows the order of burning.[75]

DIRECTION	COLOR	ELEMENT–ORGAN	SPIRIT (taboo name)	NUMBER
east	green emperor	wood-liver	Ling wei yang (Fu-hsi)	9 (3)
south	red emperor	fire-heart	Ch'ih p'iao nu (Shen-nung)	3 (2)
center	yellow emperor	earth-spleen	Han shu niu (Huang-ti)	1 (5)
west	white emperor	metal-lungs	Pai chao chü (Shao-hao)	7 (4)
north	black emperor	water-kidneys	Hsieh Kuang chi (Chuan-hsü)	5 (1)

The *Ling-pao Five Talismans* are identified in the heavens by the first row of numbers, representing stars surrounding the North Star. When implanted in the earth or in the microcosm, they are represented by the second set of numbers. Though the *Ling-pao Wu-fu Hsü* in volume 183 of the Taoist Canon identifies the Five Talismans with the mythical *Ho-t'u* from the ancient apocryphal texts, an association also made in the sixth-century *Wu-shang Pi-yao*,[76] and although the first set of numbers (9,3,1,7,5) is still associated with the *Ling-pao Five Talismans* in modern ritual, once the talismans have been "implanted" (An Chen-wen), the second set of numbers represents their earthly activity.[77] There is perhaps no more esoteric ritual in the history of religious Taoism than the Su-ch'i liturgy of the Five Talismans. Many Redhead Shen-hsiao Taoists of north Taiwan readily admit that they do not know how to perform the ritual and leave it out of the chiao festivals of renewal.

Once the *Ling-pao Five Talismans* have been implanted in the microcosm, the process of refinement is continued in the three audiences, the rituals called Tsao-ch'ao or morning audience (12 in the above list), Wu-ch'ao or noon audience (15), and Wan-ch'ao or night audience (24). Thus, in answer to my question, Chuang proposed two interpretations. In the meditations of the three audiences, the rituals are understood by the people and the lower grades of Taoists as ceremonies for sending off documents to the spiritual rulers of the heavens. But in the esoteric sense, the three audiences are interpreted as an alchemical meditation in which the five elements are refined into the three principles of life.[78]

In the earthly manifestation of the *Ling-pao Five Talismans*, wood of east is given the mystical number "3" and fire of the south the number "2" as symbols. In the Tsao-ch'ao meditation, the Taoist sees the green vapor of east and the bright red vapor of the south, that is, the essences of the elements wood and fire, combine in the empty center of the microcosm. The "3" of wood and the "2" of fire are alchemically fused in the alchemical furnace inside the Taoist's body. In the meditative tradition which

Master Chuang teaches, the empty center is called the Yellow Court, Huang-t'ing. The elements of wood and fire are fused, and become yüan-ch'i, primordial breath, a blue-green vapor personified as Primordial Heavenly Worthy, within the upper "cinnabar field" in the head of man. Thus wood's "3" and fire's "2" are fused into the first "5", the number symbolizing life breath in man.

Next, the refinement of the element earth, to which the mystical number "5" is also assigned, takes place during the Wu-ch'ao, the noon audience meditation. In the second state of meditative alchemy, the earth of center is refined into a yellow vapor, which congeals and becomes *Ling-pao Heavenly Worthy*, the personification of shen spirit in the center cinnabar field, the heart of man. Thus the second "5" is refined within the Yellow Court. Last, the element metal and the element water are meditatively brought into the alchemical furnace of the Yellow Court. In the Wan-ch'ao, the meditation of the evening audience, metal is given the symbolic number "4" and water the number "1". The white vapors of metal and the black vapors of water congeal into a pure white aura symbolized by Tao-te Heavenly Worthy, or vital essence within man, located in the lower "cinnabar field" in the belly of man. Thus the "4" of metal and the "1" of water congeal into the third "5" or the principle of vital essence within man. The meaning of the grade six Taoist's title, the "three-five surveyor of merits" is now made clear and evident. The "three fives" are the three spirits, which symbolize the three life principles, primordial breath, spirit, and vital essence.

In the final stage of the k'o-i rites of meditative union, the three principles of life are refined into the state of hun-tun, thus emptying the Yellow Court in preparation for union with the transcendent Tao. The final meditation is called Tao-ch'ang, the place where the Tao is present, or Cheng-chiao, the orthodox sacrifice.[79] The ritual consists in offering a chiao sacrifice of wine and incense to the

Three Pure Ones, Primordial Heavenly Worthy, Ling-pao Heavenly Worthy, and Tao-te Heavenly Worthy, who are, one by one, made present in the center of the Yellow Court. While externally presenting an offering of incense and wine to the Three Pure Ones, the three are internally refined and "voided," that is, reduced to the state of Hun-tun or primordial simplicity. Recalling the words of the *Chuang-tzu*, "Only the Tao dwells in the void," the final stages of the k'o-i rites end in a state of transcendent union.

In his teachings regarding the performance of a five-day chiao ritual of renewal and of the chai rites of burial, published in Chinese by the Ch'eng-wen press in Taipei, Chuang presents the meditations of union, and also the external rubrics, the mudras, mantras, melodies, and sacred dances necessary for performing Taoist ritual.[80] One short excerpt from k'o-i ritual will be chosen from the printed selections of Master Chuang's teachings as a sample of the intricacy of detail and the perfection of style required to perform the various meditative rituals of union.

6. THE FA-LU RITE FOR EXTERIORIZING THE SPIRITS. As outlined in the pages above, the k'o-i rituals of union all begin and end in the same manner. After an introduction in which the priest lights incense, sings the "hymn of ascent," and addresses the spirits to whom the ritual is directed, the meditation for emptying the spirits out of the body is performed. The rite is called fa-lu, literally, lighting the incense burner, a reference to the hand-held lu (incense burner, alchemical stove) used as the focal point of the meditation.[81] But the words fa-lu are a homonym for "exteriorizing the register," that is, sending forth all of the spirits registered as dwelling within the microcosm. The lu, or register, is the list of spirits over which the Taoist has control. The lu is given to him at the time of ordination, the rank and title of the Taoist determining the number of spirits in the lu register. Thus the grade four

Meng-wei Taoist such as Master Chuang knows the twenty-four lu of the Cheng-i sect, where the grade six San-wu Tu-kung Taoist knows only the ten or fourteen registers of the Ling-pao tradition.[82]

During the fa-lu ritual the Taoist empties out all the spirits that dwell within the microcosm, according to the list (lu) he has received at his ordination. After having exteriorized the spirits, the main body of the meditation of union takes place. That is to say, the Su-chi in which the Taoist strikes a feudal treaty with the five primordial movers, the Three Audiences in which the Three Pure Ones are refined, and the Tao-ch'ang in which union with the Tao is obtained, are performed only after the spirits have been exteriorized. After the meditation of union is finished, the master performs the fu-lu rite, which restores the register of spirits to their original place within the microcosm.[83]

As in all esoteric rituals, there are two levels on which the rite is explained. On the first level, the fa-lu is a meditation in which the Taoist builds a mandala or a pure area around himself in order to perform the chiao sacrifice and to send off the documents of petition. On the deeper esoteric level, it is interpreted as a ritual performance of the hsin-chai, the emptying the heart and the mind of all spirits, self-projections, and images that impede the contemplation of union with the Tao. This is the first of three esoteric secrets told to the novice.[84]

As to the second secret, the disciples must be instructed by the master concerning the correspondence between the various organs of the body and the spirits summoned forth during the ritual. As the year is divided into twelve months, so twelve organs of the body are selected as the special foci of ritual summoning, that is, as living quarters within the microcosm out of which the spirits are brought forth to bless and aid man. The twelve organs correspond to the twelve directions of the compass, and these in turn are imprinted as mudra on the joints of the left hand. Thus in order to summon a spirit, the Taoist must learn to press the proper joint on the inside of the left hand with the thumb, at the same time summoning the spirit from the internal organ. The tradition is oral (k'ou-chüeh) rather than written, and is explained in the following table.

MONTH (stem)	SIGN	ZODIAC	ORGAN	DIRECTION
1. tzu	rat	Aries	gall	North
2. ch'iu	ox	Taurus	liver	NNE by 3/4 East
3. yen	tiger	Gemini	lungs	ENE by 3/4 North
4. mao	hare	Cancer	big intestine	East
5. ch'en	dragon	Leo	stomach	ESE by 3/4 South
6. szu	snake	Virgo	spleen	SSE by 3/4 East
7. wu	horse	Libra	heart	South
8. wei	sheep	Scorpio	small intestine	SSW by 3/4 West
9. shen	monkey	Sagitarrius	bladder	WSW by 3/4 South
10. yu	cock	Capricorn	kidney	West
11. hsü	dog	Aquarius	pao-ko[85]	WNW by 3/4 North
12. hai	boar	Pisces	san-chiao	NNW by 3/4 West

The twelve earthly stems coordinated with the twelve directions and the twelve bodily organs.

The spirits summoned during the fa-lu ritual, which will be named below, are hidden within the Taoist's body. The Taoist master teaches the disciple how to press a joint on his left hand to summon forth a spirit. Figure 18 shows the joints on the left hand which correspond to the organs in the microcosm and the twelve stems in the macrocosm.

The various mudras on the left hand begin at the base of the ring finger with the stem tzu and travel clockwise through ch'iu, yen, mao, to the twelfth stem, hai. Each corresponds to a direction of the compass and to an organ within the microcosm of the body. In the second stage of oral instructions, the master must explain which of the

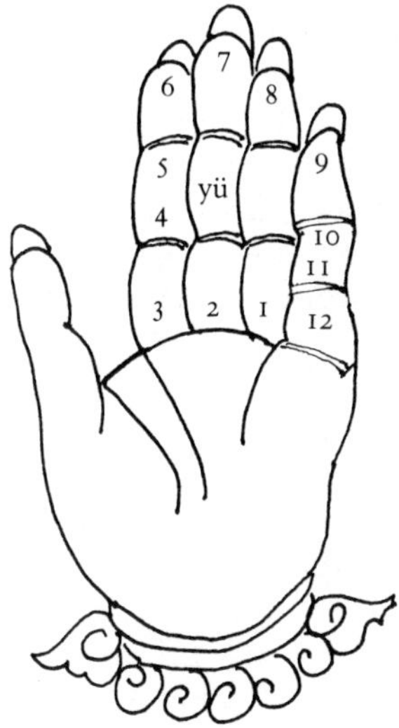

Figure 18. The left hand, showing the joints to be pressed in order to summon a spirit. By referring to the table above, the correspondence between the joint and the organ in the body can be determined.

heavenly spirits are lodged in the various organs of the body, what their appearance is, when they are to be summoned, and so forth. By pressing a joint with the left thumb, a spirit is summoned. Thus the five emperors are enfoeffed into the five central organs of the body by the systematic preparatory meditation of the young Taoist, during the many years of his training. The god of the east, for instance, with all his retainers, dwells in the liver. His is the breath of spring, the green-blue vapors that enliven nature and cause the grass and the green woods to be reborn, flowers to blossom, and life-giving rain to fall. He is summoned by pressing the mao joint with the thumb. The god of the south with his followers lives in the heart of man. He controls the bright fires of summer that redden the wheat and rice, brighten the noonday sun, and cause man to grow to maturity. He is summoned by pressing the wu joint with the thumb. The god of the west dwells in the lungs of man, a cool white breath, the spirit of autumn. Like a sharp blade of steel he cuts the autumn harvest and, after emptying the fields, leads man to war. He is summoned by pressing the yu position. The god of the north is in the kidneys of man, from whence he rules over water and acts as spirit of the freezing winter. He brings rest, the stirring of rebirth in the depths of earth's womb, the darkness of the horizon which presages dawn and new life. He is summoned by pressing the joint marked tzu. The god of the center is in the spleen, enveloped in a rich yellow vapor, the color of the loess soil. He is the source from which wood grows and in which metal hides, a power which overcomes winter's damp cold and grows forth from the ashes of fire. He is summoned by pressing the central position marked yü.

The third secret which must be taught before the disciple is allowed to perform the fa-lu rite concerns the method of summoning the special liaison of the day, who acts as the messenger between the Taoist and the courts of the heavenly bureaucracy. For each day in a cycle of sixty days, there is a special kung-ts'ao messenger, whose secret name, mantric summons, and appearance must be memorized. The teachings of Master Chuang in this regard are too lengthy to be repeated here.[86] The disciple is usually made to memorize the secret name, appearance, and cyclical day on which each kung-ts'ao messenger is summoned to facilitate execution of the meditation.

With the above three K'ou-chüeh, or oral secrets, revealed by the master, the disciple is ready to begin the fa-lu rite for exteriorizing the spirits. The oral secrets are not taught to the musicians or the lower members of the Taoist entourage but are reserved for those few disciples, usually the Taoist's own sons, destined to become Taoist masters. When done in private to initiate a meditation of inner alchemy or to cure a sick person, the fa-lu is performed without musical accompaniment of any kind. But when used during the chiao festivals of renewal or the chai rites of burial, it is always accompanied by percussion and wind instruments, the great Taoist drum being the essential signal of the inward meditations of the master. Because the circulation of breath, swallowing of saliva, and calling forth of the various spirits is signaled by the beat of the ritual drum, the master must teach the external formulae of the rite to the drummer, and to the chief and assistant cantors, the incense bearer and procession leader, who accompany him into the ritual area and chant the rite while he is performing the meditation. The disciples perform the external rubrics of orthodox ritual, while the master himself practices the meditations of inner alchemy.

The rubrics of the fa-lu meditation are clearly stated in the Sung dynasty *Wu-shang Huang-lu Ta-chai Li-ch'eng Yi*, chapters 16 and 32.[87] The Taoist and his entourage enter the sacred T'an area, the disciples through the Gate of Earth (the southwest entrance) and the master through the Gate of Heaven (the northwest entrance). A pu-hsü meditative hymn, the lighting of incense, encircling the altar, and the reading of the entrance incantation (one for a ritual offered during the day, another for a ritual offered at night) precedes the actual fa-lu meditation. The esoteric "Incantation to the Auspicious Spirits," which acts as a prelude to the meditation, is clearly described in chapter 32 of the above-mentioned canonical text, in which the Taoist first envisions the five elements as primordial movers interpenetrating the macro- and microcosms. While forming the mudras on the left hand, the master closes his eyes and sees the five internal organs, the five peaks of the external world, and the five stars in the heavens, with his own body as center of the cosmos. The five emperors are seen to be in the five organs, each with an army of soldiers and retainers, horses and chariots, dressed in the colors proper to their elements and directions. Thus the emperor of the east has an army dressed in green-blue, the emperor of the south leads an army dressed in red, the west in white, the north in black, and the center in yellow. The incantation begins with the loud command of the Chief Cantor who sings: "Let each of the ritual masters meditate upon the law!"

With these words the master begins to see the interior of the microcosm come alive with the vapors and spirits he is about to summon forth. He sees the Primordial Heavenly Worthy dwelling in the "upper cinnabar" field, in the head (that is, one of the nine sacred palaces in the head (heavens) for indwelling spirits). The Primordial Heavenly Worthy is enveloped in a blue-green mist and commands the highest of the Taoist heavens, with a myriad of heavenly worthies and retainers in attendance. The Ling-pao Heavenly Worthy dwells in the central cinnabar field in the chest, that is, the heart. He is enveloped in a yellow vapor, and is surrounded by a myriad realized spirits in the second highest Taoist heaven. The Tao-te Heavenly Worthy is envisioned in the lower cinnabar field, in the belly. He is enveloped in a white vapor and surrounded with a myriad realized spirits in the third of the Taoist heavens. While the Taoist master envisions the Three Heavenly Worthies, the Five Emperors, and so forth, the chief cantor and the other members of the entourage are singing a description of what the master envisions. When the hymn has ended, the chief cantor intones: "Sound the Taoist drum twenty-four times!"

With these words the drummer begins to strike the great Taoist drum used during the master's celebration of liturgy. The drummer first strikes the drum with eight slow blows, at the end of which the metal gong (a brass bowl) is struck once. The master grinds his teeth on the left side of his jaw once, swallows saliva, and envisions the spirits of the eight directions in the heavens. The drummer then strikes the drum again eight blows and the metal gong is rung a second time. The master grinds his four upper and four lower front teeth and swallows saliva, while envisioning the spirits of the central regions in each of the eight directions. Finally the drummer strikes the drum a third series of blows, while the Taoist grinds his teeth on the right side of the jaw and swallows saliva, envisioning the spirits of the lower regions stretching out in eight directions. Thus the three times eight or twenty-four cosmological divisions of the world, with all their realized spirits, are alerted to the master's summons. While the drum is being sounded, the master recites inwardly a secret conjuration or spell, which has several variant readings in the canonical texts but follows the same general pattern as that used by the orthodox masters of Taiwan:

The Nine Mansions of the Highest Heavens,
Are guarded by the Great One,
With hundred spirits like a forest of sentinels!
The Hun and P'o souls (in man) are united;[88]
Blue-green its going forth, dark and mysterious its return.
Like the bright rays of the sun,
Eternal life which does not grow senescent,
Suppress and destroy the heterodox and evil,
Quickly, quickly, like the highest heaven's life breath,
An imperial order!

The master thereupon kneels in the center of the sacred T'an area with the cantors and acolytes on his left and right. As the assembly of disciples sing the words of the fa-lu, the master begins his meditation. The following are the words of the text and a translation:

1. Wu-shang san t'ien	Transcendent, highest Three Heavens
2. Hsüan, yüan, shih, san Ch'i	Mysterious, primordial, original, three breaths!
3. T'ai-shang Lao-chun	T'ai-shang Lord Lao!
4. Tang chao-ch'u ch'en shen chung	Now call forth from within my body
5. San-wu kung-ts'ao	The three-five kung-ts'ao officers,
6. Tso-yu kuan shih-che	The left and right official messengers,
7. Tso-yu feng hsiang	The left and right incense bearers,
8. Yi lung ch'i li	Dragon-riding dispatch officers,

9. Shih hsiang chin-t'ung	Incense-bearing golden lads,
10. Chuan-yen san-hua yü-nü	The jade girls who carry messages and scatter flowers,
11. Wu-ti chih fu	The Five Emperors carrying the talismans,
12. Chih-jih hsiang-kuan shih-che	The special incense messenger of the day,
13. Ko san-shih-liu jen ch'u	In all, thirty-six spirits come forth!

Their coming forth is stately and elegant
Quickly they carry up the official documents
May the orthodox gods of the soil
Assemble here today to guard the altar
[variant line],
To carry out the ritual of the Tao.

While the words are being chanted by the disciples, the master envisions the heavenly worthies and the spirits within his body. One by one he summons them forth to take up their positions around the sacred area, meditating as follows.[89] ***the explanation of Chuang differs significantly from the Falu meditation of the Tainan Taoists, as described by Schipper, Lagerwey, and Ofuchi***

1. *Wu-shang san t'ien:* 無上三天

The master sees the abode of the Three Pure Ones in the head, the chest, and the belly respectively. He sees the white vapor from the lower abdomen (also called the lower cinnabar field) rise up toward the occiput in his head. Next he sees the yellow vapor from the center part of his body (the central cinnabar field, abode of the Ling-pao Heavenly Worthy) also rise upward toward the occiput. Finally he envisions the blue-green breath of the Primordial Heavenly Worthy in the Ni-wan palace in the head. The three breaths come upward into the head and rest under the scalp, waiting to be summoned forth through the occiput. The Taoist presses the joints on the left hand market wei, wu, and szu in order to summon the Three Pure Ones.

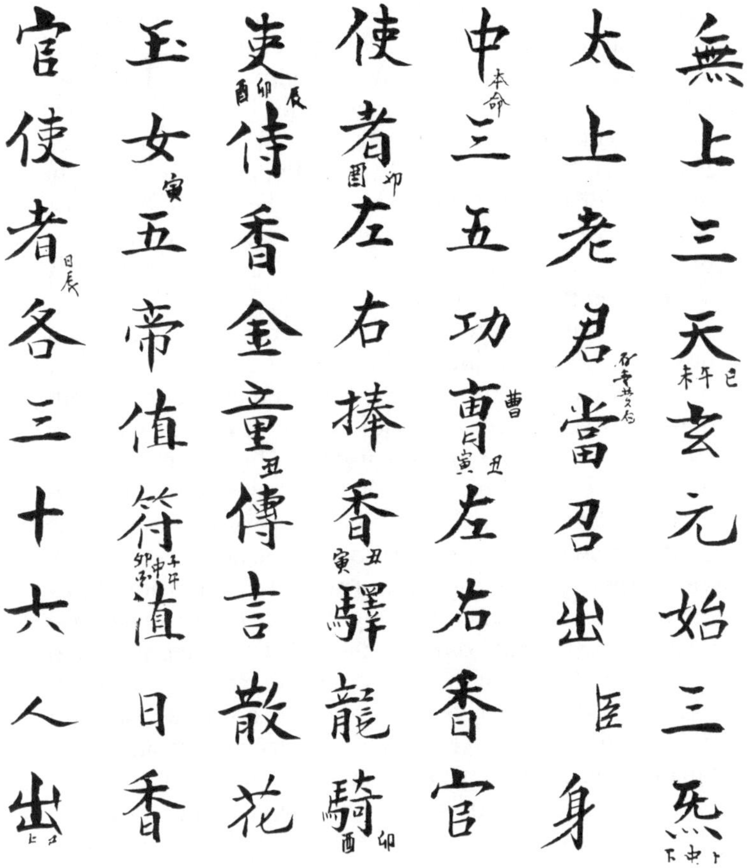

無上三天玄元始三炁
太上老君當召出臣身
中三五功曹左右香官
使者左右捧香驛龍騎
吏侍香金童傳言散花
玉女五帝值符直日香
官使者各三十六人出

Figure 19. The fa-lu rite for exteriorizing the spirits.

2. *Hsüan, yüan, shih, san ch'i* 玄,元,始,三炁
As these words are recited the Taoist presses the joint marked ch'iu on his left hand and sees the Primordial Heavenly Worthy come forth from the occiput in the center of his head. The Primordial Heavenly Worthy goes to the north wall of the sacred area, where he occupies the

very center throughout the ceremony. Next he presses the joint marked yü, in the center of the middle finger, and sees the Ling-pao Heavenly Worthy come forth. The Ling-pao Heavenly Worthy also goes to the north wall and takes up the position to the left or east of the centrally located Primordial Heavenly Worthy. Finally, he presses the joint on the left hand marked wu and sees the Tao-te Heavenly Worthy come forth. The third of the Pure Ones takes the position to the west or right of the Primordial Heavenly Worthy on the north wall.

As the Three Pure Ones come forth to take up their positions of preeminence in the ritual area, the place occupied by the emperor in court audiences, the Taoist master also envisions a splendid court of mythical animal retainers that always accompany the Three Pure Ones. In the east is the great blue dragon that represents the powers of spring. In the south is the red phoenix of summer. In the west is the white tiger of autumn. In the north is the black tortoise in its armor, the symbol of winter. The Taoist himself occupies the center, playing the role of the alchemical furnace, the central void in which the Tao of eternity is to be present. In each of the interstices—that is, the northeast, southeast, southwest, and northwest—are two lions and two herons, respectively, a total of sixteen guardian spirits. Finally over his left eye the Taoist envisions the sun with nine rays and the moon with ten rays coming forth.

3. *T'ai-shang Lao-chun* 太上老君

The third of the Three Pure Ones is especially invoked in the third phrase of the fa-lu meditation. The Taoist presses the joint marked ch'iu on the left hand and asks the intercession of Lord Lao, or Lao-tzu, in summoning forth the spirits before effecting the rite of union. In some rituals, the invocation to Lao-chun is changed to Tao-chun, a technical term for the second of the Three Pure Ones, Ling-pao T'ien-tsun. The latter invocation is found in a special version of the fa-lu used to precede the ritual chanting of the Tu-jen Ching, the canon for helping mankind pass through the stages of hell into eternal life.[90] In the latter case, the master presses the joint on the left hand marked yü when summoning the Ling-pao Heavenly Worthy.

4. *Tang chao-ch'u ch'en shen-chung* 當召出臣身中
The Taoist presses the joint on his left hand which corresponds to his pen-ming star, that is to say, his zodiacal sign and patron spirit. At the time of his ordination, a special star, a patron spirit, and a temporal see, or place of spiritual jurisdiction (chih), is assigned to each Taoist master, according to the year of his birth.[91] The patron spirit acts as a special liaison official for the Taoist's documents and prayers addressed to the three stages of the cosmos—heaven, earth, and watery underworld. At this point in the fa-lu, the Taoist calls upon his private pen-ming spirit to assist in the rite of exteriorization.

5. *San-wu kung-ts'ao* 三五功曹
The three-five kung-ts'ao refers to the liaison officials of the three stages of the cosmos (heaven, earth, and water), and the five directions (five elements, five rulers). Since the numbers "3" and "5" are consistently used for three principles of life, or the Three Pure Ones, and the five movers or the five emperors, the Taoist master now establishes control over the secret messenger spirits, the kung-ts'ao who relay messages between the three stages of the world and the supreme heavenly worthies. In the esoteric doctrines of Master Chuang, there are five secret kung-ts'ao spirits assigned to the Three Pure Ones and five assigned to the Five Emperors. The first five are summoned forth by pressing the joint marked ch'iu on the left hand. The last five are summoned by pressing the joint marked yen.

6. *Tso-yu kuan shih-che* 左右官使者
The left and right official messengers are the spirit officials who control yin and yang. In this orthodox version of ritual meditation they are named the six chia (left chest, yang) and the six ting (right chest, yin) messengers. They are, however, a far cry from the violent Six Chia spirits of chapter 4, as used in the Tao of the Left. Within the microcosm of the orthodox master, they are pure spirits who protect the emptied center or the Yellow Court from any outside distraction during the meditation of union. The chia spirits are summoned by pressing the joint marked mao, while the ting spirits are called forth by pressing the joint yu.

7. *Tso-yu feng hsiang* 左右捧香
The left and right incense-bearing spirits are lodged in the liver and the lungs (east and west) respectively. The left spirits are summoned by pressing the joint marked ch'iu, and the right spirits by the joint marked yen. This and the following invocation are not found in the Sung dynasty version of the fa-lu, but are in the sixth-century *Wu-shang Pi-yao* and the various editions of Master Chuang.

8. *Yi lung ch'i li* 驛龍騎吏
The dragon dispatch officials are lodged in the big intestine (left, yang) and the kidneys (right, yin). They are summoned forth by pressing the joints on the left hand marked mao and yu respectively.

9. *Shih hsiang chin-t'ung* 侍香金童
The golden lads, who act as the immediate forerunners of the five emperors, are housed in the liver (yang, east). They too are summoned forth by pressing the joint marked ch'iu.

10. *Chuan-yen san-hua yü-nü* 傳宮散花玉女
Immediately after the golden lads come the jade lasses, who precede the five emperors as royal court attendants. They are seen singing hymns of praise, scattering flowers, and burning pure incense before the sacred five emperors. Their residence is in the lungs (yin, west), and they are summoned forth by pressing the position marked yen.

11. *Wu-ti chih fu* 五帝值符
The emperors next come forth from their positions within the five central organs. Each is seen to hold aloft the Ling-pao talisman proper to his own jurisdiction. When the Taoist presses the joint marked mao, the emperor of the east comes forth from the liver in a green vapor. The Taoist presses the joint wu and the emperor of the south comes forth from the heart in a red vapor. The Taoist presses the central joint, yü, and the yellow emperor comes forth from the spleen in a gold vapor. The Taoist presses the joint yu and the emperor of the west comes forth from the lungs in a white vapor. Finally the Taoist presses the joint marked tzu and the emperor of the north comes forth from the kidneys in a black vapor. Each takes up his position in the sacred area, thus completing a marvelous mandala of pure spirits surrounding the Taoist in the center of the cosmos.

12. *Chih-jih hsiang kuan shih-che* 值日香官使者
The incense-bearing messenger spirit of the day is next summoned forth. This spirit is computed daily by the Taoist master from a list of sixty spirits, each of which successively takes up his or her duties in a sixty-day cycle. The sixty chia-tzu spirits are said to be the grandchildren of the San-huang, the three ancient emperors of the *San-huang Wen*, and the children of the six chia and six ting spirits who control the powers of nature. The list of the

spirits and the way of computing when each is to be summoned is one of the secrets given to the Taoist novice by his master sometime before his ordination. Without knowing how to compute the chia-tzu spirit of the day, the performance of the fa-lu is impossible.

13. *Ko san-shih-liu jen ch'u* 各三十六人出
In the last phrase of the rite of exteriorization, the Taoist summons forth the three times eight, or twenty-four spirits of the cosmos, eight each for the head, chest, and belly. Next he summons the three hun souls that represent the powers of yang in man, and the seven p'o souls that symbolize the influence of yin. Finally he calls forth the last two spirits of the microcosm, the lord yang and the lady yin. Thus thirty-six spirits are summoned forth from the body in the final invocation. With the body now emptied of all the spirits and the mind freed from any thought, even that of the highest heavenly worthies, the Taoist is ready for the meditation of transcendental union. The requirements for union, in the interpretation of Master Chuang, are fulfilled as demanded in the *Chuang-tzu*. The hsin-chai or "fast of the heart" has been accomplished by a ritual meditation. The Taoist, at the end of the fa-lu rite, has been reduced to a state of hun-tun, or primordial emptiness, ready for an encounter with the Tao of transcendence.

The written instructions of Master Chuang concerning the *fa-lu* have been published in Chinese.[92] The above brief description provides a first glimpse of the intricacies of orthodox meditation, a technique that takes years of practise to perfect. The keynotes of the meditations of the orthodox Tao of the Right are peace, simplicity, and purity. The purpose of the k'o-i rites of union is to win blessing for the people, as well as contemplative union for the Taoist master. They are an extreme opposite of the military Tao of the Left described in chapter 4 and quite different, in turn, from the popular form of Sung dynasty Thunder Magic to be described in the following chapter. The orthodoxy of a master is judged by his ability to perform meditation as described in the above pages, and to work always for the good of his fellow man, as will be seen in the final chapter.

6. Thunder Magic: Neo-Orthodoxy of the Sung

(the entire chapter represents Chuang's oral teaching)

Introduction

The stately Tao of the Right just described in chapter 5 has remained, from the time of the north-south period until the present day, the hallmark of orthodox religious Taoism. Taoists learning its meditations and classical rituals have been rewarded with the highest rank at ordination, and have performed their chiao liturgies of renewal for the imperial court as well as for the village temple. But the rituals of classical orthodoxy had one drawback in everyday use. Complete purification was necessary to perform the rites of union properly. The slightest stain on the consciousness of the adept, the presence of any impure spirit, destroyed the efficacy of the meditation of union. Furthermore, the popular Taoist orders, disregarding the meditations of purifying emptiness, summoned hosts of spirits and demons that could never be admitted to the pure area within the temple during chiao ritual of renewal. Orthodox Taoism therefore needed a new kind of ritual, one less austere and also able to control the host of unorthodox spirits developed during the ages by Taoists of sectarian bias.[1]

A second factor promoting the acceptance of a new kind of orthodoxy during the Sung period and the later Yüan or Mongol dynasty was the deep and colorful influence of the tantric Buddhist orders. As early as the eighth century A.D., tantric Buddhism had been introduced to the city of Ch'ang-an in the west of China and to Mount T'ien-t'ai in Chekiang province in the southeast of China. The esoteric Buddhist sects brought a new kind of mudra and mantra and a systematic mandala style of meditative ritual that resonated with the liturgies of orthodox Taoism. The use of pseudo-Sanskrit seed words and complicated two-handed mudras caught the imagination of the T'ang and the early Sung Taoist masters. The response of Taoism to tantric Buddhism, and to the proliferating local Taoist sects of the Sung period, was evident in the rapidly developing Thunder Magic of the mid-Sung period.[2]

As mentioned in my opening historical treatise in chapter 1, there were many schools of Thunder Magic during the Sung period. Almost all Taoist sects of the Sung period developed their own style of the new Thunder ritual. Of the many styles, three seemed to have been most successful and have come down in healthy and flourishing form to the present. These three schools are:[3]

1. Ch'ing-wei Thunder Magic, developed in west China during the early Sung period.
2. Fire-master Thunder Magic, attributed to Wang Tzu-hua during the mid-T'ang period.
3. Shen-hsiao Thunder Magic, brought to court by Lin Ling-su in 1118.

Besides these three sects, the Ch'ing-ming sect of the southern Sung period developed another form of Thunder Magic which is found in the Canon and is still influential today.[4] All Thunder Magic sects attribute the founding of the method to Hsü Hsun, a legendary Taoist said to have died in A.D. 374. Hsü was wafted up to heaven in broad daylight, but left behind twelve disciples to spread his doctrines. The story of Hsü Hsun seems to be a Sung dynasty fabrication; his name appears in the dynastic histories, but the legend about Thunder Magic and the slaying of a great serpent do not occur in Taoist writings until the mid-Sung, about 1100.

The legends told of Hsü Hsun describe the master as being a Confucian official as well as a Taoist expert.[5] A huge snake-like demon was said to be attacking the people under his administrative jurisdiction. With his twelve followers he confronted the snake and destroyed it with the power of thunder. The snake, a symbol of yin, or the demonic forces of nature, is commonly used in kung-fu and t'ai-chi physical fitness demonstrations. It is seen as an attacking creature with great mobility and indomitable resolution. In the Taoist interpretation, the black magic of the popular Mao-Shan sect and the Shen-hsiao sect make use of a snake-like spirit to harm men. The use of the snake chart will be demonstrated below in discussing the instructions of Master Chuang concerning the exorcistic use of Thunder Magic.

The paraphernalia of Thunder Magic is common to all the Taoist sects that use its purificatory ritual. A thunder block, or vajra, made of datewood is used to summon the spirits of thunder. Two-handed mudras (described below) are used to command the five orthodox thunder spirits to counteract harmful black magic.[6] Thus Thunder Magic may be seen as a form of neo-orthodoxy developed during the Sung period to counteract the spread of popular sectarian Taoists and to purify the sacred area where ritual meditation is to take place.

1. THREE STYLES OF THUNDER MAGIC

The three main styles of Thunder Magic—the Ch'ing-wei, Fire Master, and Shen-hsiao—are distinguished by clearly identifiable styles of liturgy. Each of the sects developed its own lu, or list of spirits' names. Each proposed its own style of meditation and popular ritual and held sway in a particular region in China.[7] The style of Thunder Magic taught by Master Chuang is partially derived from the Ch'ing-wei sect, from manuals originally in the collection of Wu Ching-ch'un. Besides the Ch'ing-wei style of Thunder Magic, a whole series of manuals teaching the fire-master method of Wang Tzu-hua were purchased by Lin Ju-mei at Lung-hu Shan in 1886 and brought back to

Hsinchu City in 1888.[8] The two style are similar but not identical. The differences are pointed out in the *Tao-fa Hui-yüan*, the critical treatise on Thunder Magic in the Taoist Canon.

The Ch'ing-wei style of magic derives from Mao Shan and Hua Shan, two mountains with close Taoist affiliations. In the interpretation of the meditative Mao Shan tradition, the power of thunder is stored in the five central organs and in the gall bladder. From the gall bladder it lights the alchemical furnace within the microcosm, that is, the lower cinnabar field in the belly of man. Thus all the meditations described in the previous chapter can be initiated by summoning thunder to purify the interior and "light the alchemical furnace" in a sort of adaptation from the orthodox tradition. Furthermore, the Ch'ing-wei sect claims Wei Hua-ts'un, the legendary women founder of the Mao Shan sect, as its own founder.[9] Thus its uses are meditative and are considered part of orthodox ritual as defined by Master Chuang in chapter 5 above.

The Fire-master Thunder Magic of Wang Tzu-hua originated on the southern peak Heng Shan and on Mount T'ien-t'ai in southeast China. The critical work on Wang Tzu-hua is found in the Taoist Canon, chapter 76 of the *Tao-fa Hui-yüan*. The late Sung dynasty expert Pai Yü-ch'an described the method as a kind of purifying meditation. While swallowing saliva and breathing in through the nostrils, the alchemical furnace in the lower cinnabar field (tan-t'ien) is lit and the power of thunder used to cure colds, exorcise, and purify. In the manuals brought back from Lung-hu Shan by Lin Ju-mei, the thunder of the fire master is seen to be aimed mainly at curing sickness and purifying the adept for immortality.[10] The style is called the "old" Shen-hsiao method to distinguish it from the new Thunder Magic of Lin Ling-su and other proliferations of Sung sectarianism.

The new Shen-hsiao brand of Thunder Magic is found in volumes 881 to 883 of the Taoist Canon. The style probably is rightly attributed to Lin Ling-su, the court favorite of the Hui-tsung emperor. In it, the names of the traditional spirits of the orthodox lu have been changed and the meditations of inner alchemy almost eliminated. There is a completely new and original set of talismans, mudras, and mantras, oriented toward curing sickness rather than toward use in rites of renewal or union. In the later Ming period the forty-third generation master of Lung-hu Shan, Chang Yü-ch'u, explains why the magic of Wang Tzu-hua is to be distinguished from the popular Shen-hsiao orders spreading throughout southeast China.[11] Each master, Chang says, devises his own version of the rubrics. The talismans and mantras are multiplied so that the true doctrines are lost and false versions multiplied. For contributing to this tendency the popular Shen-hsiao orders are severely criticized. Chapter 66 of the *Tao-fa Hui-yüan* concurs with the criticism, adding that the use of evil spirits to harm men was widespread in the popular Thunder Magic orders.[12] The orthodox orders' Thunder Magic, therefore, is seen as the most effective means of counteracting the use of black magic.

To Pai Yü-ch'an, the great Taoist master of the late Sung period, is attributed the achievement of purifying and making orthodox the rituals of the Shen-hsiao order. Like Lu Hsiu-ching in the fifth century, who edited out the forgeries of Ko Ch'ao-fu before publishing the Ling-pao Canon, so Pai Yü-ch'an in the thirteenth century edited the Shen-hsiao texts and gave them the aura of respectability. Pai was given the official title, "Official of the Shen-hsiao Rubric," for his strenuous efforts to bring unity into the chaos of Sung sectarianism. Nevertheless, when signing his Taoist documents and addressing the heavenly worthies in prayer, Pai did not use his Shen-hsiao title. Rather, he signed himself as a master of the Shang-ch'ing meditative tradition, knowledgeable in Thunder Magic and in the military exorcisms of the Pole Star sect.[18]

Though relieved of its earlier aberrations, the new Shen-hsiao sect is still considered to be the latest and least of the orders of Taoist brethren. As practiced in Taiwan today, new Shen-hsiao Taoism, like the aberrant form of popular Mao Shan Taoism, makes use of evil talismans to kill, injure, or harm people in the community. For this reason, the Taoists who seek to climb the various stages of perfection within the ranks of orthodox Taoism, are given Thunder Magic titles from the Ch'ing-wei sect and draw away from the simpler forms of new Shen-hsiao exorcism. The Heavenly Master at Lung-hu Shan kept manuals from all three of the dominant thunder sects and taught them to the Taoists coming for a license of ordination according to the expertise and demands of the visitors.[14]

To Master Chuang, the beginnings of Thunder Magic must be sought in the T'ang dynasty, rather than in the later Sung. The few historians who have written about Thunder Magic have found no mention of thunder rites in dated canonical texts before the Sung dynasty. Some hold that Lin Ling-su was the first to practice Thunder Magic and thus won imperial approval at court.[15] Others hold that the founders of the T'ien-hsin Cheng-fa, a branch of Thunder Magic attributed to an offshoot of the Heavenly Master sect, brought it to court a few years before Lin Ling-su.[16] Though it would be difficult to establish the existence of Thunder Magic sects before the Sung dynasty, it does seem plausible that kinds of Thunder Magic were practised on the local level before the coming of the Sung dynasty innovators. Except for the name "Five Thunder Method," which came to typify the rites of the Sung, the thunder rubrics are definitely seen in the T'ang dynasty canon.[17]

2. THE TEACHINGS OF MASTER CHUANG ON THUNDER MAGIC

The teachings of Master Chuang regarding the rites of Thunder Magic were inherited from the last of the men to instruct him in the esoteric rubrics of religious Taoism, Lin Hsiu-mei. Lin gave Chuang two manuals containing the instructions for meditation and the rubrical directions for performing thunder ritual. The first manual of preparatory meditation was the nineteen-page *Commentary on the Yellow Court Canon*. It is used in conjunction with the *Yellow Court Canon* itself and expresses philosophically the distinction between the Tao of transcendence and the meditations by which the body is prepared for its presence. The second manual, called the *Hua-shan Ch'ing-wei Sect Thunder Magic Rubrics*, was one of the manuals brought to Taiwan by Wu Ching-ch'un in 1823 and left in the Lin family collection until 1928 when it was given to Chuang. Both works are in the author's microfilm collection, listed in part 3 of the Bibliography at the end of this book. The latter manual will be translated in the following pages as an illustration of the teachings of Master Chuang on the performance of Five Thunder Magic. To introduce the meditations used by the Taoist to prepare himself to wield power over thunder, I shall attempt to summarize briefly the teachings of the first manual, in keeping with the preliminary nature of this study. It would require a full-length monograph to explain the subject adequately.

The meditation in which the Taoist sees himself in the presence of the transcendent Tao is prepared for in a series of alchemical-like processes whereby the principles of life within the body are "refined" and "joined" in the Yellow Court, which is conceived to be an empty center within the microcosm of a man's body. The Taoist does not refine or summon the ultimate transcendent Tao of the Wu-wei, for transcendent Act cannot be refined or summoned. He rather prepares the body by acts of purification and emptying for a state in which the contemplation of the Tao of Transcendence can take place. In the *Commentary on the Yellow Court Canon*, the disciple is first taught that the interpretation of the texts of interior perfection which make use of fang-chung, or sexual hygiene, are false and may not be used by the Taoist who aspires to the highest stages of spiritual perfection. The texts of interior meditation are to be interpreted as exercises in the circulation of breath and saliva and the summoning of pure spirits of the Prior Heavens. The Taoist thus distinguishes the spirits of the visible Posterior Heavens from the heavenly worthies of the eternal Prior Heavens. These latter spirits act as purifying forces for preparing the Yellow Court before the contemplation of the Transcendent. The role of Thunder Magic in the preparatory meditations is to be a stimulus and catalyst in the alchemical process of purification.

Thus, in the explanation of the *Commentary on the Yellow Court Canon*, and in chapter 76 of the *Tao-fa Hui-yüan*, the alchemical furnace is the lower cinnabar field within the belly of man.[18] The nose, which breathes in and expels air during the meditation of interior alchemy, is taken to be the "male organ" during the process of refinement, that is, the bellows which supplies wind and breath to the fire within the furnace. The mouth, which remains closed, is considered to be the female organ, or the supplier of saliva to the furnace in the belly. The saliva, however, is not ordinary material saliva alone but a mixture of the colored vapors that contain the principles of life, acting as fuel and ingredients for the alchemical process in the belly. Thus, the actual refinement is seen to take place in the lower cinnabar field and is quite unlike the Indian kundalini process of interior awakening. The various breaths of the five elements and the three principles of life are mixed with saliva and swallowed. The alchemical furnace in the belly, which has been lighted by the power of thunder, then refines and joins the various breaths into the "hierophant," or the ruddy child, the pill of longevity, or the immortal foetus, depending on the wording of the text or the choice of the translator, the words being analogous. In no sense can the final condition be taken to be the Tao of Transcendence. The ultimate Tao of the Wu-chi (Transcendent

Principle) is present only during the performance of orthodox liturgy when the Taoist has the flame pin or diadem inserted in his ritual crown, or during the meditation in the private chambers of his residence while he is in the depths of contemplation and the breathing process is stopped or contained within. At all other times, though he has indeed formed the hierophant within the Yellow Court in his own body, and though he can again join himself in union with the transcendent, the state of union is potential and not activated. Union is therefore seen to be affected by the power of thunder, and thus the Thunder Magic ritual of the Ch'ing-wei tradition is a direct descendant of the Mao Shan Shang-ch'ing sect of Wei Hua-ts'un and the *Yellow Court Canon* Tradition.

In the Ch'ing-wei tradition of Thunder Magic, the power of the thunder is first stored by a meditation which takes place each spring.[19] On the first day after the Lunar New Year in which a thunderstorm takes place, the Taoist faces the direction of the thunder and breathes in the breath of electrified atmosphere while forming mudras on both hands and reciting mantric spells. The power of the thunder is circulated throughout the organs of the body and finally stored in the gall bladder. When ready to perform the meditations of internal alchemy, the thunder is used to light the fire in the alchemical furnace in the belly. Thereupon the meditative process of refinement begins. The vapors of the elements metal and water are first joined together into seminal essence. The vapor of metal is white and is stored in the lungs. The vapor of water is black and is stored in the kidneys. Both vapors are circulated upward and mixed with saliva in the mouth. By breathing in through the nose and swallowing saliva, the mixture of breath and saliva is sent to the furnace in the lower cinnabar field, the belly, and refined into vital essence. The ultimate product is seen to be a white vapor, which is personified as the third of the Taoist trinity, the Tao-te Heavenly Worthy.

Next, the vapor of the element earth is brought forth from the spleen and mixed with saliva in the mouth. By breathing inward through the nose and swallowing saliva, the mixture is again sent downward to the furnace and refined into a yellowish vapor, the symbol of primordial spirit. From the yellowish vapor is seen to congeal the Ling-pao Heavenly Worthy, the second of the Taoist trinity. Finally the vapors of the elements wood and fire are joined to form primordial breath. The vapor of wood is drawn forth from the liver, and the breath of fire issues forth from the heart. Both are mixed with saliva and sent downward to be refined in the belly. The product is a greenish-blue vapor, which solidifies into the Primordial Heavenly Worthy. Thus all three principles of life are seen to be made present within the lower cinnabar field. In the final stage of meditation, the Taoist completely stops breathing and sees the three primordial breaths ascend upward to the "central void" which is taken to be a space between the kidneys and the heart, in the Yellow Court of the microcosm. Here, the hierophant, or the "cinnabar pill" of immortality, is formed by joining the Three Principles—primordial breath, original spirit, and vital essence—into one. The Taoist sees himself as standing in the presence of the eternal transcendent Tao as long as the meditation lasts, that is, as long as the breath is held within and contact with the external world is shut off.

It is only after perfecting the meditations of the Yellow Court that the Taoist can effectively control the power of the thunder to cure illness or expel evil. The rituals for curing illness are considered to be under the patronage of the fire master, Wang Tzu-hua, deriving from Mount T'ien-t'ai; the rites of union are thought to be sponsored by the early Han dynasty immortal, Chu Kan, a spirit honored in one of the temples of Hua Shan in west China. The Thunder Magic manuals in Master Chuang's collection are thus subdivided into manuals of curing and manuals of union. The two distinct styles of liturgy, the one oriented to meditation and the other meant for exorcisms, are each assigned a patron spirit and a ritual tradition. Both styles of Thunder Magic are transmitted by the Heavenly Master at Lung-hu Shan and were brought back by Lin Ju-mei to Hsinchu City, Taiwan, in 1888.[20] The teachings of Master Chuang concerning both styles will be set forth in the following pages.

3. MEDITATIONS FOR GAINING CONTROL OVER THUNDER. The very first step in the process of learning Thunder Magic, once the meditations of the *Yellow Court Canon* have been perfected, is the ancient method called yüeh-chien or "monthly position".[21] The method is mentioned in the *Chen-kao* by T'ao Hung-ching, thus showing that it was used at Mao Shan as early as the fifth century without any direct connection with Thunder Magic.[22] The Sung dynasty work, *Tao-fa Hui-yüan*, in chapter 77 shows it to be an essential part of the Thunder rubric.[23] Its adoption into the Ch'ing-wei sect and the fire-master sect of Wang Tzu-hua, therefore, shows the influence of Mao Shan on the two orders.

1. *Finding the gate of Life*

In order to understand the method one must first recall the Battle Chart of the Eight Trigrams, described in figure 2 above. In the battle chart, the gate of hell or the trigram ken is called "Gate of Life." The reason for the two names, opposed in meaning, can be seen in the figure 20. In the ordinary eight trigrams of King Wen—that is, the trigrams arranged in the order of change in the posterior heavens, or the order of the lo-shu—the trigram ken is found in the northeast position. Ken is thought to be the most vulnerable position for attack, that is, the direction from which the powers of evil will attack the body and make it sick. This is because the yin lines, the weak broken

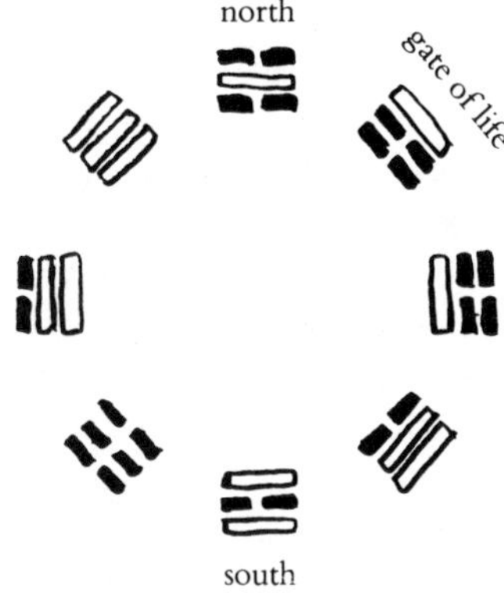

Figure 20. The eight trigrams of King Wen; the Lo-shu.

lines, are inside while the strong yang line is on the outside of the circle. If an army attacks the defender at the position ken, it is an easy matter to overcome the first strong yang line of defense, and pass through the two weak yin lines. No general would attack at the ch'ien position nor at the k'un position. The ch'ien line is invulnerable since it is three solid yang lines, while the k'un line is too obvious a place. Since it is composed of six weak broken lines, the defending general is likely to hide an army in ambush at the k'un position and defeat any attacking forces.

The position ken, however, seems strong but is in fact weak. For this reason the direction of the northeast is called the "gate of hell" or the "demon's entrance" in classical orthodox Taoist terms. A whole ritual of purification, the chin-t'an[24] liturgy, was invented to "close the devil's gate." Only after the Taoist master has sealed off the northeast position can classical liturgy be performed in the village temple. The rite of closing the "gate of hell" is therefore considered essential in the steps toward renewing the cosmos or curing sickness. Furthermore, the Ken position is considered to be the direction through which the vital essences of life flow away. Within the microcosm of the body, it is the gate through which seminal essence, primordial breath, and spirit escape, leading man inevitably from life to death. The Taoist by his meditations of inner alchemy seeks to seal off the gate of escape and keep life breaths, spirit, and vital essence within the microcosm. Thus ken is seen to be truly the "gate of life," the gate through which life can flow away or be preserved. It is very important to be able to locate the gate of life and guard it with great care.

Chapter 4 above, in which the Six Chia spirits were brought under the Taoist's control, made special use of the gate of life. Each of the rituals in which one of the terrifying Chia spirits was enfeoffed under the Taoist's control took place at the gate of life. The position from which the evil spirits were subordinated and controlled, and the subsequent position from which they were summoned to attack, was the trigram ken in the Battle Chart of the Eight Trigrams. The Taoist who uses Thunder Magic to counteract the black magic of the Tao of the Left must therefore always be aware of the location of the gate of life. (Even relationships in the Chinese society may be seen in light of the gate of life concept. As the attacking general does not attack in the weakest position, neither does one speak against a fellow man in his weakest point. Rather, one seeks to strengthen a potential weakness.)

The secret taught by Thunder Magic, borrowed from the ancient system of prognostication called yüeh-chien, is that the gate of life, or the position ken in the trigrams, changes. It is different for every month of the lunar calendar, as well as for the day and the hour. Without knowing its location, the proper performance of exorcism, blessing, or even meditation is impossible. The gate of life is at the precise position pointed to by the handle of the Pole Star constellation, Ursa Major.[25] The system is illustrated in figure 21.

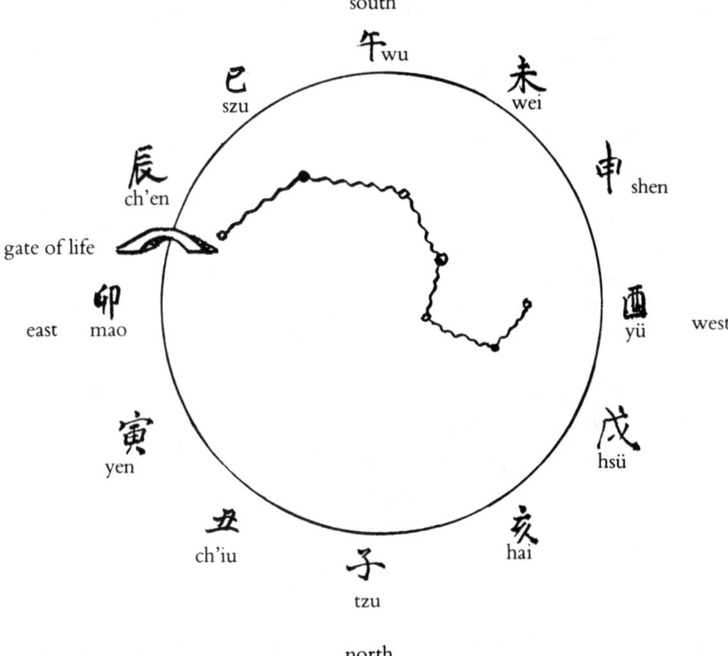

Figure 21. The gate of life is located in the direction that the handle of the Pole Star constellation, Ursa Major, is pointing.

The thunder must be summoned from the direction in which the Pole Star is pointing, in order to counteract the evil power of the Six Chia spirits or whatever other black magic is being used against the client of the Taoist master. Further, the gate of life indicates the directions from which prayer is to be initiated and the place through which the soul of a deceased person is to escape from the underworld. In the esoteric sense, it can be interpreted to be the gate of eternal life. The yüeh chien method is therefore important both in performing burial ritual and in choosing the direction from which thunder is to be summoned. The Taoist master teaches a poem or conundrum to the novice to instill the method for finding the gate of life:

In the shen, tzu, and ch'en months
When the horse points to yen
The spirit passes through mao
The three noxious breaths are at szu, wu, and wei.

In the yen, wu, and hsü months
When the horse dwells in shen
The spirit passes through yu.
The three evil breaths are at hai, tzu, and ch'iu.

In the szu, yu, and ch'iu months
When the horse passes through hai
The spirit escapes through tzu.
The three evil breaths are yen, mao, and ch'en.

In the hai, mao, and wei months,
When the horse is at szu,
The star of escape is at wu.
The three evil spirits are at shen, yu, and hsü.

The tip of the Pole Star handle is called "the horse" in the poem, and is commonly called p'o-chun in esoteric terms. The direction in which p'o-chun points is the gate of life, while the direction the open top of the dipper points is evil. A special chart is also made which shows the position of the p'o-chun star at any given time of the night and day. The novice may thus refer to the chart whenever the sky is cloudy at night or a special meditation is to be performed during the day.

The yüeh-chien method is also used in burying the dead, as mentioned above. On the evening before the interment, in the front room of the household where the coffin is kept in mourning, the Taoist prepares a special mound of rice called a ts'ao-jen, or "grass-man." A rattan mat is laid on the ground and a bushel of pure white rice is poured on top of it. The rice is shaped to resemble a man or a woman; and eyes made of stones, ears made of pomelo leaves, and so forth, are inserted into it. Around the effigy, in a circle, are laid a series of small lamps, one series for each of the eight directions, that is, the eight trigrams. Each line in the trigram is represented by a lamp. Thus the trigram ch'ien in the northwest, composed of three straight lines, receives three lamps. The trigram k'un in the southwest, composed of six broken lines, receives six lamps. The ritual area resembles the illustration in figure 22.[26]

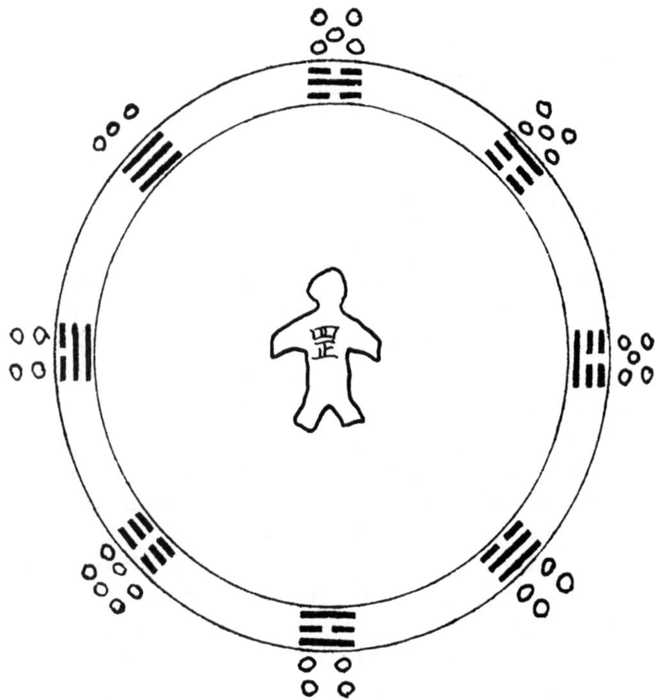

Figure 22. The ts'ao-jen and the eight trigrams represented in lamps.

The Taoist performing the rite holds a paper lantern attached to a willow branch, which represents the soul of the deceased. He dances around outside the circle twelve times, and jumps into the interior of the mandala of lamps as he passes the gate of life. He then dances around the interior of the circle twelve times, and jumps out again through the gate indicated by the Pole Star p'o-chun. Finally, he steps into the interior of the circle, and draws a secret fu talisman with the willow branch, scattering the rice in the five directions. The secret talisman is in fact the character kang 罡, the esoteric name for the p'o-chun tail of the pole star. The soul is thereby released and escapes outwards through the gate of life into the realm of the immortals in heaven.

The yüeh-chien must further be used to determine the direction that the master must face during thunder meditations when practising ritual alchemy in the privacy of his own house. Thus the month, day, and hour in which a given meditation is performed is determined by the position of the Pole Star. The power of thunder is summoned forth from the organ within the Taoist's body which corresponds to the direction in which the p'o-chun points. Thus by referring to figure 18, the direction of the thunder and the corresponding organ in the body from which it is summoned can be determined. As noted above, during the special meditation performed on the occasion of the first thunderstorm after Chinese New Year, the thunder is stored in the gall bladder, which acts as the center for most brief rites invoking Thunder Magic.[27]

Once the power over the thunder has been obtained, the Taoist must begin to practice the use of the rubrics until he has perfected the method before attempting to use it in the public forum. Thus the thunder method makes use of mudra, mantric seed word, and circulation of breath in a meditation performed by the Taoist master in the privacy of his own quarters, in preparation for the ritual use of the Thunder Magic in cures and exorcistic battles. The manual containing the rubrics for the Thunder Magic meditations is called *Shih Chuan Ch'ing-wei Ch'i Chüeh* (*The Master's Transmission of the Ch'ing-wei* [sect] *Breath secrets*).[28]

2. *Summoning the Thunder Breath.*

In the first step, preparation for drawing a talisman, one must learn to summon forth the tsu-ch'i, the ancestral (thunder) breath from the center of the microcosm. The center is to be conceived as a void between the kidneys and the stomach in the lower regions of the body; that is to say, the secret court in which the ancestral breath dwells is the Yellow Court of the center. If one does not use the ancestral breath in writing a talisman, the charm will have no effect; that is, it will not be filled with spirit (ling).

Form the left hand into the sword mudra (bend the little finger and the ring finger down so that they touch the palm of the hand. The thumb is then put under the two bent fingers so that the tips of the ring and little fingers press against the nail of the thumb. The index and middle fingers are extended straight upward.) When formed, the master uses the left hand in the sword mudra form to hold the paper on which he will draw the talisman. In his right hand he takes the brush, but does not at first write with it. Instead, he envisions the talismanic word, seeing exactly how it will be written on the blank piece of paper, balancing it by size, position and so forth. He pronounces the mantric seed word, hsü, meanwhile seeing a gold-colored ray of light diffuse over the surface of the paper. He then breathes in the golden vapor-like light, until it reaches the very gates of the Yellow Court in the center. Next, he imagines a second talismanic character on the surface of the paper and breathes forth the mantric seed word, p'i. He breathes in the vapor of the second character and mixes it with the first on the tip of his tongue, inside the closed mouth. Thereupon he swallows saliva and circulates the mixture of the first and second breath so that it too enters through the paper, its vapor is breathed into the mouth and mixed with the saliva by the tongue, while he mutters the mantric spell: "The Three Houses (Lords) have met!" As the mantra ends, he sees the three vapors now join together into a small bluish-black precious pearl in the center of the Yellow Court. The small round pearl begins to throw off light and gradually heats, becoming a reddish flame. The flame extends upward in a single thread, until it passes through the various organs of the body and ascends into the ni-wan or the ming-t'ang, the royal court of the brain. Then he sees the sun shining immediately above his left eye. The sun is round, with seven rays of light coming from it. Over his left eye he also sees the full moon, with ten rays of light issuing from it. The two spheres then join into a single while circle just inside the frontal lobe, between the eyebrows. A drop from the white sphere comes down into the mouth as a precious pearl. The Taoist then breathes vapor issuing from the pearl onto the tip of the writing brush and begins to write the talisman. The talisman is begun by drawing a hollow circle, which represents the ultimate transcendent, Wu-chi. Then while saying the magic word, k'a, he puts a dot in the center of the circle and recites the mantric spell:

The One Primordial Breath of the Prior Heavens
By ordered stages rules the myriad spirits!

Then quietly he continues to himself:

Red is so red that it seems like blood
White is so white that it looks like snow
The Path is such a path that it leads to the central void!
The dust of the world is heavy, a heavy ton of lead!

Continuing to write the talisman, he draws a second circle with a dot in the center, representing the t'ai-chi, the immanent transcendent, and from the dot in the center of the circle he sees issuing the power of the thunder. This completes the first step.

Next the Taoist employs the thunder breath, or the kang breath secret, to complete the talisman. He begins to meditate upon the power of the thunder, recalling that it must be drawn from that direction in which the kang star (p'o-chun) is pointing. Unless the direction is properly ascertained, the following rubrics may not be performed.

The Taoist closes his eyes and envisions a red star as large as a bowl of rice, above his left eye. He sees the star as a bright sun, diffusing its rays about his body. Then he sees the seven stars of Ursa Major imprinted in his own body. The four stars of the bowl are imbedded in the toes of his left and right foot and the knees of his left and right leg. The three stars of the handle are in the belly, the heart, and the tip of the tongue. The kang star, the star that points at the gate of life, is thus envisioned as embedded in the tongue of the Taoist. Alive with the shining rays of the Pole Star constellation the Taoist then uses the tip of his tongue as a brush and, on a yang day (an odd-numbered day), draws the character for yang on the hard palate, the roof of his mouth. With the character for yang completed, he breathes out through the mouth so that the breath or vapor of yang, mixed with the light of the Pole Star, shoots out and penetrates the red sun shining above his left eye. On a yin day (an even-numbered day) he draws the character yin on the hard palate and spits out the rays of yin into the red sun above his forehead. As soon as the rays from his mouth penetrate the red sun, the whole image dissolves and immediately there appears a terrifying spirit with three heads and six arms. The two center arms and the two right arms each hold a sword. The spirit is so high that it stretches upward into the sky. The spirit bends down and puts the Taoist on its shoulders, standing up so that the Taoist now is in the heavens.

Next, the Taoist draws the magic word, hung, on the hard palate and breaths out into the spirit, which he now addresses as the kang spirit, the spirit of the star that points to the gate of life. As soon as the vapor from the Taoist's mouth has touched the spirit, the following mantric spell is recited:

The Heavenly Emperor has dispatched a command!
Given to the t'ien-kang spirit to carry.
How dare the evil spirits of the five directions
Not wither away and utterly die?
One breath of the immortal flying spirit,
The myriad demons are killed in their lairs!

The Taoist then presses the hsü, yu, wei, tzu, center (yü), wu and ch'en joints on his left hand and recites:

O Red Sun spirit, the Three-Five (liaison spirits)
Come to thy aid!

The three-five liaison spirits are seen to come as supporting troops for the t'ien-kang general's victory. The Taoist again forms a magic character on the hard palate, using the tongue as a brush: the character for fire and tou (bushel) are drawn side by side and then spit out as a vapor which covers the assembling spirits. Meanwhile the Sanskrit mantra is recited three times: "Om gu gum ta li p'o k'a!" The kang spirit is seen suddenly to turn his body and, with angry eyes opened wide, bend the tip of the Taoist's ritual sword. The Taoist chants:

Oh ye (evil spirits) who seek to slay me!
Now you must flee my magic powers! (Hua-kai, that is, the keng position, north)

As soon as the recitation is finished, the Taoist breathes in through his nose the firey vapor, which is still balanced on the end of the sword. The magical breath with its power of thundering fire is drawn down into the Yellow Court in the center of the microcosm and mixed with the vapors of the Taoist's body. The breath is then exhaled, while the Taoist draws the kang talisman on the piece of paper on the table before him.

The kang talisman is a basic design used by Taoists of all orthodox traditions to sign documents or to finish off the writing of a talisman with a flourish. There are other meditative methods of writing the talisman, but the above is standard for the Taoists using the thunder rubric derived from the Ch'ing-wei tradition of Hua Shan.

3. *Using the thunder breath to cure a cold and perform exorcisms.*

The power of thunder, once infused into the body, can be used to bless a child that has a simple cold. The Taoist presses the mao position with the thumb of the left hand and sees a reddish-purple light coming from the east. He breathes the reddish-purple vapor in through both nostrils and circulates it through the body, finally gathering it into the Yellow Court in the center of the microcosm. He swallows saliva and mixes the breath with the breath of his own body. Then while uttering the word, hsü, he breathes forth the vapor and draws the kang on the palm of his left hand with the index and middle finger of his right hand. Finally he presses both hands on the head of the child, in the manner of blessing an infant or patting a child of whom one is fond. The child should quickly recover.

The thunder breath from the seven Pole Stars can be used to exorcise a demon causing a sudden disturbance or a nighttime fright in a younger member of the family. The Taoist chants the mantric words in the left column while pressing the joints on the left hand indicated in the right column:

MANTRA	MUDRA
k'uei	yen
shao	mao
ch'uan	ch'en
hang	szu
pi	face of the index finger
fu	central joint (yü), middle finger
p'iao	above the central joint

When the mantra is recited and the mudras formed, the Taoist then envisions himself as standing with the mountain of the east, T'ai-shan, directly behind his left elbow. On the mountain there is a cave. From the inner recesses of the cave a black vapor is issuing forth. The vapor is baleful, extraordinarily cold, causing the teeth to chatter when breathed in. In the following spell, sha means baleful, demonic influence. The Taoist recites the spell three times:

Heaven sha, earth sha, year sha,
Month sha, day sha, hour sha,
All you evil demonic sha vapors
Do not enter (the child's) belly!
Pains in the belly will make (him or her) die!

He then draws the kang talisman on his hard palate with the tongue and presses the mudra for overcoming the noxious black vapor; that is, he presses the lower central joint on the left side of the middle finger. The directions for performing this cure are to be passed on by oral tradition; the master does not usually transmit the directions in written form. There are in all seventy-two noxious breaths, computed according to the almanac, the birthdate of the possessed child, or the baleful directions of the yüeh-chien method explained in figure 22 above.

The Taoist can use Thunder Magic to control the rays of the sun in order to effect a cure or exorcise an evil spirit. In this method, the Taoist first presses the mao position on the left hand and meditates, seeing just above the corner of the left eye a round, red sun with seven rays of light emanating from the center. He then recites the following mantra: "Om kuo gi lai/kun t'a li p'o k'a!" The mantra must be recited continuously seven times without taking a breath. He then breathes in the seven rays of vaporous light, circulating them through the body until they reach the Yellow Court and are drawn within. In the Yellow Court they are mixed with the Taoist's vital breath and the stored breath of the thunder; finally they are breathed forth while exhaling through pursed lips, so as to form the mantric word, hsü. As the breath is slowly exhaled, he draws the kang talisman on the roof of his mouth and directs the vapor to the body of the possessed person.

On a day which falls under the influence of yin, the Taoist changes the rubrics in the following manner. He presses the yu joint on the left hand and sees just above the corner of the right eye a full, bright moon. From the moon issues ten rays of light. He then recites the following mantric spell ten consecutive times without taking a breath: "Om kuo ke lai ha/lai p'o li p'o k'a!" When finished reciting the mantra, he breathes in the ten rays of vaporous light and circulates them through the body until they enter the Yellow Court. Finally he breathes forth the vapor in the direction of the person to be exorcised while pronouncing the mantric word, hsi; then he draws the talismanic charm of the Kang spirit.

It can readily be seen that Thunder Magic is quite different from the orthodox mandala building ritual described in chapter 5. It is also quite distinct from the popular Shen-hsiao or Redhead form of thunder ritual which is described in *Kao-shang Shen-hsiao Yü-ch'ing Chen Wang Tz'u-shu Ta-fa* (*Shen-hsiao Ta-fa*) recorded in volumes 881 to 883 of the Taoist Canon. The difference between the two styles is in the meditative use of the *Yellow Court Canon* in the Ch'ing-wei Thunder Magic sect, versus the popular spirit summoning, curing, and blessing oriented rituals of the Shen-hsiao Redhead orders. The Five Thunder Magic of Master Chuang derives from the former source, and the rituals of the Redheads of Hsinchu City, as seen in the teachings of the Chang and Ch'ien clans, from the latter work.[29] It is important to note that externally the rituals appear to be almost identical. The Redhead Taoists also make use of the datewood thunder block, the talismans and mudras, and the mantric seed words. The distinction is to be found, first, in the quality of the interior meditation and, second, in the spirits summoned to Redhead ritual. In the case of the Redhead Taoists, the spirits and immortals of the popular religion and local beliefs play a central role. The devout laymen who attend the services can identify the spirits summoned by the Redheads and offer private worship, often in their own homes to the pantheon of the Shen-hsiao gods. The spirits that the Ch'ing wei Taoists summon, on the other hand, are totally esoteric and their appearance, apparel, and summons are hidden from all but the Taoist master's sons and closest disciples.

4. THE PRACTICE OF THUNDER MAGIC.

Perhaps the most perplexing enigma in the study of Taoist sects and ritual practices is the professional rivalry between the orthodox sects of antiquity and the more recent orders which originated during and after the Sung period. The rivalry is not only in the external forum where Taoists compete for the patronage of the pious faithful; it is in internal forum as well, where great magical battles are fought between competing Taoist masters. The very meditations of the various sects are subjected to the scrutiny of the opposing orders and declared to be cheng, orthodox, or hsieh, heterodox, according to the conformity of the color of the vapors to the classical texts of antiquity. Thus the late Sung Taoist, Chin Yün-chung, accuses the popular Shen-hsiao order of being wu-fa, or without real magical powers, because the color red is substituted for the vapor dark-blue used when summoning the Primordial Heavenly Worthy. Professor Noritada Kubo describes the Ch'üan-chen sect as revolutionary in his *Chūgoku no Shūkyō Kakumei* because the religious discipline and rule, as well as the vapors of internal meditation, differed somewhat from the classical orthodox style.

It is therefore most interesting to read in the texts of the Heavenly Masters from Lung-hu Shan in Kiangsi province that the Ch'ing-wei style of Thunder Magic is used to oppose the magic of various heterodox styles of ritual. The Five Thunder rubrics of the Redhead Shen-hsiao orders are diametrically opposed to the Thunder Magic of the orthodox Cheng-i sects; that is, the Ching-wei Thunder Magic in the *Tao-fa Hui-yüan* is used to oppose the Thunder Magic of Lin Ling-su and the local Shen-hsiao orders. The spells found in the esoteric texts of the Heavenly Masters say specifically: "Bind the heterodox spirits and send them back to Lu Shan and Mao Shan!"[30]

The biography of Lin Ling-su indicates, as mentioned above, that Lin Ling-su and his brand of Shen-hsiao rubrics were introduced to the court of Hui-tsung by the twenty-fifth master of Mao Shan, Liu Hun-k'ang. It seems reasonable to surmise that Mao Shan had adapted the new forms of ritual introduced by Lin Ling-su. But the opposition of the Heavenly Master sect to Mao Shan seems to have derived from another heterodox source as well. The Tao of the Left was attributed, at least from the early Ming period, to Mao Shan popular Taoists. In the nineteenth and early twentieth centuries the popular local Taoists operating in Chekiang, Kiangsu, and Fukien provinces were very often called simply "Mao Shan Taoist Masters," a term used in some parts of modern Taiwan as well. The rites of tun-chia black magic, as well as Redhead styles of popular sword-ladder climbing, trumpet-blowing exorcisms, and other such dramatic exhibitionism, became popular throughout southeast China. The Heavenly Master not only opposed these vulgar forms of popular liturgy by invoking the curses of Thunder Magic, but invented grades of ordination and Taoist perfection for the Shen-hsiao orders which led them upward into the ranks of orthodoxy. Thus, the higher stages of Shen-hsiao ordination, as administered by the Heavenly Master at Lung-hu Shan, included the titles and the registers of orthodoxy. There was no grade one Shen-hsiao ordination. Grades two and three already introduced the Redhead Taoist to monastic meditation. Instead of grade one, the aspiring master was elevated out of the ranks of heterodoxy into the more profoundly meditative orders of antiquity.[31]

The opposition between the classical sects and the modern regional orders is well illustrated by the magical battles and jousts which take place between the masters of Taiwan, using a kind of black magic known as Mao Shan snake magic. It is of course far removed from the classical Shang-ch'ing sect and the *Yellow Court Canon*. The term "Mao Shan Taoist" refers to a form of local Taoist black magic found in the southeastern provinces of China and the countryside of Taiwan. The magic employs the Six Chia spirits to attack an opposing Taoist or to cause sickness or even death to an opponent. In order to understand the principle on which the snake magic works, it is necessary to recall the Battle Chart of the Eight Trigrams, as seen in figure 20.

In the explanation of the eight trigrams of change given at the beginning of chapter 6, the trigram ken was shown to be the position of greatest weakness, while the trigram ch'ien was the source of the greatest strength. An army is invincible, and the magic of a Taoist master all powerful, which begins from the northwest position, that is, the trigram ch'ien. The peculiar rubric of Mao Shan black magic is that the circle of the eight trigrams is opened up into the form of a snake. Starting from the trigram ch'ien in the northwest position, the eight trigrams are unwound to resemble a writhing serpent. The effectiveness of the serpentine figure is seen in the mobility of the trigram ch'ien which becomes an invincible army of spirits in the hands of the Mao Shan master. The head of the attacking snake is seen to be the trigram ch'ien, which can be moved hither and thither to find the vulnerable spot in an opponent's circle of magic. The snake chart resembles the diagram in figure 23.[32]

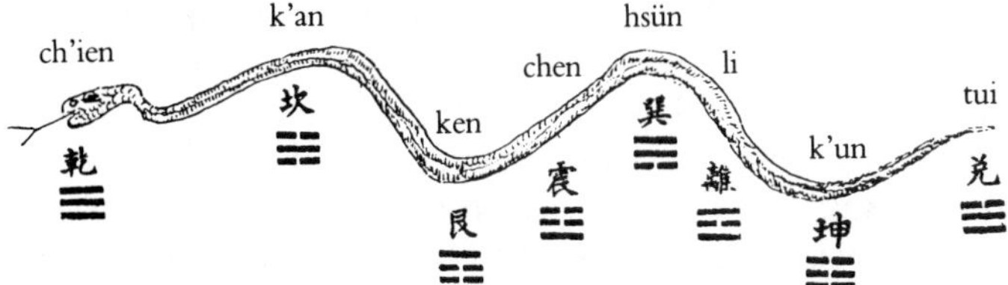

Figure 23. The Battle Chart of the Eight Trigrams unwound into the form of a serpent. The diagram also represents hills in which defending armies are hidden in ambush.

In applying the magic of the Mao Shan snake chart, the Chia spirit proper to the day, with its army of spirit soldiers, is put at the trigram ch'ien and used to attack an enemy Taoist master. It can also be used to defend the master, in which case the chart is seen as a series of rising mountains in which armies have been hidden in ambush. The k'ou-chüeh oral secrets explaining the method are as follows:

Ch'ien:	Experienced battle-trained soldiers. Attack!	(Wood conquers).
K'an:	Hidden soldiers. Ambush.	(Water conquers).
Chen:	Reserve army.	(Fire and earth conquer).
Hsün:	Reinforcements.	(Wood conquers).
Li:	Thunder brigade. Penetrate deeply.	(Metal conquers).
K'un:	Defensive army. Protect and defend.	(Water and earth conquer).
Tui:	An army of heroes. Protect and defend.	(Water and earth conquer).

The Taoist who uses either the Mao Shan method of black magic to harm a person, or a combination of the Mao Shan method with the Six Chia spirits of chapter 4, is impregnable to the defensive tactics of the orthodox Tao of the Right of chapter 5. That is, the meditative ritual of orthodox Cheng-i Taoism must cast out all impure spirits before the meditations of internal alchemy are effective. By placing one of the terrifying Six Chia spirits in the center of a sacred area where an orthodox ritual is taking place, the power of the orthodox magic is effectively destroyed. Thus the conflict between the orthodox orders and the popular local sects is a spiritual antagonism of a very basic nature. The evil spirits are indeed hsieh, in that their very presence renders orthodox magic ineffective. The master must expel all but the highest spirits of the ultimate heavens from the sacred area and from the microcosm of his own body in order to perform orthodox ritual. The fa-lu meditation is not only a pious initiation of orthodox ritual, it an absolute essential if one is to attain the ends intended by alchemical meditation. It is obvious that orthodoxy needed some sort of ritual to counteract the Tao of the Left, as well as to have a defense against all sorts of impure spirits encountered at the provincial and local levels of Chinese religious practice.

The Five Thunder Method can, therefore, be better understood in the role assigned to it by the Heavenly Masters of Lung-hu Shan. "Bind the evil spirits and send them back to Mao Shan and Lu Shan" is one of the most important adaptations of Thunder Magic to the needs of the older classical orders. That is, the rubrics of the Five Thunder Method were invoked to protect the orthodox master against the powers of magic that the classical tradition could not handle. Thunder Magic is a necessary ingredient in the fa-piao rites of announcing and the ch'ing-shen rites of invitation. The spirits of the highest pure heavens could be invited safely to the local temple only because Thunder Magic was invoked to expel and keep out the spirits of heterodoxy. Thunder Magic is used to oppose Mao Shan black magic and the tun-chia Tao of the Left in an ingenious rite of defensive purification.

5. THE DANCE OF THE HO-T'U.[33]

At the end of a chiao festival of temple renewal as described in the previous chapter, the Taoist master performs the ritual called cheng-chiao (orthodox sacrifice) or tao-ch'ang, the rite of longevous union with the eternal Tao. The rite is the culmination of the three- or five-day chiao festival and, by attending or simply watching the performance, the bystanders are granted immortality. At the very end of the rite, the Taoist master receives back from the heavenly emperors a shu-wen or imperial rescript in which the prayers of the whole community are granted, the souls released from hell in a general amnesty, and hsien-hood or immortality awarded to the village members who supported the chiao and whose names appear on the rescript. But the gift of immortality and blessing once awarded can again be lost. The powers of darkness and evil, the very serpent that is the symbol of yin, can act to destroy the blessing and pull the members of the once-renewed community back into the cycle of change. Yang can be worn away by the powers of yin, and death must inevitably conquer. The spirits that have been expelled can come back and cause ill fortune in the newly renewed cosmos.

As Hsü Hsun once killed the serpent during the third-century Chin period, so the Taoist master of the present attempts to slay the evil Mao Shan snake demon. The shu-wen memorial is carried into the sacred area by the chief cantor, who dances into the center of the temple using the lo-shu, that is, the eight trigrams arranged as the principle of change—the pattern from life to death—as he approaches the Taoist master. The chief cantor represents the power of yin, which works inexorably to drain away yang and cause cyclic change in the world of nature. The high priest, or Master of Exalted Merit, receives the rescript in an attitude of profound reverence. He then kneels and summons forth the power of the thunder, as described above. Thereupon he stands, and begins to dance the steps of the ho-t'u, the eight trigrams arranged in the pattern of permanence and immortality.

In order to understand the significance of the eight trigrams arranged in the order of the ho-t'u, compare figure 24 with figure 20.[34] In the ho-t'u arrangement of the trigrams, the trigram ch'ien appears in the south, and the trigram k'un in the north.

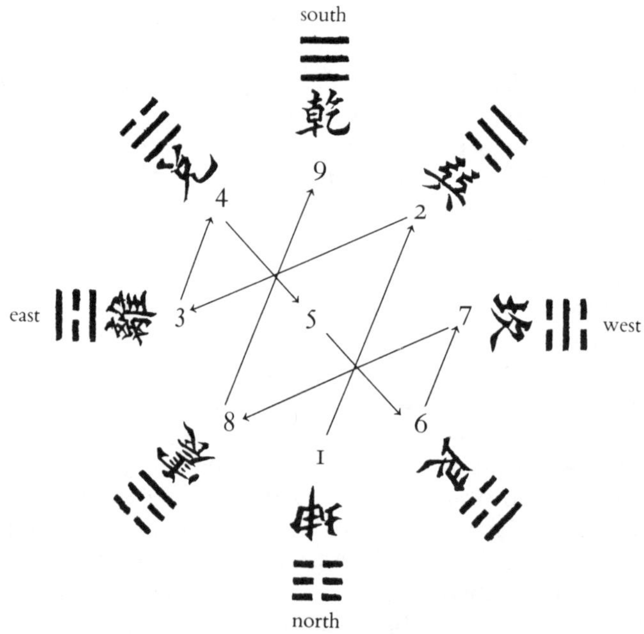

Figure 24. The arrangement of the eight trigrams in the order of the ho-t'u. In this arrangement the trigram ch'ien, or the position of greatest strength, is in the south, the ninth and last position of the sacred dance of Yü.

The Taoist master receives the shu-wen heavenly rescript and begins to dance the ho-t'u, or the magical steps of Yü the Great that the ancient ruler originally used, according to legend, to stop the floods. The sacred steps begin at the trigram k'un, marked 1 in the diagram, and continue through to the trigram ch'ien, marked 9. The master must dance the steps of Yü twelve times, one for each month in the year, and one for each of the earthly stems. As he finishes each series, he moves over thirty degrees in the circle so that all twelve directions of the cosmos are effectively sealed off with the trigram ch'ien; the ninth step of the sacred dance seals off each of the twelve directions from the attack of the serpent yin. As he seals off each direction, the Taoist master through the power of the thunder rubric assigns a spirit to guard the entrance. Thus the Mao Shan Taoist's black magic and the heterodox spirits of the provincial orders find the sacred area effectively sealed to entry. The Mao Shan serpent's magic is negated by the opposing power of the trigram ch'ien.

To insure the further safety of the shu-wen rescript and the preservation of the blessings it promises, the Taoist master, in the most esoteric of mudras and mantras at his command, appoints the six chia and the six ting spirits (chapter 4) to guard the twelve entrances of the sacred area. Thus the very spirits commanded by the power of the Mao Shan Tao of the Left are now turned around and put to work for the Tao of the Right by the power of Thunder Magic. The Taoist invokes the mighty spirit of the Pole Star handle, the kang-shen, to subdue and command the terrifying chia spirits. As he dances around the positions in the ho-t'u, he encounters the chia spirits one by one. In front of the violent and untrustworthy chia-wu spirit he falls back to the ground, visibly moved by her beauty. In front of the chi-sha general, Chia-yen, he stares in a haughty and forceful manner. By the end of the graceful dance steps the six chia spirits are subdued and obedient to the Taoist's commands. Such is the power of the Thunder rubric that the evil spirits invoked by the Mao Shan Tao of the Left now turn and attack it instead. The function of Thunder Magic as a basic tool in the rites of exorcism can thus be seen in the classical chiao rites of cosmic renewal. It has become a tool in the hands of the orthodox masters to subdue the spirits of the heterodox gods of popular Taoism.

The cycle of ritual has now turned a full revolution. From the violent chia spirits used in the Tao of the Left, Master Chuang has first turned to the classical and stately Tao of the Right, and then back again to the rites of purificatory exorcism to subdue and convert the terrifying demonic forces of heterodoxy. The spirits are indeed only projections of the master's own meditations of inner alchemy. His power over the personified forces of nature is seen to derive from a meditation in which the master has stood before the Tao of transcendence and been united, even if for a very brief moment, with the inexpressible Tao of Lao-tzu's *Tao-te Ching*. Like a Boddhisattva, the Taoist must use his power to save his fellow man from the distresses of everyday life. In so doing, the ultimate goal of his ritual is immortality for all who seek his help.

Abbreviations

CK	*Chen Kao*
CMTC	*Ch'i-men Tun-chia*
CTW	*Ch'üan T'ang Wen*
HHS	*Hou Han Shu*
HS	*Han Shu*
JAOS	*Journal of the American Oriental Society*
MHCH	*Muo-hai Chin-hu*
T	Taisho Tripitaku (*Taishō Shinshū Daizōkyō*)
TFHY	*Tao-fa Hui-yüan*
TT	Taoist Canon
WSPY	*Wu-shang Pi-yao*
YCCC	*Yun-chi Ch'i-ch'ien*

Notes

INTRODUCTION

1. See chapter 5, pt. 4, for the rules of a Taoist novice.
2. Chapter 1, note 110.
3. Though I use the term "Taoist Canon" here and in chapter 1, pt. 3, it must be noted that the Chinese term *Tao-tsang* was used to identify the lists of canonical books composed by Lu Hsiu-ching and others in the Fifth and Sixth centuries, and did not refer to an actual printed canon until the reign of the emperor T'ai-tsung (A.D. 976–997), in the Sung dynasty. The first printed Buddhist Canon was also published during emperor T'ai-tsung's reign. The extant version of the Taoist Canon was printed during the following Ming dynasty, as explained in the text. Before the Sung and the Ming dynasties, then, the Taoist Canon was a list of books considered to be canonical, rather than a printed collection which could be purchased, as today. Until the present century, the canonical books had to be laboriously copied out by hand, as transmitted from master to disciple.
4. Taoist Canon (TT), vols. 877, 878.
5. Chapter 1, notes 176–179; chapter 5, notes 20–21.

CHAPTER ONE

1. Pp. 1–3 represent the opinions of Master Chuang on the history of religious Taoism. The remainder of chapter 1 will attempt to show the historical foundations for Chuang's thinking, and to distinguish historical fact from legend.
2. The twenty-four registers or lu that distinguish the orthodox Meng-wei or the Cheng-i Heavenly Master sect, of which Master Chuang is a member, are found in the Taoist Canon (abbreviated TT), vol. 877, *Tai-shang San-wu Cheng-i Meng-wei Lu*. See chapter 5 for a full discussion.
3. The *Yellow Court Canon* (*Huang-t'ing Ching*) is one of the basic texts of the Shang-ch'ing Mao Shan sect, treated in chapter 1, notes 92–112. The text is found in TT, vols. 130–131, 189–190, and 679, chapters 11–12.
4. The Ch'ing-wei sect is treated in chapter 1, notes 135–139, and chapter 6, notes 12–13. The meditative and magic practises of Ch'ing-wei magic as taught by Master Chuang are the subject of chapter 6, pts. 2 and 3.
5. The Pei-chi or Pole Star sect has not been studied by western historians. Its lu, or registers, are found in TT, vol. 879. The legendary founder of the order is Chu-ko Liang, though the mountain and its military form of magic are not mentioned until the sixth century compilation *Chen-kao* (TT, vols. 637–640), chapter 14. The Six Chia magic attributed to the order is the subject

of chapter 4 below. Since the style of magic that uses the Six Chia spirits became popular at Mao Shan in the late Sung and early Ming dynasties, present-day Taoists who practice the more violent forms of military black magic are often called Mao Shan Taoists. Taoist forms of kung-fu and T'ai-chi ch'üan physical fitness exercises are said to derive from Wu-tang Shan.

6. The Shen-hsiao order is discussed at the end of this chapter; see notes 155–164 below. The opinions of Master Chuang concerning the order are stated there, and in note 7.

7. The registers, or lu, of some Shen-hsiao orders contain harmful talismans and forms of black magic meant to cause illness or even death. On this basis, the order is sometimes classified as heterodox. Examples of the talismans that can be used to cause as well as to cure headaches, arguments, and divorce between husband and wife, are found in the *Chuang-lin Hsü Tao-tsang* (Taipei: Ch'eng-wen Press, 1975), pt. 4, chapter 24, pp. 6931–6959.

8. Local Taoists who came to Lung-hu Shan to purchase a license of ordination from the Heavenly Master were almost always given the registers of the Shen-hsiao order. See John Keupers, "Taoist Exorcism," in *Buddhist and Taoist Studies* (Honolulu: University of Hawaii Press, 1977), chapter 5. The great Sung dynasty Taoist Pai Yü-ch'an devoted much of his life to rectifying the heterodox practices of the Shen-hsiao Taoists. See notes 161–173 below.

9. See chapter 2 below, notes 10 and 20.

10. The teachings of Master Chuang are divided into three genre, or styles, of liturgy—the military Tao of the Left treated in chapter 4, the literary Tao of the Right discussed in chapter 5, and Five Thunder Magic, which is treated in chapter 6. This later form of Sung neo-orthodoxy is the orthodox Taoists' response to the sectarianism of the Sung dynasty's popular Taoists. By learning the orthodox version of thunder magic, the popular Taoists were led upward into the ranks of orthodoxy. See chapter 5, notes 19–22.

11. Fu Ch'in-chia, *Chung-kuo Tao-chiao Shih* (*The History of Taoism in China*) (Taipei, 1966), pp. 48–53; *Dokyo no Jittai* (Anonymous work, Kyoto, 1975), pp. 26–32. In Master Chuang's opinion the historians who consider the possessed mediums or wu (sometimes called shamans) to be predecessors of orthodox Taoism are in error. Medium possession is allowed by the popular or local Shen-hsiao orders and the Lü Shan Redhead Taoists, but not by the classical orders described in the following pages.

12. Szu-ma Ch'ien, *Shih-chi*, Ch'in Shih Huang Pen-chi, 37th year.

13. Szu-ma Ch'ien, *Shih-chi*, Hsiang Yü Pen-chi, tells of Chang Liang's part in the founding of the Han. For canonical biographies, see TT, vols. 141, 558, 992.

14. TT, vol. 142, chapter 18, p. 1a, line 5.

15. Seidel, Anna, *La Divinisation de Lao Tseu dans le Taoisme des Han* (Paris, 1969), pp. 34–50; *Han Shu* (HS), Biography of Han Wu-ti, chapter 6, p. 32a; 103 B.C., 4th–5th month.

16. Master Chuang insists on the primacy of the apocryphal *Ho-t'u* and the *Lo-shu* in the transmission of the secrets of orthodox Taoism. The *Ho-t'u* is symbolic of the chart of the Prior Heavens, the eight trigrams of Fu Hsi, and the Ling-pao Five Talismans described in chapter 5. The *Lo Shu*, the magic square of the Posterior Heavens, or the visible world of change, is symbolic of earth, the eight trigrams of King Wen, and rituals of purification. These two

ancient charts are mentioned but not defined in pre-Han sources. Thus the *Ho-t'u* is mentioned in the *Lun-yü*, chapter 9, and the *Shu-ching*, *Ku-ming* chapter (Legge, vol. 3, p. 12). The *Ho-t'u* and *Lo-shu* are central themes of the *Ku Wei Shu*, the ancient apocryphal texts, which probably date from the mid-Han period. *I-sho Shū-sei*, a critical work on the apocryphal texts by the Japanese scholar Yasui Kozan is now being published, vols. 2, 3, and 5 appearing in Tokyo in 1975. Citations from the *Ku Wei Shu* used in the following pages are taken from the above and from the *Muo-hai Chin-hu* (MHCH), a critical Ch'ing dynasty work on the apocryphal texts. The *Ho-t'u* is an essential part of the orthodox Master's lu, or register, appearing as the tenth in a list of twenty-four registers; see TT, vol. 877, chapter 3, p. 1, and p. 4b, line 6 to p. 7b, line 4. See also notes 123 and 128–130 for T'ang dynasty ritual involving the *Ho-t'u*. The *Ho-t'u* is quite diverse; its various forms will be studied in notes 17–38.

17. *Han Kuan-i*, hsia, p. 1a; *Hou Han Shu* (HHS), vol. 112, shang, p. 2b; HHS, vol. 17, p. 6a.

18. HHS, vol. 112, shang, pp. 11b, 14b; vol. 112, hsia, p. 1b; vol. 60, shang, p. 5b; vol. 109, hsia, p. 4a. Scholars are seen to study the *Ho-t'u* and *Lo-shu*, in HHS, vol. 112, shang, pp. 1a, 1b, 11b, 14b; vol. 112, hsia, p. 1b; vol. 60, shang, p. 5b.

19. The apocryphal texts were condemned during the north-south period by the emperor Wu of Chin, A.D. 267; Hsiao Wu-ti of the Sung in 457; and Hsiao Wen-ti of the northern Wei. The apocrypha were destroyed during the reign of Sui Yang-ti, 604–617. See an earlier work of Yasui Kozan, *I-sho* (Tokyo: Mei-toku Press, 1969), pp. 49–50.

20. MHCH, p. 4238; *Ku Wei Shu*, chapter 13, *Ch'un-ch'iu Ming-li Hsü*, p. 1b, lines 3–7.

21. *Dokyo no Jittai*, p. 25; TT, vol. 575; TT, vol. 770, chapter 25, p. 1a, lines 3–10.

22. The modern Taoist masters do not know of any connection between the ancient apocryphal texts and the rituals of orthodox Taoism. Yasui Kozan, *I-sho* (Tokyo, 1969), pp. 37–50, shows how the apocrypha came to be considered a source of dissent and revolt. One can surmise that the Taoists of the north-south period and the Sui were forced to disassociate such central texts as the *San-huang Wen*, the *Ho-t'u*, and the *Ling-pao Five Talismans* from the condemned apocrypha.

23. *Li-chi*, *Yüeh-ling* chapter; MHCH, pp. 4056–4058; *Huai-nan-tzu*, vol. 3, pp. 5b–6a. The Taoist version of the ritual is the *Su-ch'i*, described in chapter 5 notes 81–87.

24. *Dokyo no Jittai*, p. 26; MHCH, pp. 4056–4058; TT, vol. 183, shang, pp. 15a–b.

25. MHCH, pp. 4599–4604; *Ku Wei Shu*, chapter 32, *Ho-t'u Chiang-hsiang*.

26. *Ku Wei Shu*, *Ho-t'u Chiang-hsiang*, chapter 32, p. 8b, line 11 to p. 9a, line 3. MHCH, p. 4600, line 9 to p. 4601, line 2. The preceding fragment describes the Yellow River as bending in nine places and guided by nine stars. The two descriptions are complementary: the *Ho-t'u* described with five stars is symbolic of the five elements, while the chart with nine stars depicts the eight trigrams plus the role of emperor or ruler in the center, as in MHCH, p. 4286, *Ku Wei Shu*, chapter 15, p. 6b. The fragment describes Fu Hsi carving

the book of changes, based on the eight trigrams, and using the same with the center position to establish the nine provinces. MHCH, p. 4252, *Ku Wei Shu*, chapter 13, p. 8b, lines 2–4, describes the *Ho-t'u* as being a magic chart depicting the rivers, mountains, and provinces of China, for the use of rulers.

27. MHCH, p. 4093; *Ku Wei Shu*, chapter 5, *Chung Hou*, p. 4a, lines 3–5, describes the spirit of the Yellow River. The horselike dragon that carries the *Ho-t'u* out of the river is used as a motif of religious art in the much later Sung period. Sung and Ming dynasty commentaries on the *I-ching* often picture the dragon-horse coming out of the Yellow River with a series of fifty-five spots on its back, and the tortoise coming out of the Lo River with forty-five lines on its carapace. The *Ho-t'u* is taken to be a symbol of the eight trigrams of Fu Hsi and the *Lo Shu* the symbol for the eight trigrams of King Wen. See my *Taoism and the Rite of Cosmic Renewal* (Pullman: Washington State University Press, 1972), chapter 3, which describes the commonly held teachings of the Taiwanese Taoists regarding the *Ho-t'u*. Such systematized treatments of the two charts are also found in the popular t'ung-shu almanacs and the manuals of feng-shui geomancy. The relationship of the *Ho-t'u* to the *Ling-pao Five Talismans* is known only to those few masters acquainted with the Taoist Canon.

28. MHCH, p. 4602, lines 3–4. The gloss for the corrupt apocryphal text interprets Pao Shan to be Mao Shan.

29. *Ling-pao Chen-wen*, see TT, vol. 191, Lu Hsiu-ching, *Ling-pao Chung-chen Wen*, p. 1a, line 10; p. 7a, line 4, *Wu-fang Chen-wen*; TT, vol. 183, *Ling-pao Wu-fu Hsü*, p. 10a, lines 7–8. See also note 36 below.

30. MHCH, p. 4602; *Ku Wei Shu*, chapter 32, *Ho-t'u Chiang-hsiang*, p. 9b, lines 4–5.

31. Ibid., line 5, refers specifically to the ch'ih-niao, the red bird or the phoenix, a symbol of the south, seen on the temple rooftops when a *Ho-t'u* is about to be revealed. Confucius denies any knowledge of the red bird or its significance in line 9 of the apocryphal text, thus pointing out Ho-lü's falsehood. P. 9b, lines 6–8, of *Ho-t'u Chiang-hsiang* contain the poem translated immediately below.

32. The modern versions of the *Yüeh-chüeh Shu* bear only fragmentary evidence of the above poem; the *Szu-pu Ts'ung-k'an*, *Szu-pu Pei-yao*, and *Szu-pu K'an Yao* editions now have only fifteen chapters of an original sixteen. That the poem did once belong to the *Yüeh-chüeh Shu* is seen in the quotation taken from the *Chen Cheng Lun*, note 33 below. The missing *Yüeh-chüeh Shu* text is quoted in the gloss of the MHCH, p. 4603, line 7 to p. 4604, line 6.

33. *Taishō Shinshū Daizōkyō*, (*Taisho*), vol. 52, *Chen Cheng Lun*, p. 2212a–c; TT, vol. 183, shang, p. 9b, line 9 to p. 10a, line 8. *Wu-shang Pi-yao* (WSPY), TT, vol. 777, chapter 83, p. 13b, line 5. In this last text, the chart given to Yü is called the *Ling-pao Five Talismans*.

34. The *Chen Cheng Lun* (*Taisho*, vol. 52, p. 2112) is probably a T'ang dynasty text, attributed to the monk Hsüan Yi. An even earlier version of the *Yüeh-chüeh Shu* apocryphal story is found in the fourth-century *Pao-p'u-tzu* of Ko Hung, *Nei-pien*, chapter 13, p. 56, lines 4–7. Ko Hung states that the *Ling-pao* tradition derives from the magic charts given to Yü, called *Cheng-chi*, *P'ing-heng*, and *Fei-kuei Shou-chih*. The first two terms refer to the Pole Star, while the latter are the "flying horse and turtle books or charts"; see the critical

work of Max Kaltenmark, "Ling-pao; note sur un terme du Taoisme religieux," *Mélange Publies par l'Institut des Hautes Études Chinoise*, 2, 14 (Paris, 1960), pp. 559–588.

35. *Taisho*, vol. 52, #2112, p. 564b–c.

36. *T'ai-shang Ling-pao Wu-fu Hsü*, TT, vol. 183, pp. 6a–11b, line 4. The text is considered by most scholars to be one of the earliest in the Taoist Canon, dating probably from the time of Lu Hsiu-ching, mid-fifth century. A lengthy version of the apocryphal story is given, linking the *Ho-t'u* of Yü the Great with the *Ling-pao Five Talismans*. The words of the text are the basis for the *Su-ch'i* ritual, explained in chapter 5, notes 81–86. For a fuller treatment of the *Ling-pao Wu-fu Hsü*, see the critical treatment of Ch'en Kuo-fu, *Tao-tsang Yüan-liu K'ao* (*A Critical Study of the Origins of the Taoist Canon*) (Peking, 1963), p. 64.

37. TT, vol. 183, shang, p. 11, lines 1–2. The text is similar to the reference found in the *Pao-p'u-tzu*, note 34 above.

38. Ch'en Kuo-fu, pp. 62–66.

39. De Groot, J. J. M., *The Religious System of China* (Leiden, 1910), vol. 6, pp. 1187–1268.

40. Fu Ch'in-chia (Taipei, 1972) suggests in the *Chung-kuo Tao-chiao Shih* (p. 57, line 8) a possible relationship between the Yellow Turbans and the later Redhead Taoists found at the local level throughout China. See note 11 above.

41. The Taoists do not distinguish themselves by the popular Redhead and Blackhead titles, but rather by the official lu or register given to each master at the time of ordination. Thus Redhead can refer to any of a number of popular Taoist sects, including the San-nai Lü Shan sect, the Shen-hsiao sect, the Lord Lao sect, and many others. Taoists who specialize in exorcism cures and do not know the classical registers of antiquity are called Redhead by the people of modern Taiwan. To the Taoists themselves, the two terms Blackhead and Redhead serve to distinguish Taoists who follow the canonical tradition from all others.

42. It is possible to distinguish a definite literary bent in the early Heavenly Master sect in west China, as opposed to the more military Yellow Turbans of east China. Fu Ch'in-chia suggests in his *Chung-kuo Tao-chiao Shih*, p. 57, line 8, that the Redheads of later times are the descendants of the Yellow Turbans of the Han.

43. Another theory holds that the *T'ai-p'ing Ching* was given first to a late first century B.C. fang-shih, Kan Chung-k'o, from the text in chapter 75 of the *Ch'ien Han Shu*, the biography of Li Shun-lieh. The relationship between the earlier Han dynasty book and the later *T'ai-p'ing Canon* of Yü Chi is discussed by scholars.

44. TT, vols. 746–755, the present canonical text, has only 119 chapters. See note 46, below.

45. HHS, chapter 60.

46. Wang P'ing, *T'ai-p'ing Ching Ho Hsiao* (Shanghai, 1960); in this excellent work, the author attempts to restore some of the missing chapters. Ch'en Kuo-fu, pp. 82–83; Fukui, Kojun, *Dokyo no Kisoteki Kenkyu* (Tokyo, 1958), pp. 62–86.

47. See note 113 below; the tenth master of Mao Shan, Wang Yüan-chih, was a practitioner of the *T'ai-p'ing Ching* style of ritual.

48. See note 44 above. Ling-pao Taoism has since the fifth-century collations of Lu Hsiu-ching been considered a part of the orthodox tradition. The *T'ai-p'ing Canon*, though allied with the more popular Redhead styles of Taoist ritual, seems to have had a deep influence on both orthodox and popular Taoist cults.

49. Chang Tao-ling is canonized as a patron saint of all Taoists, whatever the sect or order to which a particular master owes allegiance. He is variously credited with writing the *Ling-pao Five Talismans*, as well as the twenty-four registers of the Cheng-i Meng-wei order.

50. *Wei Shu*, Lieh-chuan, chapter 8; HHS, chapter 105.

51. Ch'en Kuo-fu, pp. 98–100.

52. The literary documents sent off by the masters of the Cheng-i sect, the Ling-pao sect, and the other classical orders seem to have derived from the practices of Chang Tao-ling. For Chinese versions of these documents as used by Master Chuang, see *Chuang-lin Hsü Tao-tsang* (Taipei, 1975), vol. 19.

53. The *Shen-hsien Chuan* of Ko Hung in ten volumes is frequently quoted in encyclopedias such as the *T'ai-p'ing Kuang-chi* and the *T'ai-p'ing Yü-lan*. It is found in the *Han Wei Ts'ung-shu*, ed. by Ch'eng Jung, 1592 (Taipei: Hsin-hsing Press, 1959), vols. 38–39, but is no longer extant in the present Taoist Canon as a single work. The biography presented here is taken from the Ming dynasty *Li-shih Chen-hsien T'i-tao T'ung-chien* (*Mirror of Perfected Immortals*), TT, vols. 139–149. See Ch'en Kuo-fu, vol. 2, p. 233.

54. The term "chi-chiu," libationer of wine, occurs five times in the *Yi-li* as a ceremony and later in Han times at the title of an official, appointed at the village level. The converts of the first Heavenly Master sect were most probably of the village-gentry class, and the terms "chi-chiu," "kung-ts'ao" (liaison official), "tu-chiang" (chief cantor, person in charge of classic texts) were borrowed by the leaders of the sect from the language of provincial officialdom.

55. See *Taisho*, vol. 52, *Kuang-hung Ming-chi*, 2103, *Erh-chiao Lun*, p. 141b, line 12; the Buddhist author attributes the entire Ling-pao Canon to Chang Tao-ling. The passage seems to be in error; rather only the early five talismans deriving from the apocryphal tradition and the yin-yang five element rituals of the *Li-chi* were utilized by the early Heavenly Masters.

56. TT, vol. 563; the *Cheng-i Fa-wen T'ien-shih Chiao Chieh K'o-i*, an early document that can probably be dated to the reign of Ts'ao P'ei, ca. 226 (p. 17a, lines (5–6), summarizes the doctrines of the first Heavenly Masters. The twenty-four chih or episcopal sees, the doctrine of the Three Pure Ones as personifications of the three principles breath, spirit, and vital essence (p. 12a, lines 8–9) and the teachings outlined in the above paragraph are found in the passage.

57. TT, vol. 142, chapter 18, pp. 1–25. See p. 2a, line 1, for the influence of the *Ho-t'u* and *Lo-shu* on Chang Tao-ling.

58. See Ch'en Kuo-fu, p. 233, and note 53 above. For other Taoist biographies, also attributed to Ko Hung, see Max Kaltenmark, *Le Lie-sien tchuan* (Biographies légendaires des immortels taoiste de l'antiquité), (Peking, 1953).

59. *Wei Shu*, chüan 8, biography of Chang Lu.

60. Stein, Rolf, "Remarques sur les movements Taoisme Politico-religieux au IIe Siecle Ap. J.C." (*T'oung-pao* 50, 1963), pp. 1–78.

61. *Wei Shu*, chuan 8; HHS, chapter 101.

62. Levy, Howard, "Yellow Turban Religion and Rebellion at the End of the Han," JAOS, 76, 4 (1956), pp. 214–227.

63. See Stein, note 60 above, for the following distinction. Henri Maspero, *Le Taoisme* (Paris, 1967), pp. 149–169, holds that the two movements were the same.

64. The *T'ai-p'ing* literature influenced the literary as well as the military styles of Taoist ritual. It is used in many of the later Ling-pao rites and deeply influences the tenth master of Mao Shan, Wang Yüan-chih; see notes 113–114 below. Its use by the Yellow Turbans was definitely associated with the military nature of the sect. Later military Taoists did not necessarily use the *T'ai-p'ing* materials in their rituals, but present-day Taoist movements continue to classify themselves as literary or military and divide the sacred T'an area used for Taoist ritual into east or literary and west or military divisions. Similarly, Chuang's elder son A-him is being trained in the military Tao of the Left (chapter 4) and in t'ai-chi, kung-fu, and other methods of physical self-defense. The younger A-ga is being trained in the literary Tao of the Right (chapter 5). The two ministries are kept distinct, the military style being a part of the Pole Star or Wu-tang Shan registers (lu) of transmission, the literary style being a part of the orthodox Cheng-i or Meng-wei registers. One Taoist master can learn both styles, but need not know both for a classical ordination.

65. The three colors hsüan (dark black or purple), yellow, and white are a basic part of the transmission of the Meng-wei registers and meditations. See chapter 5, the fa-lu meditation, notes 104–114. The colors are also used in the meditations of the *Yellow Court Canon* of the Mao Shan Shang-ch'ing sect.

66. See note 56 above for an early Taoist reference to the colors. Also, *Taisho* 52, 2110, *Pien-cheng Lun*, p. 536c, lines 21–23, for a Buddhist discussion of the basic Taoist colors attributed to the Meng-wei sect.

67. See Ch'en Kuo-fu, p. 88, line 2, for the T'ai-p'ing colors.

68. TT, vol. 639, *Chen Kao* (CK), chapter 13, p. 6a, line 3. The masters of the T'ang period were ecumenical or catholic in their use and interpretation of the various styles of meditation, as described below. The sectarian movements of the Sung period changed the colors to red, yellow, and white, as can be seen in the YCCC, TT, vols. 677–702, chapter 10. These latter color configurations become typical of the Redhead orders, as seen for instance in the liturgical inventions of Lin Ling-su (notes 155–156).

69. Both the orthodox Blackhead Taoists and the popular Redhead Taoists now use the two styles, military and literary, in their rituals. It would be wrong, therefore, to associate military with popular and literary with orthodox Taoist ritual. Rather, the popular Redhead orders tend to stress the exorcistic battle against the evil forces of yin, while the orthodox Blackhead orders emphasize the meditative aspects of union with the Tao. Conflict is basically outside of the spirit of religious Taoism, and the orthodox movements of the Sung dynasty will be seen below to attempt to draw the sectarian movements back into ecumenical harmony.

70. Ko Hung, *Pao-p'u-tzu*, chapter 19 lists the basic Taoist manuals known in the area of Mao Shan, southeast China, of his day.

71. The Meng-wei registers and the liturgies of Ling-pao Taoism are

slighted by the eccentric Ko Hung, who was more interested in methods of alchemical immortality than in the popular rituals later propagated by his grandnephew Ko Ch'ao-fu. T'ao Hung-ching in the *Teng-cheng Yin-chüeh* (TT, vol. 193, hsia, pp. 6a–23b) states that the twenty-four registers were known from the end of the Han period, having been popular in Szechuan with the first Heavenly Masters. See *Fa-lu*, chapter 5, sect. 6; also notes 86–88 below.

72. Ch'en Kuo-fu, pp. 106–107. The bibliography of Lu Hsiu-ching, *San-tung Ching-shu Mu-lu* (list of books and canons in the *San-tung* (*Three Arcana*), is no longer extant. References in both Buddhist and Taoist literature prove that it did exit. Thus, according to Ch'en (p. 106), the first Taoist Canon was in existence by the time of Lu Hsiu-ching. Within the next several decades the canon had been expanded to its present seven sections; see Ch'en Kuo-fu, pp. 107–108; Fukui Kojun (Tokyo, 1958), pp. 164–170.

73. WSPY, TT, vols. 768–779, published between 561 and 581, shows the basic format of Taoist liturgy to be clearly established. See the discussion of Taoist ritual in chapter 5, notes 94–97.

74. The Su-ch'i ritual, found in WSPY, is modeled after the *Yüeh-ling* chapter of the *Book of Rites*. See chapter 5, notes 81–86.

75. Scholars agree that the *San-tung* (*Three Arcana*) were brought together by the time of Lu Hsiu-ching, if not by the great Taoist master himself. Since Lu was a Ling-pao Taoist, the viewpoint of the Ling-pao sect can be seen in the naming of the three sections, a bias which has confused later scholars piecing together the elements of fourth- and fifth-century Taoist movements. In the following paragraphs I have followed the explanation of Chuang, derived from his own collection of documents and the oral traditions of Lung-hu Shan and Mao Shan which he represents. This interpretation differs from the accepted Buddhist version of the first canon; see *Kuang-hung Ming-chi*, *Taisho*, vol. 52, 2103, *Erh-chiao Lun*, p. 141b, lines 16–22. In this version the legendary Ko Hsüan is made founder of the Shang-ch'ing tradition, Chang Tao-ling founder of the Ling-pao tradition, and Pao Ching founder of the San-huang texts.

76. For the foundation of the Mao Shan Shang-ch'ing sect, see notes 84–88. This paragraph reflects the teachings of Master Chuang, and the commonly accepted canonical version of the first three Taoist orders; see Ch'en Kuo-fu, pp. 1–101.

77. The following chart differs from that of Ch'en Kuo-fu, p. 28 fold-out, who shows the present content of the *Three Arcana* as allegedly put together by the early Ling-pao Taoist masters. The *Three Arcana* were named after the *Shang-ch'ing* texts, the Ling-pao scriptures, and the *San-huang Wen*. A chart made according to the names given to the *Three Arcana* would read:

Shang-ch'ing canon	*Ling-pao* canon	*San-huang Wen* canon
Yang Hsi	Ko Hsüan	Pao Ching
Hsü Mi	Ko Ch'ao-fu	Ko Hung
Hsü Hui		

Three Arcana

Lu Hsiu-ching

78. The history of religious Taoism before the formation of the Ling-pao and the Heavenly Master sect is legendary. The three reputed founders, marked in section 2 of the chart with asterisks, have little foundation in historical texts.

79. I believe, as I have maintained thus far, that the *San-huang Wen* must be classified with the Ling-pao tradition; there was no major order of San-huang Taoists, as there was an order of Meng-wei Heavenly Master sect or Ling-pao Taoists. Rather, the *San-huang Wen* were one stage in a series of documents or registers given to the Ling-pao sect Taoists, and later to all Taoists in the ecumenical period of the T'ang. See chapter 5, note 42; and TT, vol. 772, WSPY, chapter 35, p. 2a, where the *San-huang Wen* is seen as one in a series of texts given to Taoist masters. I have therefore listed the Meng-wei order as the third source for the *San-tung* Canon, the Ling-pao order in my opinion being the source for the *San-huang Wen*.

80. Ko Ch'ao-fu multiplied the Ling-pao scriptures for profit. See notes 90–91 below. Thus the popularity of the Ling-pao chiao and chai rituals can probably be dated from this period.

81. Ch'en Kuo-fu, pp. 31–101.

82. The legendary lady Wei Hua-ts'un was reputed to be a Meng-wei Taoist libationer (see notes 93–94).

83. Chapter 5, pt. 6.

84. Because the T'ang emperors patronized Taoist liturgy, the tendency of T'ang dynasty masters was definitely toward the development and propagation of the grand liturgies of renewal or chiao and the chai rites for the dead. See the discussions of Wang Yüan-chih, Chang Wan-fu, Szu-ma Ch'en-cheng, and Tu Kuang-t'ing below. Both the stress on mystic contemplation of union for the highest ranks of Taoist masters, and the demands of emperors and people for the colorful rites of renewal diverted the Taoist masters from the heady dangers of metaphysical dispute, which divided the Buddhist sects of the T'ang. Ritual ecumenism typified the Taoist movements of the period.

85. See T'ao Hung-ching, CK, chapter 19, who relates from hearsay the attempts of the elite of the southern kingdoms to acquire the Shang-ch'ing scriptures (notes 93–108).

86. TT, vol. 193, hsia, *Teng-chen Yin-chüeh* (chüan hsia), pp. 5b–6a; p. 13a, lines 8–10; p. 23a, lines 4–6.

87. TT, vols. 768–779. WSPY; all of the chiao and chai rituals in this sixth-century text begin with the fa-lu and end with the fu-lu.

88. TT, vol. 193, hsia, p. 6a, lines 6–9.

89. Ch'en Kuo-fu, pp. 62–71.

90. Ibid., p. 67.

91. Ibid., pp. 68–70.

92. Ch'en Kuo-fu, pp. 31–62; CK, chapter 19.

93. The existence of Wei Hua-ts'un is doubted by some scholars. The events of her life as recounted in the hagiographies of the Taoist Canon are at best legendary. Ch'en Kuo-fu, pp. 31–32.

94. The *Yellow Court Canon* is mentioned as a single volume by Ko Hung in chapter 19 of the *Pao-p'u-tzu*. It is expanded into two volumes with the revelations of Wei Hua-ts'un, the earlier *wai chüan* or supplement containing directions for meditation, and the later *nei-chüan* or esoteric (inner) volume containing the new lu or list of spirits' names proper to the Shang-ch'ing order.

95. The work of Ch'en Kuo-fu contains all the references from the Taoist Canon for the biographies of the various Mao Shan masters discussed below. The notes will cite Ch'en's work alone rather than make cumbersome references to the entire Canon. See Ch'en, pp. 32–34, for the biography of Yang Hsi.

96. Though a number of scholars hold that Yang Hsi's revelations were by means of a planchette and possessed-medium visions, it seems to me that this theory must be rejected. First, the possessed medium is neither coherent nor in control during a trance, where the writings of Yang Hsi were so beautiful that they aroused the admiration of the meticulous T'ao Hung-ching as he collated them more than a century later. Second, the system of meditative alchemy worked out by the Mao Shan masters is too well defined to have been composed by the random meanderings of a planchette or a medium. Either the Shang-ch'ing scriptures were received by Yang Hsi from the son of Wei Hua-ts'un (Ch'en, p. 32, line 3) or were composed by Yang and the two Hsü's. Third, the masters of the Shang-ch'ing and the Meng-wei traditions have consistently banned the rites of the possessed mediums from their liturgies and considered mediums in trance subjects for exorcism. The Mao Shan doctrines are intended for meditations of union rather than medium possession, according to the teachings of Master Chuang.

97. CK, chapter 19. The gist of the story recounted by T'ao Hung-ching, here summarized, is that the esoteric doctrines of the Shang-ch'ing sect were successfully defended from the incursions of the sixth-century literati. The Mao Shan revelations were collected and hidden in the arcanum of Taoist esoterica to become the highest and most cherished form of meditative practice reserved for the Taoist masters alone. See chapter 5, note 20.

98. TT, vol. 640; CK, chapter 19. Chapter 19 must be considered hearsay, since it was collated by T'ao from oral evidence some 150 years after the dissemination of the Shang-ch'ing documents.

99. CK, chapter 19, p. 11a, lines 5–8.

100. CK, chapter 19, p. 11a, line 4.

101. CK, chapter 19, p. 11b, lines 5–12a, line 4.

102. CK, chapter 19, p. 12b, lines 9–13a, line 1.

103. CK, chapter 19, p. 13b, lines 6–7.

104. CK, chapter 19, p. 14b, lines 5–7.

105. CK, chapter 19, p. 15a, lines 9–15b, line 1.

106. The literati interest in the Shang-ch'ing scriptures was not so concerned with the rituals of religious Taoism as with the new meditative manuals for attaining longevity and immortality, or with the blessing accruing from keeping sacred objects, as in the case of Ma Lang. Even T'ao Hung-ching himself can be seen more as a master and scholar than as a ritual expert. The trend away from scholarly collation of canonical scriptures and toward the performance of classical ritual in the public forum can be seen in the following Sui and T'ang periods.

107. Ch'en Kuo-fu, pp. 29–30 (foldout).

108. Ibid., p. 41, lines 10–12. CK, chapter 19, p. 15a, lines 9–10.

109. CK, chapter 13, p. 13b, lines 2–6.

110. CK, chapter 19, p. 1b, lines 4–7.

111. TT, vol. 193, *Teng-chen Yin-chueh*. Only three chüan of an original

twenty chapters remain to this important sixth-century work. The first chapter, shang, names the spirits of the microcosm, and the third chapter, hsia, gives a primitive version of the fa-lu rite for sending the spirits out of the body.

112. The purpose of the *Yellow Court Canon* meditations is gradually to refine the spirits within the microcosm until finally the state of void or hun-t'un is reached. See my "Buddhist and Taoist Notions of Transcendence," in *Buddhist and Taoist Studies I* (Honolulu, 1977), chapter 1.

113. Ch'en Kuo-fu, pp. 47–50.

114. Ch'en Kuo-fu, p. 49, lines 2–11.

115. The opinion expressed here is my own. The Taoist masters were hard pressed by the Buddhist monks in the metaphysical disputes held at the imperial court. Whether from the influence of the *Lao-tzu Tao-te Ching* and the *Chuang-tzu*, which did not support philosophical debate or contention, or the immense success of the Taoist masters in the sphere of liturgy and popular ritual, the great Taoist masters of the T'ang period produced very little metaphysical disputation. The majority of T'ang dynasty records in the Canon are concerned with ritual or with alchemy and hardly at all with philosophical speculation. The great debates between the Buddhists and the Taoists and the work of political Taoists, such as K'ou Ch'ien-chih of the north-south period, have been left out of the present discussion as not germane to the teachings of Chuang.

116. Ch'en Kuo-fu, pp. 52–59.

117. *Ch'uan T'ang Wen* (CTW), chapter 924, works of Szu-ma Ch'eng-chen. The CTW, a Ch'ing dynasty compilation, is generally considered unreliable; that is, many of the passages attributed to T'ang authors have not been authenticated. The passage quoted in the following note seems to be canonical and therefore acceptable as a T'ang period doctrine.

118. CTW, chapter 924, p. 13b, line 7; *Chuang-tzu*, chapter 4, line 28. See TT, vol. 704, *Tso-wang Lun* (A treatise on "Sitting in Forgetfulness").

119. TT, vol. 899, *Tao-fa Hui-yüan* (TFHY), chapter 76, p. 3b, line 9. This Sung dynasty text, attributed to Pai Yü-ch'an (see notes 161–173), states that the thunder magic of the Ch'ing-ching style involving the pole star to control thunder was taught to the T'ang dynasty thunder-magic expert Wang Tzu-hua through the help of Szu-ma Ch'eng-chen. The tale is probably legendary, since there is little evidence for the actual systematization of the style before the Sung dynasty. See notes 136–139.

120. Ch'en Kuo-fu, p. 55, line 5.

121. Eight works are attributed to Chang Wan-fu in the Ming canon. See TT, vols. 77, 563, 990, 278–290, 198, 48, 878, and (bis) 990.

122. TT, vol. 990. *Chuan shou San-tung ching-chieh Fa-lu lieh shuo*, shang.

123. TT, vol. 990, shang, pp. 3b–19a, for the moral precepts (chieh), Cheng-i registers, *San-huang Wen*, and the Ling-pao writs; TT, vol. 878 *Chiao San-tung Chen-wen wu-fa, Cheng-i Meng-wei Lu Li-ch'eng Yi*, for the twenty-four registers, including p. 10a, line 2, *Ho-t'u;* TT, vol. 990, *Tung-hsüan Ling-pao Tao-shih shou San-tung ching-chieh Fa-lu tse jih li*, pp. 4b–5b for the order outlined here, including "*Precious Ho-t'u*," p. 5, line 3, and Shang-ch'ing scriptures, p. 5b, line 7.

124. That is to say, the authentic T'ang dynasty texts in the extant Taoist Canon all bear the same ritual content outlined by Chang Wan-fu, i.e., moral

precepts, *Lao-tzu Tao-te Ching*, *Cheng-i Meng-wei* twenty-four registers, *San-huang Wen* and Ling-pao scriptures including the *Ho-t'u* register, and the Mao Shan Shang-ch'ing scriptures. These basic documents are therefore taken to be the core of orthodox religious Taoism, as taught by Master Chuang in modern Taiwan.

125. See Harvard-Yenching Index series, vol. 25, p. 135.

126. CTW, chapter 929.

127. TT, vol. 565, *T'ai-shang Cheng-i Yüeh-lu Yi.*

128. TT, vol. 976–983, *Tao-men K'o-fan Ta-ch'uan Chi*, attributed to Tu Kuang-t'ing, has many passages citing and using thunder magic texts; by the end of the T'ang period, therefore, the thunder rites were already known at least at the local level. The text was edited, however, by disciples of Tu Kuang-t'ing, which may put the actual composition of the text at a later date. See notes 132–139 below, on thunder magic.

129. TT, vol. 565, *T'ai-shang Tung-shen T'ai-yüan Ho-t'u San-yüan yang hsieh Yi.*

130. Chapter 5, part 6, notes 94–125.

131. The influence of Ch'an Buddhism was felt most deeply in the Ch'üan-chen sect of the Sung period. The vajrayana or tantric Buddhist rites are reflected in the seven or more Taoist sects that practiced thunder magic. With a few exceptions, the majority of the Sung dynasty innovators were drawn into the ranks of Taoist orthodoxy, as will be seen below.

132. TT, vol. 324, *T'ai-shang Ch'ih-wen Tung-shen San-lu*, and TT, vols. 631–636, *Chin-suo Liu-chu Yin*, both authenticated T'ang dynasty texts.

133. TT, vol. 324, *T'ai-shang Ch'ih-wen Tung-shen San-lu*, Li Hsiang-feng, A.D. 632. Wrongly attributed to T'ao Hung-ching, the text shows the clear use of left-handed mudras (p. 14b, lines 2–10), pseudo-Sanskrit mantras (p. 15a, lines 2–7), and the datewood blocks used to control the spirits of the pole star and of nature in general. The datewood block is later used exclusively for thunder magic.

134. The Ch'ing-wei sect is in direct descent from Mao Shan through the western peak Hua Shan in Shensi. The manuals of Li Ch'un-feng (TT, vol. 324, p. 24b, line 4) show the relationship to the style of magic described in the *T'ai-shang Ch'ieh-wen Tung-shen San-lu*, Hua Shan. TFHY, TT, vol. 883 and following, chapters 1–56 describe the registers and rubrics proper to the sect. See notes 138–139 below.

135. See chapter 6, pts. 1 and 2.

136. TFHY, TT, vol. 899, chapter 76, p. 3b, line 9, states specifically that Wang Tzu-hua learned Ch'ing-ching style thunder magic from Szu-ma Ch'eng-chen sometime before the An Lu-shan rebellion. The term "Ch'ing-ching" is identified with the "old" Shen-hsiao style of thunder magic, that taught by Pai Yü-ch'an in the remainder of chapters 76 and 77. This style is visibly different in content and manner from the "new" Shen-hsiao style of the Sung innovator Lin Ling-su, for which see 155–160 below. It would be technically inaccurate, therefore, to associate the orthodox Taoism of the great Sung master Pai Yü-ch'an (deriving from the semilegendary Wang Tzu-hua) with the popular public rituals of Lin Ling-su, for which see TT, vols. 881–883, for comparison of styles.

137. TT, vol. 899, chapter 76, p. 3a, lines 7–8.

138. *Biographies of Tsu Shu are in TT. vols. 75 and 149. Oral tradition throughout modern China call her a late T'ang dynasty Taoist.*

139. The closeness of Ch'ing-wei Taoism to the masters of Chen-yen Buddhism in west China seems to be confirmed by the similarity in ritual, mudras, and mantras between the Buddhist tantric sect and the Taoist thunder magic. The goddess Marishi-ten is identified in the manuals of the present Heavenly Masters with Tou-mu, the mother goddess of the pole star. The Taoist version of the Goma (Huma) ritual builds a purificatory fire dedicated to Tou-mu (Marishi-ten) and the Kang Shen (Fudō Myō-ō).

140. Kubo, Noritada, *Chūgoku no Shūkyō Kaikaku* (Tokyo, 1967), pp. 7–8.

141. Kubo, pp. 12–13.

142. Chin Yün-chung, *Shang-ch'ing Ling-pao Ta-fa*, chapters 4, 10.

143. Kubo, pp. 40–52.

144. Kubo, pp. 134–150.

145. Kubo, pp. 71–86.

146. The sixty-fourth generation Heavenly Master still grants licenses of ordination to the Taoists of the diaspora from his headquarters in Taipei.

147. *Dokyo no Jittai*, pp. 138–139.

148. Ibid., p. 139, lines 7–8.

149. Ibid., pp. 151–154.

150. *Dokyo no Jittai*, pp. 144–151; Akizuki Kanei, "La secte de Hiu Souen et le Tsing-ming tchong-hiao tao," *Dokyo no Kenkyu*, vol. 3 (Tokyo, 1968), pp. 197–146 (article in Japanese).

151. Akizuki Kanei, p. 220, line 11.

152. *T'ai-shang Chu-kuo Chiu-min Tsung-chen Mi-yao*, TT, vol. 986, hsü, p. 2a, line 7.

153. *Shang-ch'ing T'ien-hsin Cheng-fa*, TT, vols. 318–319. For pseudo-Sanskrit seed-word mantras, see chapter 1, p. 2a, line 10; pole-star exorcism using the Kang spirit (as in chapter 6), see chapter 2, lines 2–10, et passim; fu talismans summoning directional thunder, chapter 3, p. 11b; using the pole star to control the five thunder spirits, chapter 6, pp. 1a–19b; control of the liu-chia and liu-ting spirits, chapter 7, pp. 3a–5a, line 6.

154. The *T'ien-hsin Cheng-fa* utilizes both Cheng-i Heavenly Master sect materials with the Pei-chi Pole Star sect exorcisms in a style of ritual designed for curing colds and bestowing popular blessings. The meditations of the Ch'ing-wei Thunder Magic sect are distinguished from this and the other popular thunder magic orders by contemplative style and content.

155. *Sung Shih*, vol. 21, Pen-chi, p. 10a, line 8; vol. 421, pp. 12b–14a (*Po-na Pen* edit.).

156. *Li-shih Chen-hsien T'i-tao T'ung-chien*, TT, vol. 148, chapter 53, pp. 1a–16a, line 2; see p. 2b, lines 2–4, where Lin in said to receive five thunder magic from the Heavenly Master sect. Brilliant but eclectic, he seems to have pieced together his new Shen-hsiao magic from many sources, orthodox as well as popular. His colleague, the more orthodox Wang Wen-ch'ing, is generally credited with the written materials in the Canon concerning the Shen-hsiao version of ritual. TT, vol. 148, chapter 53, pp. 16a–21a. TT, vol. 900, chapter 76, p. 3a, line 7.

157. *Shang-ch'ing Ling-pao Ta-fa*, TT, vol. 963, chapter 10. In this early thirteenth-century work, the meticulous Chin Yün-chung defends the three

early orders, Mao Shan's Shang-ch'ing sect, Lung-hu Shan's Cheng-i sect, and Ko-tsao Shan's Ling-pao sect, against all newcomers to the ranks of religious Taoism in the Sung. Chin seems especially upset about the Shen-hsiao sect, calling its rituals wu-fa (without power, or without darma) in chapter 10, p. 7b, line 8. He also knows Pole Star and Thunder Magic, while promoting the three ancient orders above all others (pp. 41–19b).

158. Chapter 21, p. 8b, line 3 to 22a, line 5. Chin Yün-chung explains in this lengthy passage why the colors blue, yellow, and white are orthodox (descending from the time of Lu Hsiu-ching and Tu Kuang-t'ing) and why the substitution of the color red is a mistake, or heterodox. The use of red vapor or other noncanonical or nontraditional vapors is not only a mistake but vitiates the very purpose of meditative alchemy. Not only the Shen-hsiao order of Lin Ling-su was erroneous in this regard before the work of Pai Yü-ch'an (a contemporary of Chin who corrected many of the aberrations in the Shen-hsiao texts), but such texts as the *Yun-chi Ch'i-ch'ien* (TT, vols. 677–702, chapter 10) also substituted the colors red, yellow, and white for the traditional green, yellow, and white meditation of union with the Tao. Chin Yün-chung's point is that the sequence of meditative vapors is in fact a form of reflective alchemy, bringing about union with the Tao. Those who mistake the colors are not performing meditative alchemy leading to union but making a substitute for classical liturgy, for less than orthodox motives.

159. See TT, vols. 881–883, *Kao-shang Shen-hsiao Yü-ch'ing Chen-wang Tz'u-shu Ta-fa*, for an example of Shen-hsiao liturgy. The lu or list of spirits' names, and the various ritual formats, are quite different from the chiao or chai rituals of union. For modern examples of Shen-hsiao rituals after the influence of orthodoxy, see *Chuang-lin Hsü Tao-tsang* (Taipei, 1975), pt. 4, vols. 21–25.

160. The great Mao Shan center descended from the heights of orthodox splendor and Shang-ch'ing meditative ritual to the lower forms of black magic and popular exorcism sometime between Wang Yüan-chih in the early T'ang period and the popular Lin Ling-su during the Hsüan-ho reign of the Sung. Black magic (chapter 4), climbing the thirty-six sword ladder, and other popular dramatic exorcism is associated with Mao Shan magicians in modern Taiwan and previously throughout southeast China. For an example of Mao Shan popular magic, see *Chuang-lin Hsü Tao-tsang*, pt. 3, vol. 20, pp. 5779–5835 (Chinese text).

161. TT, vol. 148, chapter 48, p. 16b, line 9 to p. 18a, line 7.

162. *Pai Yü-ch'an Ch'uan-chi* (*The Complete Works of Pai Yü-ch'an*) (Taipei: Tzu-yu Press, 1969), pp. 1–63.

163. One of Pai's three official titles was Shen-hsiao San-shih (official propagator of Shen-hsiao Taoism); see TT, vol. 148, chapter 48, p. 17a, line 4.

164. TT, vol. 898, (TFHY), Ch'en Hsiang-chen, *Lei-t'ing Kang-mu Shuo* (*An Outline of the Thunder Magic Sects*), chapter 66, p. 1a–10a.

165. The Ch'ing-wei sect is associated with the Tung-chen or Mao Shan style of magic and with vajrayana style Buddhist ritual (Sanskiritized characters). TT, vol. 898, chapter 66, p. 2a, lines 8–10 to p. 2a, line 5, identifies six kinds of sanskiritized thunder magic, including Tung-chen, Ch'ing-wei, Ling-pao, and Tung-shen, the earliest version of which is associated with

Mao Shan. See TT, vol. 884, chapter 1, p. 1a, line 4, where Pai Yü-ch'an claims Tz'u-hsü Yüan-chun (Lady Wei Hua-ts'un) as founder of the order; see chapter 6 for the ritual of the order.

166. TT, vol. 898, chapter 66, p. 2b, line 6 to p. 3a, line 5.

167. Lin Ling-su is credited with teaching and spreading a popular form of local Shen-hsiao Taoism, but the style had many variations. See note 180.

168. The documents which Lin Ju-mei brought back from Lung-hu Shan in 1886 (see chapter 2) indicate that the Yü-fu style of thunder magic is thought to be proper to the Cheng-i Heavenly Master sect. The Blackhead Taoists of north Taiwan call themselves Yü-fu Taoists.

169. See TT, vol. 879, for a complete list of the Pole Star registers.

170. TT, vol. 898, chapter 66, p. 9a, lines 4–7.

171. TT, vols. 963–972.

172. TT, vol. 900, chapter 76, p. 3a, lines 1–2.

173. The actual date of the adaptation of this practice is difficult to determine. The present system seems to have been firmly established by the late Sung or early Yüan period, though the grading of Taoists by the number and kind of registers they know is seen as early as the sixth-century; WSPY, chapter 35.

174. Ch'en Kuo-fu, pp. 175–179.

175. Selections from the Tao-chiao Yuan Liu and other Mi-chueh are published in the Dokyo Hiketsu Shusei, Tokyo: 1979.

176. See note 168 above. *Yü-fu* or Jade Pavilion is the esoteric title for the Cheng-i Heavenly Master sect.

177. The grading from a lowly grade nine to a highest grade one is an obvious imitation of the imperial mandarinate system. It is difficult to trace the titles of the registers as used today earlier than the Sung dynasty; see note 173 above.

178. See *Dokyo no Jittai*, pp. 165–187.

179. Chuang considers the Ch'ing-wei sect to have originated at Hua Shan in the late T'ang period. See notes 138–139 above.

180. TT, vol. 988, *Tao-men Shih-kui*, pp. 10–11, esp. p. 11a, lines 8–10.

181. See *Taoism and the Rite of Cosmic Renewal*, chapter 5.

182. TT, vol. 1016, *The Collected Sayings of Po Yü-ch'an*, a Ming dynasty work, attributes to Pai Yü-ch'an derogatory statements about the northern Lü Shan order. See TT, vol. 1016, chapter 1, pp. 8b–9a.

183. The wrath of Pai Yü-ch'an is directed against the possessed Wu or medium rituals associated with heterodoxy and vulgar spirits by the traditional orthodox orders, as noted in note 182. The Redhead Taoists of Taiwan often act as interpreters for the possessed mediums, and thus both are often called Shen-hsiao Taoists. The reason for this anomaly can be seen in note 184. The Heavenly Masters consistently gave Shen-hsiao registers to all local Taoists coming for an ordination or license.

184. The Shen-hsiao registers are kept in fifth place, after the four traditional orders—Mao Shan, Ch'ing-wei, Pole Star, and Cheng-i—as can be seen in the *Tao chiao Yuan-liu*, note 175 above. Concerning the present practice in Taipei of giving Shen-hsiao ordinations to all local Taoists and foreigners who ask for ordination: a common title for such licenses is Wan-fa Tsung, a sort of "bringing together of all traditions" in a late twentieth-century ecumenism.

185. *Dokyo no Jittai*, p. 187.

186. Not only Taiwan, but other Chinese communities in southeast Asia have experienced a renewal of festival custom in the latter half of the twentieth century despite secular industrialization. The popularity of kung-fu and t'ai-chi exercises in the Chinese community of Honolulu is a visible sign of a deeper movement among college-age youth to recover the festive and customary practices of their cultural roots. Chinese religious custom appears to be a means of community identification, and Taoist liturgy is a part of a cultural legacy.

187. See note 115 above.

CHAPTER TWO

1. *Wu-shih Chia-p'u* (*History of the Wu Clan*), 23 folio pages, author's microfilm collection, p. 21.

2. *Hsinchu Ts'ung-chih* (*An Historical Gazette of Hsinchu*) (Hsinchu city archives, 1946), p. 141.

3. *Hsinchu Ts'ung-chih*, biography of Lin Chan-mei, p. 231.

4. Hsinchu city, Ch'eng-huang Temple records, courtesy of Cheng Hung-yüan.

5. *Hsinchu Ts'ung-chih*, pp. 401–402.

6. *Hsinchu Hsien-chih* (*Hsinchu County Gazette*) (Hsinchu, 1955), biography of Lin Ju-mei, vol. 9, pp. 9–10.

7. The Mao Shan *Ch'i-men Tun-chia*, the subject of chapter 4, bears the colophon "Lin Shih-mei, 1851, Westgate Villa," thus making Lin Ju-mei about sixteen years old when the book was brought into the family by an elder brother.

8. Field notes, November 1972. Three oral sources testified to the adoption: Ch'en A-kung, the son of Ch'en Chieh-san; the funeral-wreath maker and son-in-law of Lin Hsiu-mei, Mr. Huang; and Chuang himself.

9. *Hsinchu Hsien-chih*, vol. 9, p. 9.

10. Diary of Lin Ju-mei, Shu-wen document from the library of Chuang-ch'en Teng-yun. Microfilm copy in the author's possession. The date was confirmed by the Hsinchu county archives, courtesy of Mr. Liu Chin-mei.

11. The talisman was originally kept in the red lacquer box hanging over the main altar of the Ch'eng-huang deity, Hsinchu city. In 1969 it was removed to the private residence of Lin Ju-mei's maternal grandson, T'ung, with the datewood thunder block and other paraphernalia of Lin Ju-mei.

12. *Hsinchu Hsien-chih*, vol. 9, p. 10. 1886–1888, 1906–1910.

13. The documents of Ch'en Chieh-san have been partially published in the *Chuang-lin Hsü Tao-tsang* (Taipei, 1975), pt. 3, vol. 19.

14. Ch'en Chieh-san, *Wen-chien* (author's microfilm collection), title page. The descendant of one of the four Taoists, Ch'en Ting-feng, still performs in Hsinchu city today. See chapter 3.

15. Ch'en Chieh-san, *Wen-chien* (author's microfilm collection), p. 22–23, lists eight grades of perfection for women Taoists. Compare TT, vol. 989, *San-tung Hsiu-Tao Yi*, p. 9a, line 5 to p. 11a, line 10, for canonical evidence of Taoist titles of ordination given to women.

16. The Chinese reckon a child to be already nine months old at the time

of birth, and add a year to its age at the time of the Chinese New Year Festival. Thus Chuang was sixteen in 1926.

17. Author's field notes, Nov. 6, 1972. The Ch'eng-huang temple committee, the funeral wreath maker Huang, and Ch'en A-kung recall the event. Master Chuang is noncommittal on the subject.

18. See Sung Yin-tzu chu, *Huang-t'ing Wai-ching* (Taipei: Tzu-yu Press, 1959); and *Huang-t'ing Ching Chu*, from the library of Lin Hsiu-mei, author's microfilm collection.

19. TT, vol. 636, CK, chapter 2, p. 2b, lines 4–5.

20. The Teachings of Master Chuang are published in the *Chuang-lin Hsü Tao-tsang* (Taipei, 1975), Chinese text. This twenty-five–volume collection contains only the tradition of the chiao festival of renewal (chüan 1–50), the chai liturgies of burial (chüan 51–71), the mi-chüeh rubrics meant for oral transmission (chüan 72–82) and the Shen-hsiao and Lü Shan versions of Taoist ritual (chüan 82–103). Being prepared for publication are the teachings of Master Chuang on Thunder Magic (chapter 6) and the military Tao of the Left (chapter 4).

CHAPTER THREE

1. Since the role of the Taoist, whether Blackhead or Redhead, is associated with sickness, death, or the rectifying of natural disaster, the very ministry of the Taoist elicits unpleasant associations. In the ministry of internal alchemy, bodily exercise, and gymnastics, however, the associations are pleasant and definitely of positive value. The taboo against mentioning the Taoist, therefore, applies only to those masters who specialize in exorcism or burial. One of the major themes in chapter 3 is the association of the elite classes with meditative ritual, as opposed to the popular public ritual of curing, exorcism, and burial. Every Taoist in this chapter will be seen to seek enough affluence to practise private meditation and leave the ministry of public ritual.

2. The practitioners of medium possession and their interpreters are usually said to be members of the Lü Shan sect, or more exactly, the Lü Shan San-nai (Three Sisters) sect. There seems to be little relationship between the Lü Shan sect condemned by Pai Yü-ch'an in chapter 1 and the Fukien-based Lü Shan Three Sisters sect so popular in Taiwan. The Taiwanese Lü Shan Taoists are considered a branch of the Shen-hsiao order, because they are given Shen-hsiao titles of ordination when they approach the Heavenly Master for a license. See chapter 1, notes 184–185.

3. British Museum, OR/12673. This collection of Taoist ritual manuscripts was brought to London in 1872 from Fukien, and contains rituals identical to those used by the Taoists of Tainan city in southern Taiwan.

4. The Fu Jen University library copy of the Canon loaned to the project by the Rev. Yves Raguin, S. J., was used by Chuang during a portion of the study. The *Wu-shang Pi-yao* (TT, vols. 768–779) was the basis for much of Chuang's instruction in chapter 5 below.

5. See bibliography of works in Japanese for the titles. Chuang was delighted with the work of Maspero and amazed that a foreigner could derive so much from the Canon.

6. Oct. 16, 1972. See chapter 6, notes 46–48.

7. Oct. 15, 1972.
8. Dec. 2, 1967, field notes.
9. Nov. 22, 1969, field notes. The child was our daughter, Maria.
10. U.S.$12.50.
11. See my "Orthodoxy and Heterodoxy in Taoist Ritual," where this rite is described in more detail. N.T.$20 is the equivalent of U.S.$50; *Religion and Ritual in Chinese Society* (Stanford, 1974), pp. 325–336.
12. The Su-ch'i is described in chapter 5, notes 81–87. The text can be found in *Chuang-lin Hsü Tao-tsang* (Taipei, 1975), vol. 5, pp. 1321–1379.
13. Chapter 6, note 48, and chapter 1, notes 25–38.
14. See chapter 4, for the ritual of the six chia spirits.
15. See note 13 above.
16. Dec. 5–10, 1970.
17. The rituals of renewal are performed according to the time of the day that corresponds to the purpose and title of the rite. Thus the Su-ch'i usually starts before midnight, the Morning Audience before dawn, the Noon Audience before noon, and the Night Audience before sunset.
18. See chapter 6, pt. 1, sec. iv.
19. The mother goddess of the Pole Star, Tou-mu, is also patron of the military arts and under her sanskrit name Marishi-ten she reigns as one of the patron spirits of Ninjitsu military techniques in Japan. The Heavenly Master maintains the registers of Marishi-ten and transmits the popular Rite to the Pole Star, Pai-tou, in her honor.

CHAPTER FOUR

1. The Tao of the Right will be the subject of chapter 5. The Taoist master usually begins the novice's instruction with the playing of the musical instruments and by having him assist at classical ritual as an acolyte. The meditations of inner alchemy are reserved for the exclusive inner coterie, including the master's own sons, who are to receive a title of ordination.
2. The ministry of military Taoism is divided into two separate titles: first, the spiritual ministry of exorcism and breath control; and second, the external practice of t'ai-chi ch'uan, kung-fu, ch'i-kung, and the other techniques of self-defense and bodily exercise and health. Since these latter techniques are also used in rituals of exorcism and purification, the young Taoist is required to perfect himself in military techniques.
3. The two ministries, wen or literary and wu or military, are preserved as distinct ritual styles by the masters of orthodox Taoism in Taiwan.
4. The mudras, mantras, and meditations are usually a part of the k'ou-chüeh or oral secrets passed on by the master. Chuang's library of written instructions was indeed rare among the Taoists of Taiwan. The manuals in Chuang's collection are listed in the bibliography, and are in the author's microfilm files.
5. As will be seen below, the title *Ch'i-men Tun-chia* (*Marvelous Method for Hiding or Commanding the Six Chia Spirits*), is a deliberate falsification of the actual contents of the manual. The title should read *Register* (lu) *of the Six Chia Spirits*.

6. See chapter 2, note 1.

7. The manual is named after Mao Shan in Kiangsu province, but belongs in genre or style of magic to the tradition of Wu-tang Shan; see chapter 1, note 5. The preface states clearly that legendarily the founder of this style of military magic is Chu-ko Liang, and the area of composition is Wu-tang Shan in Hupei province. Chuang's book is a Ming dynasty compilation from earlier sources. There are a dozen or so mentions of tun-chia magic in the Ming dynasty canon, as in TT, vols. 576, 580, 857, 873.

8. See below, figure 1, for the *Pa-chen T'u*.

9. *Ch'i-men Tun-chia*, Chu-lin Press (Hsinchu, 1957); this is the pamphlet purchased at the temple.

10. This passage, including the quotes and the explanations, are taken directly from vol. 1 of the four-volume *Ch'i-men Tun-chia* register. References in the following pages will be given to specific charts or sections; CMTC, 3a.

11. CMTC, 3b–4a.

12. CMTC, 5a–5b, for the figures and diagrams.

13. CMTC, 6a–6b, for part 3. Note that figure 5 is a *ho-t'u*, as in chapter 6, note 48.

14. CMTC, pp. 7a–8b, including the instructions for making the seal.

15. CMTC, pp. 9a–10b.

16. CMTC, pp. 11a–15b, for the talismans and conjurations.

17. CMTC, pp. 16a–19b, for the twenty-eight constellations.

18. CMTC, pp. 9a–9b, for the great standard.

19. CMTC, pp. 21a–23b, for the lu or description of the six chia spirits.

20. CMTC, pp. 23b–24a, for the layout of the altar.

21. The following pages are a translation of the entire second volume of Chuang's manual, with field notes taken in 1969, 1970, and again in 1972 with Chuang in Hsinchu City. The manual is in the author's microfilm collection.

22. CMTC, vol. 2, 5a–5b; field notes, Oct. 12, 1972.

23. The above rubrics are used by the Redhead Taoists for the K'ai-kuang or "opening the eyes" ceremony to bless a new statue, or initiate a chiao rite of renewal. The rite definitely belongs to the popular style of Taoist ritual as opposed to the stately Tao of the Right, in chapter 5.

24. See *Sui Shu*; Lieh-chuan; the fourth son of Sui Wen-ti, was reduced to the state of a commoner for practising Tso-tao.

CHAPTER FIVE

1. *Chuang-tzu*, chapter 4, p. 1, line 26; TT, vol. 207, *Chai-chieh Lu*, p. 1b, line 1; p. 1b, line 3; TT, vol. 704, *Tso-wang Lun*.

2. TT, vols. 768–779, WSPY, chapter 52.

3. WSPY, chapters 53, 54.

4. WSPY, chapter 50.

5. TT, vol. 704, T'ang, Szu-ma Ch'eng-chen, *Tso-wang Lun*; TT, vol. 641, *Tao-shu*, chapter 2, pp. 1a–8b, *Tso-wang Lun*.

6. See *Chung-kuo Hsüeh-chih* (Tokyo, 1968, vol. 5), Li Hsien-chang, pp. 213–224; TT, vol. 878, Chang Wan-fu, *Chiao San-tung Chen-wen*. *Sui-shu*,

Ching-chi Chih, Tao-ching Shu-lu for an early definition of Taoist ritual and chiao; quoted by Li Hsien-chang, p. 214.

7. See TT, vol. 209, *Chi-tu Chin-shu*, chapter 2, p. 2a, line 8 to p. 35a, line 4, for an exhaustive list of chiao and chai liturgies, according to daily scheduling of rituals. Compare *Chuang-lin Hsü Tao-tsang* (Taipei: Ch'eng-wen Press, 1975) 25 vols., pt. 1, vols. 1–50, for a modern five-day chiao as performed by Master Chuang in Taiwan.

8. See note 7 above. The chiao of modern Taiwan follow the general order of the classical fifth- and sixth-century chiao, but add many of the popular and dramatic Sung dynasty rituals attributed to the Shen-hsiao Redhead order. For a description of Redhead ritual, see John Keupers, "Taoist Exorcism," in *Buddhist and Taoist Studies* (Honolulu, 1977), vol. 1, chapter 5.

9. Chiao thus retains its earliest meaning, the offering of wine and incense in a sort of "pure" sacrifice at the end of each k'o-i orthodox ritual of union.

10. *Chuang-lin Hsü Tao-tsang*, pt. 1, chapters 32–39, for examples of ching or canonical readings; compare TT, vols. 527–529 for similar canons dedicated to the Pole Star. The formats of the canons are similar to the sutras read by Buddhist monks, and are obvious imitations of Buddhist ritual chant.

11. *Chuang-lin Hsü Tao-tsang*, pt. 1, chapter 50.

12. Li Hsien-chang, pp. 225–231. See note 6 above.

13. *Lao-tzu*, *Tao-te Ching*, chapter 42.

14. See Saso, Michael, "Buddhist and Taoist Notions of Transcendence," *Buddhist and Taoist Studies* (Honolulu, 1977), chapter 1.

15. *Huang-t'ing Ching Chu* (Taipei, 1959), hsia, p. 21b, line 6. There are two accepted theories of the location of primordial breath. The more commonly accepted version locates the blue-green primordial vapor in the chest; the elite esoteric version (from the *Yellow Court Canon* and the Mao Shan Shang-ch'ing tradition) puts the residence of the Primordial Heavenly Worthy in the Ni-wan palace of the brain (the microcosmic equivalent of the heavens). The two theories are not contradictory but complementary—that is, the blue-green vapor of primordial breath is refined in the yellow court (the mystical crucible) from the primordial vapors of wood (green, liver) and fire (red, heart). Once refined in the yellow court, the spirit of primordial breath, Yüan-shih T'ien-tsun, resides in the Ni-wan. In the orthodox religious interpretation taught by Master Chuang, the principles are interpreted to be spirits. The spirits are to be refined, or exteriorized, until the final state of Hun-tun simplicity is achieved, Hun-tun being the state of hsin-chai or hsü void, which precedes union with the transcendent Tao of the Wu-wei.

16. Kaltermark, Max, "Ling-pao: Note sur un terme du Taoisme Religieux," *Mélanges Publies par l'Institut des Hautes Études Chinoises* 2 (Paris, 1960), pp. 559–588.

17. The above paragraphs relate the basic cosmology of religious Taoism, as taught by the Heavenly Master sect and transmitted by Master Chuang. See TT, vol. 563, *Cheng-i Fa-wen T'ien-shih Chiao-chieh K'o-i*, pp. 13b–21b.

18. See Saso (Honolulu, 1977), ch. 1, p. 25, table 1.

19. See *Chi-lu T'an-ch'ing Yüan-k'o* (Lung-hu Shan, 1886), collection of the Heavenly Master (microfilm), pp. 31a–33b.

20. Ibid., p. 33b. *Tao-chiao Yüan-liu*, pp. 127–132.

21. Taoists lower than grade six do not know the meditations of union, and are not given the oral secrets for performing the fa-lu (pt. 6 below).

22. Chapter 6, notes 12 and 13.

23. Field notes, Nov. 1972, (Hsinchu City, Taiwan).

24. Field notes, Oct.–Nov. 1972. The WSPY (TT, vol. 768–779) was used by Chuang throughout the lessons, loaned by Rev. Yves Raguin, S. J. of Fu Jen University, Taipei.

25. WSPY, paraphrase of chapter 24, p. 2b.

26. WSPY, chapter 24, p. 3a, line 10 to p. 3b, line 6.

27. WSPY, chapter 24, p. 4a, lines 5–7 to p. 4b, line 6.

28. "Lung-han" is the esoteric term for the state of primordial chaos, or Hun-tun; thus the period of gestation from the transcendent Tao to the T'ai-chi is seen to be completed in five stages, presaging the Ling-pao five talismans, and ritually enacted in the Su-ch'i; notes 30–33 below.

29. WSPY, chapter 24, p. 4b, line 3.

30. WSPY, chapter 24, p. 4b, lines 3–4. Thus a feudal treaty is made between the Taoist and the heavenly worthies, using the five talismans as symbol of enfeoffment.

31. The talismanic writings of the fang-shih seem to have preceded the coming of Buddhist sutras and sanskrit from India; the Taoists of the north-south period claimed a Taoist origin even to the Buddhist teachings. See Fukui Kojun, *Dōkyō no Kiso teki Kenkyū* (Tokyo, 1963), pp. 267–283, the *Hua-hu Ching* controversy; also *Dokyo no Jittai*, pp. 75–78.

32. WSPY, chapter 24, p. 4b, lines 7–10.

33. Ibid. The process is performed in ritual meditation during the Su-ch'i ritual, on the first evening of the five-day chiao, in Chuang's version of the liturgy. See *Chuang-lin Hsü Tao-tsang*, part 1, chapter 20.

34. WSPY, chapter 24, pp. 7b–15a, line 6.

35. This phrase and the following (note 36) are to be identified, in Chuang's interpretation, with the *Ho-t'u*, in the *Ling-pao Five Talisman* form.

36. Another term for the *Ho-t'u*, or the *Ling-pao Five Talismans*.

37. The twenty-four solar interstices, which correspond to the twenty-four registers of the Meng-wei or Cheng-i sect teachings; see TT, vol. 878, *Cheng-i Meng-wei Lu*.

38. The term means "union with the Tao." Thus the chen-jen means the man who has realized union through the Ling-pao ritual meditation.

39. The influence of the T'ai-p'ing canon is seen in the concluding line of the WSPY text. The *Ling-pao Five Talismans* bring the "Great Peace."

40. Field notes, Dec. 1967; Nov.–Dec. 1970; Oct.–Nov. 1972. The order of instruction is outlined in WSPY, chapter 35, p. 2a–b.

41. The WSPY, a Ling-pao text, puts the *San-huang Wen* in third place; the Meng-wei or Cheng-i tradition of Master Chuang puts the doctrines of the Three Pure Ones (San-ch'ing) in this spot. Though the ritual order is the same, the colors of the vapors and the directions are different; see WSPY, chapter 38. The San-huang vapors are brown, white, and green, while the San-ch'ing vapors are green, yellow, and white. The descriptions of the San-huang are also significantly different (see chapter 43, pp. 7b–8a). The ritual that Chuang calls Tao-ch'ang or Cheng-chiao (*Chuang-lin Hsü Tao-tsang*,

pt. 1, chapter 48) is otherwise the same as WSPY, chapter 49, *San-huang Chai*, with only the names of the San-huang changed to the San-ch'ing. Thus the difference in emphasis between the two orders, the Ling-pao order of WSPY and the Meng-wei order of Chuang, is minimal, the emphasis shifting from the *San-huang Wen* to the *San-ch'ing* in the third stage of meditative alchemy. See notes 73–75 below.

42. The present order of the Heavenly Master sect at Lung-hu Shan, as can be seen in the references cited in note 19 above, uses the chart supplied here by Master Chuang, rather than the order of WSPY, chapter 35. That is, the San-ch'ing or the ritual of the Three Pure Ones supplants the *San-huang Wen* as the third step in the order of transmission. See notes 20 and 21, where the present practise is outlined more clearly. The Ch'ing-wei Thunder Magic registers are inserted from the Sung dynasty on, between the highest Yellow Court Canon, and the lower Meng-wei and Ling-pao registers. Thus, for Chuang, the *Yellow Court Canon* is the highest, after which comes the Ch'ing-wei Thunder Magic register, the Meng-wei registers, and finally the Ling-pao registers.

43. The esoteric secrets are technically passed on only from father to son, as can be seen in the *Hsüan-tu Lü-wen*, TT, vol. 78. Possession of the canonical texts, however, constitutes the right of the disciple to seek a master and to receive instruction in Taoist legerdemain. Thus possession of the *K'o-i* texts presupposes transmission and allows the scholar access to the k'ou-chüeh oral explanations of the master.

44. Field notes, Oct.–Nov. 1972. Chuang explicitly allowed the *Chuang-lin Hsü Tao-tsang* to be published for the sake of preservation. The *Mi-chüeh* written transmission of oral secrets are in the author's microfilm collection and are being prepared for publication. See the bibliography for the Thunder Magic titles and holdings of the Heavenly Master.

45. WSPY, chapter 35, p. 6a, line 10 to p. 8a, line 5.

46. Thus the *fang-chung* sexual hygiene techniques are forbidden by the higher grades of esoteric Taoism.

47. WSPY, chapter 38, quoting the *Ming-chen K'o*, p. 11b, lines 1–6.

48. WSPY, chapter 46, p. 7a, lines 3–6.

49. Chuang did not observe this precept, except when performing ritual meditation.

50. Chuang was not given a grade two ordination, but was kept at a grade four by Lin Hsiu-mei; see chapter 2.

51. WSPY, chapter 46, p. 14b, lines 1–3.

52. WSPY, chapter 47, p. 3a, lines 1–8.

53. WSPY, chapter 47, p. 3a–3b.

54. The five organs plus the gall bladder.

55. Saso, *Taoism and the Rite of Cosmic Renewal* (1972), chapter 2.

56. Ong-ia (Amoy dialect) or Wang-yeh rite for expelling the demons of pestilence. This ritual belongs to the Shen-hsiao style of ritual, and is performed throughout Taiwan, especially in the coastal fishing villages.

57. Ninth lunar month, ninth day, in honor of Marishi-ten, or Tou-mu, mother goddess of the Pole Star. See the Bibliography, author's microfilm collection.

58. Though some of the Taoists in southern Taiwan perform the Su-ch'i ritual without the Three Audiences and the Cheng-chiao, or by reversing the

required order, the process of ritual alchemy requires that all five of the K'o-i rites of union be performed in succession. Thus at least three days and nights are required to perform a chiao.

59. See *Chuang-lin Hsü Tao-tsang*, introduction, pp. 16–17, for the list of rituals. Also, TT, vol. 209, as in note 7 above.

60. The ritual items marked with an asterisk derive for the most part from the Shen-hsiao style of liturgy for which Lin Ling-su was so famous. The rituals are dramatic and entertaining to watch. The unmarked rituals or "canons" do not require an ordained Taoist to perform, and can be read by lay experts or local fang-shih if a Taoist is not present.

61. The Fen-teng has been exhaustively treated by K. M. Schipper, *Le Fen-teng, Rituele Taoiste* (1975).

62. *Ch'ung-pai*, reinviting the spirits, varies with each Taoist master. For Chuang's version, see *Chuang-lin Hsü Tao-tsang*, pt. 1, chapter 21.

63. These texts are not included in the Ming-dynasty canon.

64. For the Buddhist influence in these texts, see Kamata, Shigeo, *Chugoku Bukyo Shiso Shi Kenkyu* (1965), pp. 53–56.

65. The version of the Cheng-chiao used by the Taoists of southern Taiwan and the Shen-hsiao tradition is different from that used by Chuang in the Meng-wei tradition. For Chuang's version, see note 41 above.

66. The rite for climbing the thirty-six sword ladder is popular throughout Taiwan, and must be ascribed to the Shen-hsiao dramatic tradition. Volume 50 of the *Taisho Tripitaka* shows cases of Buddhist and Taoist monks of the T'ang period competing in the height of sword ladders and the sharpness of blades used in display of supernatural powers. The rite probably comes from India and is not a part of the orthodox tradition.

67. See Keupers, John, "Taoist Exorcism," *Buddhist and Taoist Studies I*, chapter 4, for a description of this rite.

68. Even the most orthodox of Taoist masters must accede to the wishes of the local populace in performing the chiao festivals of renewal. See Schipper, p. 11.

69. The Shen-hsiao order in particular was accused of changing both the content and the externals of chiao ritual, as described in chapter 1 above. Aside from the usages of the Shen-hsiao order, however, the program of the chiao as performed by Chuang has remained relatively unchanged since the T'ang period.

70. The following order is used by the Taoists of Honolulu in the annual P'u-tu celebrated at the Kuan-yin temple, and the Lum-sai Ho-tang.

71. See Pang, Duane, "The P'u-tu ritual," *Buddhist and Taoist Studies I*, chapter 5.

72. TT, vol. 282, *Wu-shang Huang-lu Ta-chai Li-ch'eng I*, chapter 17, p. 7a, line 9.

73. The Latin term is used in theology to describe the sacramental rites of Roman Catholicism. The proper execution of the words and the intention (ex opere operato) and the devotion and perfection of the priest performing the rite (ex opere operantis) are distinguished in Taoist grades of perfection.

74. *Chuang-lin Hsü Tao-tsang* (1975) Pt. 3, vol. 19, pp. 5367, 5441.

75. Ibid., pt. 1, vol. 5, pp. 1355–1361; WSPY, chapter 53, pp. 1b–2b.

76. WSPY, chapter 83, p. 13b, line 5.

77. Thus, the numbers of the *Ling-pao Five Talismans* do not correspond to the equivalent symbols used in the Three Audiences. This discrepancy can only partially be accounted for by Chuang's explanation. The following sets of numbers are used in the two systems:

Symbol:	east	south	center	west	north
Su-ch'i:	9	3	1	7	5
3 Audiences:	3	2	5	4	1

According to Chuang's interpretation, the numbers of the Su-ch'i are symbolic of the primordial gestation of the Ling-pao Five Talismans, as described in the WSPY at the beginning of the chapter. The numbers of the Three Audiences are symbolic of the workings of the five elements in the visible world of the "posterior heavens," that is, within the microcosm. It is also possible that the first set of numbers represents the Ling-pao tradition, while the second set derives from the Meng-wei tradition, and the *Yellow Court Canon*.

78. The explanation of meditative alchemy in the following paragraph can be found in the *Shang-ch'ing Ling-pao Ta-fa* of Chin Yün-ching, TT, vol. 963–972, chapter 21, pp. 5b–9b. It is also found in the *Huang-t'ing Ching Chu*, chapter chung, and hsia, 8b–22b.

79. The explanation of the Tao-ch'ang given here belongs to the Meng-wei or Cheng-i Heavenly Master sect tradition. See note 41 above.

80. *Chuang-lin Hsü Tao-tsang* (1975), 25 volumes.

81. The fa-lu occurs throughout the WSPY, and in all of the early canonical passages describing the k'o-i rites of union. It can thus be safely established as one of the earliest rites in orthodox Taoist liturgy. The *Teng-chen Yin-chüeh* of T'ao Hung-ching, an early sixth-century text (TT, vol. 193, hsia, pp. 61–32b) describes the rite and associates its use with Han-chung, the area in Szechwan where the first Heavenly Master spread his doctrines.

82. TT, vols. 877–878 contain the various lu, or registers, used since the T'ang dynasty and continuing in the oral transmission of the Taoist masters until the present. The lu transmitted by Master Chuang is identical with the text of the *T'ai-shang San-wu Cheng-i Meng-wei Lu*, TT, vol. 877; Chang Wan-fu, (TT, vol. 900), and Tu Kuang-t'ing, (TT, vol. 566).

83. The fu-lu is found in the passages described in note 81, and always accompanies the k'o-i ritual meditations as the concluding rubric.

84. The three oral "secrets" listed here are not found in writing, but are included in the mi-chüeh doctrines taught by the master in preparation for chiao ritual. Field notes, Oct.–Nov. 1972.

85. Pao-ko, and san-chiao below, are terms from Chinese medicine. In religious Taoism pao-ko refers to the shoulders, or the lymphatic glands, and san-chiao to the "three tubes" in the belly.

86. For the Chinese text, see *Chuang-lin Hsü Tao-tsang*, pt. 1, chapter 49, the *Ch'u-chüan* or novice's manual used to teach the names and cyclical days for summoning the kung-ts'ao messengers.

87. TT, vols. 278–290, *Wu-shang Huang-lu Ta-chai Li-ch'eng I*, chapter 16, pp. 2b–5a; chapter 17, pp. 7a–8a, line 8; chapter 32, pp. 11b, line 6 to p. 12b, line 10. The text used is from *Chuang-lin Hsü Tao-tsang*, pt. 1, chapter 48,

Tao-ch'ang, pp. 3755–3757. The explanations of Chuang are from oral notes, Dec. 1970, Oct.–Nov. 1972, and from the written manual *Ch'u-chüan* cited in note 86 above. Comparative notes can be found in the *Tao-tsang Chi-yao*, vol. 4, k'ang, chapter 7, pp. 27a–28b. The earliest use of left-handed mudras as indicated in the text can be found in the Sung dynasty work *Ling-pao Ling-chiao Chi-tu Chin-shu* (TT, vol. 210), chapter 9, p. 4a, line 7 to p. 4b, line 2.

88. The Six Chia spirits used by the orthodox Tao of the Right are not the same as the terrifying demons described in chapter 4.

89. The following pages are oral tradition, and are not found in written form with such clarity of detail in the published Taoist canon.

90. *Tao-tsang Chi-yao*, vol. 4, chapter 7, p. 27a.

91. *Chi-lu T'an-ch'ing Yüan-k'o*, Lung-hu Shan, 1886, collection of the Heavenly Master. Ordination manual, microfilm collection of the author, pp. 39–45.

92. *Chuang-lin Hsü Tao-tsang*, pt. 1, chapter 14, p. 3874.

CHAPTER SIX

1. Extreme caution must be taken not to identify with one side or the other in the controversy over the orthodoxy of the Thunder Magic orders. The teachings of Master Chuang regarding the various expressions of tantric Taoism are based on the criteria of meditative union and observance of the lu registers of antiquity. Thus in rejecting the popular Shen-hsiao style of magic attributed to Lin Ling-su, Chuang did so simply because the rituals of the order were devoid of the meditative alchemy transmitted in the *Yellow Court Canon* tradition and because the registers (lu) of the Shen-hsiao Taoists summoned spirits considered impure, unorthodox, or improper to the meditations of union. Ch'ing-wei Thunder Magic will be used by Chuang at the end of the present chapter to purify the microcosm and macrocosm in order to make orthodox ritual effective.

2. The vajrayana or tantric Buddhist sects of the T'ang period had a deep influence on Shingon and Tendai Buddhism in Japan, but seemed to diminish in importance in China after the Yüan or Mongol period, when it was patronized by the Mongol emperors. The mudras and pseudo-Sanskrit mantras of Taoist Thunder Magic are obvious imitations of the vajrayana sects (see note 6).

3. TT, vols. 884–941, *Tao-fa Hui-yüan* (TFHY), is the classical canonical treatise on Thunder Magic, containing descriptions of the various sects that flourished during the late T'ang and the Sung. The dynastic histories do not take notice of Thunder Magic sects before the Sung period.

4. Akizuki Kanei, "La secte de Hiu Souen et le Tsing-ming tchong-hiao tao," *Dōkyō no Kenkyū* (1968, article in Japanese), chapter 3, pp. 197–246.

5. TT, vol. 197, *Hsü Chen-chun Hsien Chuan*; and TT, vol. 200, *Hsi Shan Chen-chun Pa-shih-wu Hua Lu*. Both are Sung dynasty works.

6. Compare TT, vol. 900, TFHY, chapter 96, pp. 35a–38a, with *Taisho* 21, # 1265, p. 295a and b; # 1269, p. 297, et passim.

7. The Ch'ing-wei sect, a descendant of the Mao Shan order, flourished in west China, Hua Shan, and the city of Ch'ang-an. The "old" Shen-hsiao or "fire-master" sect flourished on Heng Shan, the southern peak, and Mount

T'ien-t'ai. The popular Shen-hsiao order flourished in Chekiang and Fukien and is prevalent in modern Taiwan.

8. See Bibliography, author's microfilm collection.

9. TFHY, TT, vol. 884, chapter 1, p. 1a, line 5; Tz'u-hsü Yüan-chun is Wei Hua-ts'un; see TT, vol. 884, chapter 2, p. 6b, lines 7–8, Tz'u-hsü Wei Yuan-chun, Hua-ts'un.

10. See Bibliography, author's microfilm collection. Chapter 1, notes 162–163.

11. See chapter 1, note 181. TT, vol. 988, *Tao-men Shih-kui*, p. 11a, lines 8–10.

12. TT, vol. 898, TFHY, chapter 66, p. 9a, line 4.

13. TT, vol. 900, TFHY, chapter 76, p. 3a, lines 1–3.

14. *Chi-lu T'an-ch'ing Yüan-k'o* (Lung-hu Shan, 1886), pp. 33–39.

15. Michel Strickmann, "The Thunder Rites of the Sung–Notes on the Shen-hsiao Sect and the Southern School of Taoism," *Tōhō Shūkyō*, no. 46 (1975), pp. 15–28. (Article in Japanese, tr. Abe Michiko.)

16. K. M. Schipper, *Le Fen-teng, Rituel Taoiste* (1975), p. 39, note 12.

17. TT, vol. 324, *T'ai-shang Ch'ih-wen Tung-shen San-lu*, Li Ch'un-feng, (colophon, A.D. 623). TT, vols. 621–635, *Chin-suo Liu-chu Yin*, T'ang, Li Hsiang-feng.

18. TT, vol. 900, TFHY, chapter 76, p. 9a, lines 5–8.

19. *Hua-shan Mi-chüeh*, Fukien, Ch'ing-yün Kuan; author's microfilm collection, from the library of Wu Ching-ch'un.

20. See Bibliography, author's microfilm collection, for the titles of the Thunder Magic manuals of the Heavenly Master. For the following passage, the manual *Ch'ing-wei Ch'i-chüeh*, with the commentary of Master Chuang, Oct.–Nov. 1975, is used as reference.

21. HS, death of Wang Mang. Wang Mang is seen to climb the palace pavilion and face the *Yüeh-chien* position before death. HS, chapter 99, p. 27a.

22. TT, vol. 638, CK, chapter 9, p. 1a, lines 5–8.

23. TT, vol. 900, TFHY, chapter 77, pp. 13b–14b.

24. See Saso, *Taoism and the Rite of Coasmic Renewal*, pp. 67–72.

25. See note 20 above. The following passages are taken from the manual, with Chuang's commentary, fieldnotes, Oct.–Nov. 1972.

26. See *Chuang-lin Hsü Tao-tsang*, pt. 2, chapter 7, p. 4462, illustration.

27. Saso, "Orthodoxy and Heterodoxy in Taoist Ritual," *Religion and Ritual in Chinese Society* (Stanford, 1974), pp. 331–333.

28. See note 20 above. The following passages are taken from the manuscript, pp. 1a–10b.

29. See *Chuang-lin Hsü Tao-tsang*, pt. 4, chapter 16.

30. *T'ai-i Pei-yü K'ao-hsieh Mi*, and *Chu Shuai Chiao Hsieh Fu-mi* (Lung-hu Shan, 1886), collection of the Heavenly Master, author's microfilm files. Both of these texts refer to Mao Shan and the southern Lu Shan as centers for heterodox medium possession. The latter text says specifically, on p. 26a, lines 2–5, that the art of medium possession and the spirits used by the Mao Shan and Lu Shan Taoists are to be exorcised. The passage is parallel to that of Pai Yü-ch'an, in TT, vol. 1016, chapter 1, pp. 8b–9a, except that the words "Lü Shan," i.e., the northern peak, are changed to "Mao Shan and Lu Shan," as centers for heterodoxy in late Ch'ing dynasty south China.

31. *Tao-chiao Yüan-liu* (microfilm edition), p. 131.

32. Oral tradition, field notes, Oct. 31, 1972. Canonical tradition, TT, vol. 197, chapter shang, p. 27, woodblock print.

33. The dance of the *Ho-t'u* described here is the rite used by Chuang in chapter 3 note 15 to counteract Tun-chia black magic. The dance was performed by Chuang on Oct. 16, 1972, in the Jade Emperor temple, Hsinchu City, as described in the following pages.

34. The *Ho-t'u* dance steps, and the other variations of the "steps of Yü" (Yü pu) are illustrated in *Hua Shan Mi-chüeh*, author's microfilm collection, pp. 2–13, (from the Hua Shan collection of Wu Ching-ch'un).

Select Bibliography: Taoist Sources

1. Citations from the *Cheng-t'ung Tao-tsang*

The extant Taoist Canon, *Tao-tsang*, was published during the Cheng-t'ung reign years of the Ming period (1436–1450) in 1,057 chüan, with a supplement of 63 chüan added in 1607, during the Wan-li reign years. The full 1,120 volumes were first published in 1924–1926 by the Commercial Press of Shanghai, and an inexpensive photo-offset edition was marketed by the I-wen Publishing Company in Taipei, 1962. The citations follow the numbers and order of the Harvard-Yenching Institute Sinological Index Series, No. 25 (Taipei: 1966).

VOLUME NUMBER	TITLE
16–17	*Shang-ch'ing Ta-tung Chen-ching.*
67	*Ling-pao Wu-liang Tu-jen Ching Fu-t'u.*
72	*Shang-ch'ing San-tsun P'u-lu.*
73	*Tung-hsüan Ling-pao Chen-ling Wei-yeh T'u.*
75	*Ch'ing-wei Hsien-p'u.*
77–78	*Szu-chi Ming-k'o.*
78	*Hsüan-tu Lü-wen.*
122–131	*Hsiu-chen Shih-lu.*
138	*Lieh-hsien Chuan.* (*Shen-hsien Chuan*, a text missing from the *Tao-tsang*, is found in *Han-Wei Ts'ung-shu*; see the following listing for Taoist hagiographies.)
139–148	*Li-shih Chen-hsien T'i-tao T'ung-chien.*
149	Supplement to the above.
153–158	*Mao-shan Chih.*
160	*Hsi-yü Hua-shan Chih.*
167	*Huang-t'ing Nei-ching, Huang-t'ing Wai-ching.*
183	*T'ai-shang Ling-pao Wu-fu.*
190	*Huang-t'ing Nei-ching Yü-ching Chu.*
191	*T'ai-shang Tung-hsüan Ling-pao Chung Chien-wen.*
193	*Teng-chen Yin-chüeh.*
200	*Hsü Chen-chun Hsien Chuan.*
	Hsi Shan Hsü Chen-chun Pa-shih-wu Hua Lu.
208–263	*Ling-pao Ling-chiao Chi-tu Chin-shu.*
278–290	*Wu-shang Huang-lu Ta-chai Li-ch'eng I.*
302–311	*Ling-pao Yü-chien*
318–319	*Shang-ch'ing T'ien-hsin Cheng-fa.*
319	*Shang-ch'ing Pei-chi T'ien-hsin Cheng-fa.*

323 *Shang-ch'ing Liu-chia Ch'i-tao Mi-fa.*

324 *T'ai-shang Ch'ih-wen Tung-shen San-lu.*

332 *T'ien-t'ai Shan Chih.*

337–339 *Kuang-ch'eng Chi.*

563 *Cheng-i Fa-wen Tien-shih Chiao-chieh k'o-ching.*

564 *Cheng-i Ch'u-kuan Chang-i.*

565 *T'ai-shang San-wu Cheng-i Meng-wei Yüeh-lu Chiao-i.*
T'ai-shang Cheng-i Yüeh-lu I.
T'ai-shang Tung-shen San-huang I.
T'ai-shang Tung-shen T'ai-yüan Ho-t'u San-yüan Yang-hsieh I.

566 *T'ien-shin Cheng-fa Hsiu-chen Tao-ch'ang She-chiao i.*

572 *Yang-sheng Yen-ming Lu.*

575 *T'ai-shang San-huang Pao-chai Shen-hsien Shang-lu Ching.*
San-huang Nei-mi Wen.
San-huang Nei-wen Yi-mi.

576 *Mi-tsang T'ung-hsüan Pien-hua Liu-yin Tung-wei Tun-chia Chen-ching.*

579 *Pei-tou Chih-fa Wu-wei Ching.*

580 *T'ai-shang Ch'u San-shih Chiu-ch'ung Pao-sheng Ching.*
Huang-t'ing Tun-chia Lu-shen Ching.
T'ai-shang Lao-chun Ta Ts'un-szu T'u Chu-chüeh.

631–636 *Chin-suo Liu-chu Yin.*

637–640 *Chen-kao.*

641–648 *Tao-shu.*

677–702 *Yun-chi Ch'i-ch'ien.*

704 *Tso-wang Lun.*

746–755 *T'ai-p'ing Ching.*

760 *I-ch'ieh Tao-ching Yin I Miao-men Yu-ch'i.*

761 *Lu Hsien-sheng Tao-men K'o-lieh.*

762–763 *Tao-chiao I-shu.*

768–779 *Wu-shang Pi-yao.*

780–782 *San-tung Chu-nang.*

868–870 *Pao-p'u-tzu Nei-p'ien.*

876 *T'ai-shang Cheng-i Fa-wen Ching.*
T'ai-shang San-t'ien Nei-chieh Ching.

877 *T'ai-shang San-wu Cheng-i Meng-wei Lu.*

878 *T'ai-shang Cheng-i Meng-wei Fa-lu.*
Cheng-i Fa-wen Shih-lu Chao-i.

879 *T'ai-shang Pei-chi Fu-muo Shen-chou Sha-kuei Lu.*

881–883 *Kao-shang Shen-hsiao Yü-ch'ing Chen-wang Tz'u-shu Ta-fa.*

884–941 *Tao-fa Hui-yüan.*

963–972 *Shang-ch'ing Ling-pao Ta-fa.*

976–983 *Tao-men K'o-fan Ta-ch'üan.*

984–985 *Tao-men T'ung-chiao Pi-yung Chi.*

988 *T'ai-p'ing Yü-lan.*
Tao-men Shih-kuei.
Tao-shu Yüan-shen Ch'i.

989 *T'ai-shang Ch'u-chia Chuan-tu I.*
San-tung Hsiu-Tao I.
Chuan-shou Ching-chieh I Chu-chüeh.
990 *Cheng-i Hsiu-chen Lieh-i.*
Chuan-shou San-tung Ching-chieh Fa-lu Lieh-shuo.
Cheng-i Fa-wen Fa-lu Bu-i.
1003 *Cheng-i Fa-wen Hsiu-chen Yao-chih.*
1004 *Tung-hsüan Ling-pao Wu-kan Wen.*
1005 *Wu-yüeh Chen-hsing Hsü Lun.*
Kao-shang Shen-hsiao Tsung-shih Shou-ching Shih.
T'ai-shang Tung-shen San-huang Chuan-shou I.
1016 *Hai-ch'iung Pai Chen-jen Yü-lu.*
1040 *Shang-ch'ing T'ien-kuan San-t'u Ching.*
Shan-ch'ing Ho-t'u Nei-hsüan Ching.

2. OTHER WORKS IN CHINESE

Anonymous *Ku-wei Shu* (The Ancient Apocryphal Texts), *Muo-hai Chin-hu* Collection, Taipei: Wen-yu Press, 1969.

———. *Tao-chiao Yüan-liu* (The Origins of Religious Taoism, Yüan period manuscript), Taipei: In press, 1977.

Chang Hsin-wei. *Wei-shu T'ung-k'ao* (A Critical Study of Authentic and Unauthentic Texts), Taipei: Shang-wu Press, 1970.

Ch'en Kuo-fu. *Tao-tsang Yüan-liu K'ao* (A Critical Study of the Taoist Canon), Peking: Chung-hua, 1963. 2 vols.

Chou Chao-hsien. *Tao-chia yü Shen-hsien* (Taoism and Spiritual Perfection), Taipei: Chung-hua Press, 1970.

Chuang-ch'en Teng-yün and Michael Saso. *Chuang-lin Hsü Tao-tsang* (The Chuang-lin Supplement to the Taoist Canon), Taipei: Ch'eng-wen Press, 1975. 25 vols.

Fu Ch'in-chia. *Chung-kuo Tao-chiao Shih* (The History of Taoism in China), Taipei: Shang-wu Press, 1966.

Fu Tai-yen. *Tao-chiao Yüan-liu* (The Origins of Religious Taoism), Shanghai: Chung-hua Press, 1922.

Hsiao T'ien-shih, ed. *Pai Yü-ch'an ch'uan-chi* (The Complete Works of Pai Yü-ch'an), Taipei: Tzu-yu Press, 1969.

Oyanagi, Shigeta, and Ch'en Pin-ko. *Tao-chiao Kai-shuo* (An Outline of Religious Taoism), Taipei: Shang-wu Press, 1966.

Sun K'o-kuan. *Sung-Yüan Tao-chiao chih Fa-chan* (The Developments in Religious Taoism During the Sung and Yüan periods), Taichung: Chung-yang Press, 1965.

———. *Yüan-tai Tao-chiao chih Fa-chan* (The Growth of Taoism During the Yüan period), Taichung: Chung-yang Press, 1968.

Wang Ming. *T'ai-p'ing Ching Ho-hsiao* (A Reconstruction of the Full T'ai-p'ing Ching), Shanghai: Chung-hua Press, 1960.

Yen I-p'ing, *Tao-chiao Yen-chiu Tz'u-liao* (Materials for the Study of Religious Taoism), Taipei: I-wen Press, 1974. 2 vols.

3. UNPUBLISHED MATERIALS FROM THE *Cheng-i Tz'u-t'an* COLLECTION

給籙壇靖元科 三山滴血派 龍虎山師傳法派 正乙預修給籙元科 清微傳度科範一宗 職籙壇靖治炁心印 (Ordination manual of the Heavenly Master), Lung-hu Shan: 1886.
漢祖天師傳諸帝諱 (Taboo Names of the Heavenly Rulers).
朱帥勦邪三限符 梵文 五雷呪符 (Thunder Magic talismans).
大梵斗奏告符(Pseudo-Sanskrit mantras and charms).
太乙北獄拷邪秘 (Pole Star sect exorcisms).
禮斗玄功訣(五雷拜斗法)(Thunder Magic Pole Star rites).
龍虎山秘傳手訣 (Two-handed mudras).
大氣字催生符秘 (Talismanic aids for birth).
大生氣字治病符秘 (Talismanic cures).
小氣字治病符訣 (Talismanic cures).
秘授呪棗治病訣要 (Mantric cures).
王帥芰治大法符秘 (Master Wang style talismanic cures).
王帥三限治邪符秘 (Master Wang exorcistic cures).
驅邪治病秘篆 (Exorcistic cures).
師傳清微氣訣林修梅(全眞派)藏本 (Ch'ing-wei Thunder Magic rubrics). (Lin Hsiu-mei collection)
黃庭經解(峽西棲雲山道士劉一明解) (Notes for the Yellow Court Canon).
黃庭內外景科儀(林修梅庚戌年授籙) (Ritual of the Yellow Court Canon).
華山秘訣(Hua Shan esoteric rubrics).
茅山奇門遁甲(林士梅 咸豐元年授) (Mao Shan Ch'i-men Tun-chia).
內外天罡訣 (Esoteric rubrics, Thunder Magic).

4. A BRIEF BIBLIOGRAPHY OF THE BASIC WORKS OF JAPANESE SCHOLARS ON TAOISM

Fukui, Kōjun, *Dōkyō no Kiso-teki Kenkyū* (A Fundamental Research in Religious Taoism), Tokyo: Shoseki Bunbutsu Ryutsu Kai, 1952.

Kamada, Shigeo, *Chūgoku Bukkyō Shisō-shi Kenkyū* (A Study of Chinese Buddhist Thought), Tokyo: Shunshu Sha, 1969. Pt. 1, The interaction of Buddhist and Taoist Thought, pp. 9–249.

Kubo, Noritada, *Chūgoku no Shūkyō Kaikaku*, (China's Religious Reformation, a Study of the Founding of the Ch'üan-chen Sect), Tokyo: Hōzōkan, 1966.

———, *Dōkyō to Chūgoku Shakai* (Taoism and Chinese Society), Tokyo: Heibonsha, 1946.

———, Dōkyō Shisō no Hensen (The Development of Taoist Thought), *Seikai Shi no Kenkyū*, Tokyo: Yamagawa Shuppansham, 1965.

Obuchi, Ninji, *Dōkyō Shi no Kenkyū* (A History of Religious Taoism), Okayama: Okayama University Press, 1964.

Oyanagi, Shigeta, *Rō-sō no Shisō to Dōkyō* (The Thought of Lao-tzu and Chuang-tzu and Religious Taoism), Tokyo: Morikita Shoten, 1942.

Yoshioka, Yositoyo, *Dōkyō Kyōten Shiron* (A Treatise on Taoist Canonical Texts and their date of earliest citation), Tokyo: Taishō University, 1955.

———, *Dōkyō to Bukkyō, I* (Buddhism and Taoism, Vol. I), Nihon Gakujitsu, 1959; Vol. II, Tokyo: Toshima Shobō, 1970.

———, *Eisei e no Negai: Dōkyō* (The Search for Long Life: Taoism), Kyoto: Tankosha, 1970.

———, *Dōkyō no Jittai* (Religious Taoism in Practice), Peking: 1941; This excellent and little known work was republished in Kyoto: Hōyū Press, 1975, in an anonymous limited edition.

Selected books written since 1980

Anderson, P., *The Method of Holding the Three Ones; a Taoist Manual of Meditation,* London: Curzon Press, 1980

Boltz, Judith, *A Survey of Taoist Literature*, Berkeley: 1987

Girardot, Norman, *Myth and Meaning in Early Taoism,* Berkeley: 1983

Kohn, Livia, *Early Chinese Mysticism,* Princeton: 1992

Lagerwey, John, *Taoist Ritual in Chinese Society,* New York: 1987 (and passim, many scholarly works in French)

Mair, Victor, (Ed.), *Experimental Essays on the Chuang-tzu,* Honolulu: 1983

Palmer, Martin, *Taoism,* Element Books (England), 1991

Robinet, Isabelle, *Taoist Meditation,* SUNY: 1993

________ *Taoism, Growth of a Religion,* Stanford, 1997

Saso, Michael, *Blue Dragon White Tiger*, Honolulu: 1990

________, *Gold Pavilion, (Taoist Meditation),* Tuttle: 1995

________, "The Taoist Body and Cosmic Prayer," in *Religion and the Body*, Sarah Coakley (ed.) Cambridge: 1997

Schipper, Kristofer, *The Taoist Body*, Berkeley: 1993

Wong, Eva, *Taoism*, Boston: Shambala Press, 1997

(for a chronicle of Taoist Studies, see Anna Seidel, *Cahier d'Extreme Asie*, 5, 1989-90, and Franciscus Verellen, in *Journal of Asian Studies*, 54, 1995, pp.322-46)

Index and Chinese Characters

Index and Chinese Characters

Well-known place names and mantric seed words have been omitted from the index. The characters for the Fa-lu mandala meditation occur in the text. Titles occurring in the bibliography have not been repeated in the index. The names of all but the major figures appearing in chapter three have been changed.